Transport modelling for a complete beginner

Yaron Hollander

Transport modelling for a complete beginner
by Yaron Hollander

Disclaimer

The book contains the views of the author regarding the practice of transport modelling. It does not intend to provide complete guidance for transport modellers, planners, engineers, analysts or anyone else.

Professional knowledge and practices evolve continuously and vary with time, place and perspective. Readers of this book must always rely on their own professional judgement, experience and knowledge, as well as on advice from various experts, when deciding whether, when and how to use the advice included in this book.

In using any information from this book, the user should consider the safety, security, legality and professionalism of their actions. Anyone who uses material from this book must also seek professional advice that is tailored for the situation where it is being used, since the ideas described here are general.

Neither the author, publisher or anyone else involved in producing this book can be held responsible or accept liability for any damage or harm that may result from using any of the ideas presented in this book.

Contents

An introduction by Luis Willumsen

My own introduction

Part I: the rules of transport modelling

1	**Why we use transport models**	**2**
	1.1 The scope of a transport model	2
	1.2 Using models as input for project design	7
	1.3 Using models as input for project appraisal	12
2	**The building blocks of transport models**	**18**
	2.1 Trips and travel demand	18
	2.2 Networks	19
	2.3 Zones	23
	2.4 Matrices	32
	2.5 Scenarios	35
	2.6 Costs	38
	2.7 Demand segmentation	43
	2.8 The value of time	47
3	**The four-stage concept**	**49**
	3.1 The hierarchy in a transport model	49
	3.2 A matrix view of a four-stage model	53
	3.3 A tree view of a four-stage model	56
	3.4 The composite cost	59
	3.5 Model hierarchy and travel behaviour	61
	3.6 Adding time choice	65
	3.7 Tour-based models	66
	3.8 Other limitations of the four-stage concept	68

Chapter 1   Chapter 2   Chapter 3

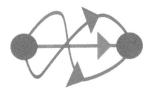

4   Calibration, validation and application   70
4.1   The role of model parameters   70
4.2   The calibration process   74
4.3   Model validation   76
4.4   Goodness of fit   77
4.5   Application of a calibrated model   81
4.6   Using a model built somewhere else   83
4.7   Aggregate and disaggregate models   85
4.8   Data sources   87

5   Anything from planes to bikes   93
5.1   Multi-modal and uni-modal models   93
5.2   The feeder mode   94
5.3   Models for car travel   95
5.4   Models for freight transport   98
5.5   Modelling travel by taxi   101
5.6   Modelling bus travel   101
5.7   Modelling rail travel   103
5.8   Modelling cycling   108
5.9   Modelling travel by motorcycle   113
5.10   Modelling walking   114
5.11   Models for air travel   117
5.12   Modelling self-driving vehicles   118

6   More on trip generation   119
6.1   Trip ends and trip rates   119
6.2   Demand growth scenarios   122
6.3   Production and attraction   122
6.4   Will the total demand change?   126
6.5   Land use and transport interaction   129
6.6   Limitations of trip generation models 134

Chapter 4   Chapter 5   Chapter 6

7   More on mode split   136
   7.1   Mode split before or after distribution   136
   7.2   Split between public transport modes   138
   7.3   Stated Preference and Revealed Preference   138
   7.4   The mode constant   144
   7.5   Allowing trips by more than one mode   149
   7.6   Limitations of mode split models   152

8   More on matrix development   154
   8.1   Distribution or destination choice   154
   8.2   Balancing a demand matrix   157
   8.3   Matrix conversions   158
   8.4   Conflicts with observed traffic   160
   8.5   Trips inside a zone   163
   8.6   Understanding the demand matrix   164
   8.7   Limitations of matrix building processes   169

9   More on network models   172
   9.1   Road networks and route networks   172
   9.2   From the matrix to the network   175
   9.3   Route choice for public transport users   180
   9.4   Route choice for road users   183
   9.5   The level of network detail   186
   9.6   Junction modelling   190
   9.7   Traffic micro-simulation   193
   9.8   Dealing with parking   196
   9.9   The monetary cost of car travel   200
   9.10   Model convergence and iteration   205
   9.11   Short-term prediction   208
   9.12   The outputs from network models   211
   9.13   Limitations of network models   215

Chapter 7   Chapter 8   Chapter 9

Part II: the culture of transport modelling

10   Why we really use transport models   **219**
    10.1   The political and organisational context   219
    10.2   The practical side of model scoping   224
    10.3   Abuse and misuse of transport models   227
    10.4   The expectations from transport models   236

11   So is it accurate?   **237**
    11.1   The tricky business of model accuracy   237
    11.2   Why models aren't prediction tools   239
    11.3   Why models aren't comparison tools   254

12   Good modelling practice   **262**
    12.1   Successful modelling   262
    12.2   Looking for evidence   263
    12.3   Starting the modelling work   270
    12.4   Scheduling modelling activities   271
    12.5   Allocating modelling tasks   273
    12.6   Defining scenarios   275
    12.7   Dealing with uncertainty   277
    12.8   Explaining different choices   279
    12.9   Showing detailed outputs   280
    12.10 Showing controversial outputs   281
    12.11 Spending money   282

Chapter 10   **Chapter 11**   **Chapter 12**

13		**The future of transport modelling**	**285**
	13.1	Where do we go from here	285
	13.2	Self-driving vehicles	285
	13.3	New forms of shared travel	288
	13.4	New data sources	289
	13.5	Artificial intelligence	293
	13.6	Data-driven decision making	295
	13.7	Faster and prettier modelling	297
	13.8	Online modelling	298
	13.9	DIY modelling	300
	13.10	Open-source models	302
	13.11	Same old tricks	303

Chapter 13

An introduction by Luis Willumsen

I was fortunate to be able to read a draft version of this book. My immediate reactions were surprise and admiration. My surprise came since only on reading it, I realised that a book like this should have been written 25 years ago; the fact that it only comes out now is a peculiar reflection on our profession. My admiration came because Yaron has managed to explain some of the most advanced concepts in transport modelling, and to add new insights, in a down-to-earth manner without using a single mathematical equation.

The title of this book is quite unassuming. This is a good guide for beginners, but not only for them. It should be read by students, planners and economists, or those just interested in modelling; but also by most modelling practitioners and academics. The book dissects the transport modelling process with forensic detachment and sheds light on many gaps in our knowledge, misuses of technical concepts, and the sometimes unrealistic nature of the assumptions underpinning our practice.

A disclosure: I have known Yaron for over a decade, during which we have worked together on several projects. He has an eye for detail and for unwarranted assumptions. Yaron has substantial experience in public and private sector projects; as such, he has been exposed to the mentality of official guidance and public consultation processes, but also to the inquiring minds of financial institutions and rating agencies. This book conveys the insights gained from this experience, and these lessons are relevant, even urgent, to a wide range of professionals who use the outputs of transport models.

The first part of the book is devoted to "the rules of transport modelling" whilst recognising that, in fact, there are none. This section takes most of the volume of this book and is particularly useful to the beginner, but experienced practitioners too will find in it some deep insights on topics they thought were straightforward. These include demand segmentation, model validation, and handling difficult issues with taxis, walking and cycling. The treatment of mode choice, dealing with junctions, the challenge of modelling parking, and the handling of multi-modal trips are particularly helpful for both complete beginners and skilled practitioners.

The second part of the book will be the most controversial and also the most valuable. Yaron deals with the culture of transport modelling, which is rarely mentioned in any other book or guidance document. The review of the real reasons behind the use of transport models, and the arguments about the accuracy of model outputs, deserve some serious reflection. They may even justify the re-writing of sections in other popular books.

The last chapter, on the future of transport modelling, is a good pointer to the difficult tasks ahead. Our world is changing faster than it did a decade ago, and we are facing new challenges. Some of our most "solid" approaches, like the way we treat car ownership and the most common data collection methods, will be questioned and replaced in the future. Yaron identifies the most critical of these and points to useful ways forward without delivering a simplistic recipe, as there really is none.

Professional ethics are at the centre of this important book. This is a topic only sometimes discussed in project meetings, but recent litigation cases against modelling consultancies, as well as challenging books by Bain and Flyvbjerg, bring this topic to the fore. Despite pressures from clients, the public and other stakeholders, we must accept that two modellers will make different assumptions, use different approaches and reach different results. Recognising the subjective nature of modelling is a first step towards adopting a more rigorous view on the accuracy of model outputs and a more watchful stance when these pressures arise.

The book makes extensive use of colour and naïve figures to illustrate concepts and practices. Rather than distracting, these illustrate a playful approach to serious matters; they help understanding these concepts in most cases, and will provoke your thinking even if not. Overall, this thoughtful book gives a well-balanced introduction to modelling to a reader with no previous knowledge. To a more experienced reader, reading the book may be at times painful; but it is a good kind of pain, the one that induces us to improve our ways.

Dr. Luis Willumsen is co-author of "Modelling Transport" (with Prof. Juan-de-Dios Ortúzar), now in its fourth edition, and author of "Better Traffic and Revenue Forecasting". His career as an advisor on travel demand analysis spans nearly 40 countries over four decades.

My own introduction

Hello! Thank you for having enough interest in my book to read the first paragraph. Even if you stop here, you already are part of a rare species.

Your first question must be who this book is for. Let's start with the geographical aspect: the information in this book isn't specific to any particular part of the world. Much of my own work has been in England, but I've also done transport modelling work in the USA and about 10 other countries. The principles described in this book are relevant everywhere. When I talk about practices which vary between countries, I'll make it very clear.

I wrote this book with many types of readers in mind, including town planners, property developers, politicians, investors, policy advisors, and managers of transport projects. You may be working in a local authority, a transport agency, a company that considers investing in transport infrastructure, an operator of transport services, a company that provides services in the transport sector, or a consultancy that works with all of these. Maybe you have a role in a decision-making process, where you need to judge whether some suggested transport improvements make sense.

In my work I've met many members of the public who campaign for or against various transport projects, and cannot afford to hire expensive consultants. If you're one of them, you definitely are part of the audience I've aimed for. You may find interest in this book also if you're simply someone who's interested in understanding how authorities make big decisions about transport infrastructure. Or you may be a journalist writing about transport policy, or a professional in a field which has some links to transport planning.

I hope this book is also useful to students in transport courses and in related areas such as economics, civil engineering, data science, geography, urban and regional planning. Such readers might want to know what transport modelling is all about, or even consider working in this field at some point.

There isn't a single mathematical formula in this book. It does talk about the theory behind transport modelling, which can sometimes get quite complex, but it's in plain English only. To understand this book you don't need any previous knowledge, only the ability to tolerate my poor graphic design skills.

This book doesn't cover any specific software package for transport modelling. To some extent it covers all of them, because I'll talk a lot about the things you need to consider when choosing your modelling technique. But I don't call any of these software packages by name; I don't talk about how to use specific tools; and I don't give any instructions regarding which button you need to push and when.

This book doesn't describe innovative, super-clever models that only a small bunch of people would understand. I focus on the types of models which are commonly used already. But this book does include lots of new ideas. There's a lot of information here which you won't easily find in other books.

The first part of the book, which includes chapters 1 to 9, introduces the key principles of transport modelling. These principles are presented in a way that is specifically aimed at readers with no prior knowledge at all. If you become confident in these principles then you'll find it quite straightforward later to go deeper into more specific types of modelling.

"Auntie Tilda? We're coming to see ya."

The second part of the book, which includes chapters 10 to 13, talks about more strategic topics. This part is about the management of transport modelling work, the way model outputs are communicated, and the professional environment where this is done. This is where I suggest which common modelling practices are good and which ones, in my view, are not. The second part of the book is meant to help you ensure that transport investment decisions in your professional environment are fair, effective and evidence-based.

So much is happening in the world of transport modelling, that I couldn't include everything in the book. There are some methods and processes in modelling which I haven't included, to keep things simple enough.

The same visit to auntie Tilda, but in modelling talk. We'll see later how to read this.

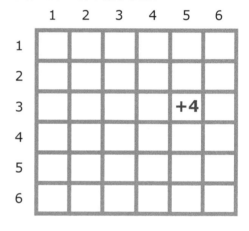

My recommendation is that you read the whole book and don't skip sections. I wish I could put on a cool face and say you're welcome to read only the bits you fancy. But in practice, there's a lot of terminology to go through, so I organised the book such that each chapter uses the terminology I introduced in earlier chapters. If you come across a term that you don't understand, anywhere in this book, then it's probably because you skipped the section where it's explained.

If you have comments or suggestions on anything in this book, please don't hesitate to get in touch on yaron@CTthink.com. I'd be curious to hear your feedback, if it is polite and professional. But please don't email to tell me the drawings in this book are silly; I know this already.

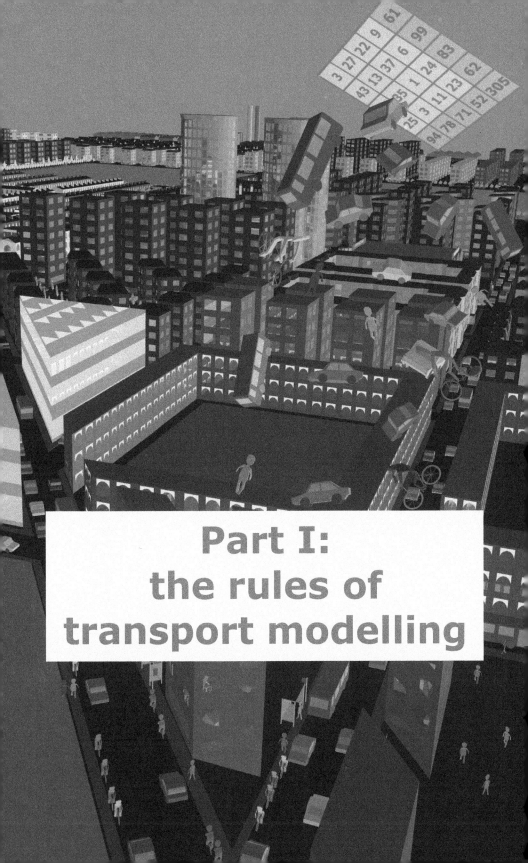

**Part I:
the rules of
transport modelling**

Chapter 1
Why we use transport models

1.1 The scope of a transport model

I've split this book into two parts. This chapter starts part I which focuses on the theory of transport modelling. Please don't be put off by the scary word "theory"; you won't find any mathematics or philosophy here. It's just that practitioners model the transport system in a specific way, based on some assumptions and principles, which together form a theoretical framework.

Some principles of transport modelling are very common, so the first part of the book explains them as they are. This part does explain the strengths and weaknesses of these principles, but it accepts that this is how things are usually done. Debating these principles more seriously is something I leave for the second part of the book, which goes in more detail into the practices of real-world projects which involve transport modelling.

Transport models are very often used to produce forecasts of how the transport system will operate in a new situation. But both "the transport system" and "a new situation" are terms that are worth explaining. Let's start with the latter.

The "new situation" is the reason why we want to do some modelling. There can be different types of new situations that may justify transport modelling work. Examples for such situations are presented in figure 1.

Figure 1: modelling all kinds of "new situations"

| A new road, bridge or tunnel are built | A road, bridge or tunnel are improved | An existing road is closed |

A new public transport service opens

An existing public transport service is modified

An existing public transport service closes

Changes are made to freight and delivery services

Changes are made to air services and airports

Changes are made to waterborne transport and ports

Infrastructure for pedestrians is built or changed

Infrastructure for cyclists is built or changed

Parking provision is changed

Restrictions on specific vehicles are introduced or removed

Ticketing, fares or taxes are changed

There are some population changes in the area

New houses or offices are built somewhere, so people need to travel there

People change their preferences and they start using the transport system in a different way

You should note a few important things about this "new situation" which we sometimes wish to model...:

■ It sometimes involves changes to transport infrastructure and facilities, but sometimes not.

■ It sometimes involves changes to transport services, but sometimes not.

■ Sometimes the only change is that time passes, so there are some natural changes to the population or employment in the area.

■ Sometimes we're interested in modelling a future situation, but sometimes we want to know how things would be if the change happened now.

In all these cases, the model can be a source of insight to help understand the new situation or prepare for it. It's not guaranteed that modelling work will help, and there are definitely cases where I wouldn't recommend doing any modelling. But the point for now is that for each type of "new situation" shown in figure 1, transport models can often give us some analytical help. Later in this book we will discuss how helpful the model may be for specific situations.

The "transport system" covered in the model could include, for example, the streets in a specific urban area, or the network of bus routes across town, or all the highways and motorways in the entire country. There are comprehensive models where the "transport system" includes all the main roads, urban and interurban rail routes, buses and lories, cars and taxis, bikes and motorbikes, across a very large area. By contrast, there are also cases where "the transport system" in a model only covers one junction or one station.

Deciding what counts as the "transport system" in the model can be described as the **model scoping** problem. The model generally needs to cover the transport infrastructure and/or transport services that will be affected by the "new situation". So the scope of the model depends on the kind of expected change, investment or intervention, which made us want to do some modelling. Figure 2 gives some more detail on what this means.

4

Figure 2: the scope of a model

Model scoping question	Example
Current versus future	
We always include in the model existing transport services and infrastructure, but often we also decide to include planned future changes. In this way we can use the model to turn these changes on and off, and look at how well things work with and without the change.	If we consider adding a third lane to a street which currently has two lanes, we would build two versions of the model, one with two lanes in the relevant place like now, and one with three lanes. We would keep everything else in the model the same.
Behavioural responses	
Transport models try to represent human behaviour when it comes to deciding where, when and how to travel. There are many types of human behaviour that could be relevant, but it's better if our model focuses on a small number of behaviour types that are most relevant to our work. Otherwise we might need an extremely complex model which would require some serious research.	Many cyclists would prefer not to cycle through a park where the ground is very muddy on days with bad weather. In specific studies, the ability to model this would be critical. But for most models, it's not worth spending time developing an ability to identify how the weather affects the routes that cyclists take. Modellers need to decide how important this is.
Relevant modes of transport	
We often start modelling because we plan some improvements to specific modes of transport. Naturally, these modes should be part of what we model. But if the change will also affect other modes then we may want to model them as well.	If we build a new bus station which makes it nicer to travel by bus, we may want to include in the model the modes that potential bus users use now, like cars or bikes. Without including them, it's difficult to analyse how drivers and cyclists may become bus users.

Model scoping question	Example

Geographical scope

It's only natural that the area where we plan a transport improvement should be covered by the model. But how large should the modelled area be? The general rule is that the model should cover the whole area where there may be considerable changes. This includes not only the changes we introduce directly but also changes that would happen as a result.

Think about a plan to build a segregated cycle path along a major road, which will reduce the amount of road space that cars can use. To examine this plan, we will want to model the road where the segregated cycle path is constructed, but also parallel car routes because they are likely to experience an increase in car traffic as cars will be looking for new routes.

Level of detail

When we create a model for a certain area, we need to decide whether it needs to include every single back street, each bus stop, each individual platform in a big railway station, and so on. There isn't a specific level of detail which is right or wrong. More detail allows us to have a closer look into very specific places, but it also makes the model sensitive to information that we don't always have.

If we model the extension of a tram route into a new area, then including detail of every tram stop will allow us to analyse the specific places that passengers go to, but the quality of the analysis will depend on the data we have about all these places.

I tend to split the uses of a transport model into two slightly different types, based on whether the outputs are used for project design or for project appraisal. Each of the two following sections focuses on one of these. There is a significant overlap between these two reasons for using transport models, and it is very common to build models for both purposes at the same time. But I still find it helpful to introduce them one by one, to keep things simple.

1.2 Using models for project design

One of the main reasons we use transport models is to produce some of the figures that engineers and planners need to design detailed solutions for transport problems. A few examples for how models help with the design of transport improvements are described in figure 3.

The following symbols are used in figure 3:

 Examples of decisions that need to be made

 Examples of information that can help make the decision

 Examples of information which may be available without a model

 Examples of additional insight that a model can potentially add

Figure 3: using models for project design

Type of improvement	How models help the design	
Roads, streets, highways, motorways		How many traffic lanes are needed
		The amount of traffic and how it splits between cars, vans, buses and trucks
		The amount of traffic by each type of vehicle, as observed in recent surveys on specific roads
		The estimated amount of traffic by each type of vehicle, also in a future situation when more people travel in the area
New roads, road bridges or tunnels		Is there a need for signalised junctions where the road connects to existing roads
		The number of people travelling between the places that will be connected by the new road
		The number of people travelling to and from these places, based on a survey conducted before the new road is built
		The estimated number of people travelling to and from these places, also in a future situation where the new road has attracted more people to the area

Traffic calming and restrictions		At what times of day the restrictions will apply
		The amount of traffic affected by this policy at different times of day
		The amount of traffic as observed in surveys at different times of day
		The estimated amount of traffic also in a future situation when people change their travel behaviour
New public transport stations or station improvements		How many ticket gates are needed
		The number of passengers going through the station at peak time
		The number of passengers using an existing station
		The estimated number of passengers also in the future situation, after these improvements are introduced
Tolling, ticketing, taxing and user charging		How much to charge
		The revenue that can be collected
		An estimated revenue, calculated using assumptions of who will pay and how much
		An estimated revenue, calculated in a systematic way, considering how people decide how much they are willing to pay for their travel

New public transport routes or route improvements		How many services to run during rush hours
		The time of day with the highest number of passengers
		The number of passengers using an existing route
		The estimated number of passengers also in a future situation when the wider area has gone through regeneration
Air services and airport improvements		What terminal size is needed
		The number of passengers going through the terminal per day during holiday periods
		The estimated number of passengers based on assumptions on how they choose their airport
		The number of passengers, derived from analysis of airport choice patterns
Waterborne transport and port improvements		What length of a taxi rank is needed at the passenger terminal
		The number of boat passengers that continue their journey by taxi
		The number of boat passengers continuing by taxi today

		The number of boat passengers continuing by taxi after these improvements are introduced
Changes to freight and delivery services	? ?	The number of staff needed for roadside vehicle checks
		The locations with the highest freight traffic
		Freight traffic as observed in recent surveys on some key roads
		Estimated freight traffic for all roads in the area
Infrastructure for pedestrians and cyclists	? ?	The number of green light seconds for cyclists in a signalised junction
		The proportion of cyclists going straight, right or left at the junction
		The number of cyclists observed recently on some specific paths
		An estimated cycling route for each cyclist using the relevant junction, before and after the improvement
Development of housing and employment	? ?	The size of bus station required at a new development
		The proportion of residents regularly travelling by bus
		The proportion of bus users in other places in the area where development took place already
		The estimated proportion of bus users also in this specific development, once it is complete

11

The examples over the last few pages show various cases where models may give more specific and more comprehensive inputs into the design process, compared with the information that is available without a model. Information provided by a model does not simply reflect the current situation; it can be adjusted to a future situation, after some improvements were made or after other changes may have happened.

In addition, model outputs can cover an entire area, not only specific points where current data is available. Figures produced by models are based on a consistent analysis of how everyone in the relevant area makes their travel choices; the model takes into consideration everything which has been included in the scope of the model, in a systematic way.

1.3 Using models for project appraisal

Transport models are one of the sources of input into the appraisal of possible solutions to transport problems. The word appraisal is one of the many names of the process of checking what's the best solution to a transport problem or a transport need. The appraisal of alternative options is a critical process because transport improvements can be very expensive. The appraisal process needs to ensure that the money paid for transport infrastructure or services is a better investment than other things that could be done with this money.

The appraisal of potential transport projects is sometimes called "the feasibility study" or "the transport assessment". The document that describes the likely impacts of the project, both positive or negative, and the strengths and weaknesses of the different options, is sometimes called "the business case". The work to understand all these considerations is sometimes called "the cost-benefit analysis". There are various other terms used in the appraisal process, and very often a mixture of all these terms is used, so in this book I refer to all of them under the name "project appraisal".

Appraisal of possible transport solutions is sometimes done before there's a detailed engineering design of the possible solutions, but sometimes it's done when the alternative solutions

12

are designed already. A good appraisal is an iterative process, or in other words, parts of it are normally repeated several times. An iterative appraisal process starts before there is a lot of detail, to provide some initial ideas of what alternatives need to be considered, and is then refined when the ideas develop. Whenever more detail becomes available on what exactly is being planned, the appraisal results become more conclusive. Sometimes the appraisal shows that some ideas still need improving and then parts of the process need to start again.

Modelling can have an important role in all stages of this iterative appraisal process. An example is given in figure 4.

The appraisal of a transport project relies on both quantitative and qualitative evidence. I'll discuss this in more detail in part II of this book. For now it's worth mentioning that, naturally, models mainly have a role in the quantitative elements of the appraisal. The quantitative appraisal work aims to identify, for each possible option that is being considered, all the following: costs, income, benefits and disbenefits (yes, this is a word!). More on each one of these, and the relevance of modelling for each one, is presented in figure 5.

Benefits are measured in various different units, including minutes or grams or the number of people enjoying the benefit. But most appraisal approaches have a way of converting the benefits from all these different units into money, so that all benefits can be summed up into a total monetary value. Disbenefits, too, are converted from various different units into money. In the appraisal, the total disbenefits are subtracted from the total benefits, to see if the overall impact is positive or negative.

Figure 4: an example of how modelling helps the appraisal

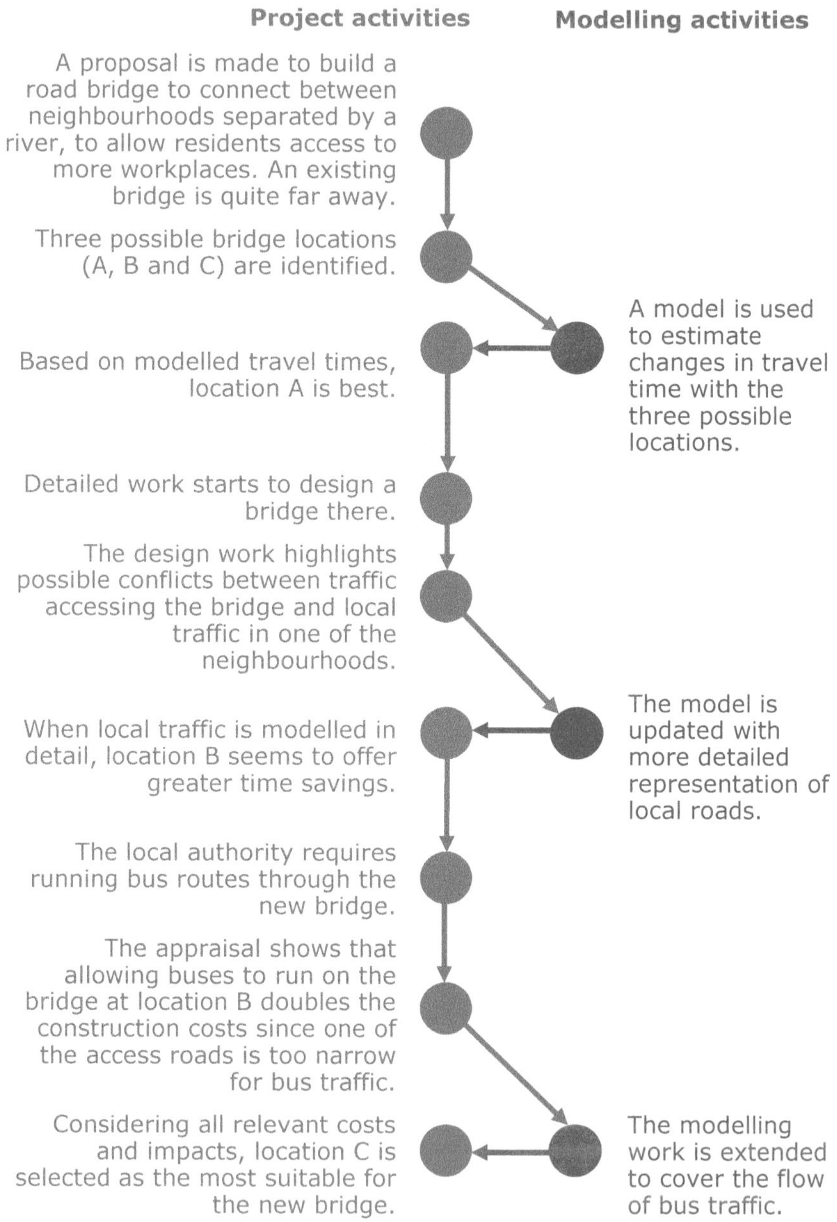

Project activities	Modelling activities

A proposal is made to build a road bridge to connect between neighbourhoods separated by a river, to allow residents access to more workplaces. An existing bridge is quite far away.

Three possible bridge locations (A, B and C) are identified.

A model is used to estimate changes in travel time with the three possible locations.

Based on modelled travel times, location A is best.

Detailed work starts to design a bridge there.

The design work highlights possible conflicts between traffic accessing the bridge and local traffic in one of the neighbourhoods.

The model is updated with more detailed representation of local roads.

When local traffic is modelled in detail, location B seems to offer greater time savings.

The local authority requires running bus routes through the new bridge.

The appraisal shows that allowing buses to run on the bridge at location B doubles the construction costs since one of the access roads is too narrow for bus traffic.

Considering all relevant costs and impacts, location C is selected as the most suitable for the new bridge.

The modelling work is extended to cover the flow of bus traffic.

Figure 5: modelling and appraisal

	What is it	How models help
Costs 	The amount of money needed to pay for construction, maintenance and various other expenses.	Models feed into the work to plan and design the necessary solutions, but the cost of each solution is estimated without using the model.
Income 	Money that can be earned using the agreed solution, such as public transport fees, the revenue from a toll road, or the tax that car users pay for their fuel.	The model provides important inputs, such as the amount of traffic on a tolled lane or the number of passengers buying tickets. To calculate the income, additional stages are needed outside the model, for example adding the impact of inflation.
Benefits 	The benefits from a private sector investment is similar to the income, since it's done for profit. When public money is invested, there are other outcomes that count as benefits.	The appraisal will examine a long list of potential benefits. Some of them are calculated using models, and others don't. Important types of benefit which we calculate using models are listed in figure 6.
Disbenefits 	Any impact which counts as a benefit when it's positive, counts as a disbenefit when it's negative.	The list of potential disbenefits is the same as the list of potential benefits. If the impact is good then it's a benefit, otherwise it's a disbenefit. See figure 6.

Figure 6: benefits that models help us estimate

Benefit or disbenefit	How models help estimate it
Travel time 	One of the main benefits from investing in transport infrastructure is reducing travel times. There are also situations where there's an increase in congestion, and therefore a travel time disbenefit. Estimated changes in travel times, either positive or negative, are a direct output from many transport models, which goes directly into the appraisal.
Environmental impacts 	Many transport improvements aim to reduce air pollution and greenhouse gas emissions, mainly from road traffic. Models have an important but indirect role in estimating emission levels in different situations. For example, they estimate the number of vehicles travelling at different speeds. This can be used in a separate spreadsheet to calculate the overall amount of fuel consumed and the resulting concentrations of gasses like NO_2, PM_{10}, NO_x and CO_2.
Noise 	Similar to environmental impacts, changes in the level of noise are calculated outside the model but they use information from the model. Model outputs that influence noise levels include the amount of traffic, the proportion of heavy vehicles in traffic, and speeds in different places.
Physical activity 	When people are physically active as part of their travel, they tend to become healthier and also more economically productive. The impacts of more physical activity aren't estimated using models, but if a model is capable of estimating the change in the level of activity (for example, an increase in the number of bike trips) then some available parameters can be used outside the model to convert this into a benefit in the appraisal.

Benefit or disbenefit	How models help estimate it
Accidents	We know that generally if people travel more or longer then there are more accidents. Models help estimate the total number of kilometers or miles travelled by all people in the study area, so if this number changes then it can be translated into an estimated change in the number of accidents. The total number of travelled kilometers can be reported by the model separately for different types of roads, vehicles or railways. For each type we use its own typical number of accidents per kilometer.

There's a "chicken and egg" relationship between modelling and appraisal. To scope the modelling work properly, you need to know what benefits or disbenefits will have a critical impact on the appraisal results. Using the example from figure 4, if the issues with local traffic and buses were known in advance, it would be easier to ensure from the start that the model examines them in sufficient detail. But very often, sensitive or contentious issues reveal themselves only after the project team examines the model outputs, or even later, when the model outputs are shared with external stakeholders.

Therefore, the most effective projects consider both the modelling and the appraisal together, starting from a very early stage of the project. Then they continuously check that the scope of the modelling work remains consistent with the needs of the appraisal, as the work evolves. I will return to this topic later.

Chapter 2
The building blocks of transport models

2.1 Trips and travel demand

Transport modelling has its own language, and it's difficult to discuss anything with modelling specialists without knowing at least the basic terminology. In this chapter I go through some of the key words used in modelling work. These words reveal a very specific way of viewing the transport system, as a world that is made of **zones**, **matrices**, **generalised costs** and whatnot.

These definitions describe things that don't exist in the real world. They are simplified conventions that allow us to analyse the complex transport system within a reasonable effort. That's why you should use the modelling language only if it helps you. You'll sometimes want to know things that the modelling terminology isn't helpful for, in which case you may choose to seek solutions that aren't based on standard modelling. There's nothing wrong with this, but for now let's stick to the standard.

A basic unit used in transport models is a **trip** or a **journey**. A trip and a journey are two words for the same thing. Many models estimate the number of trips that people make, and then they estimate how and where these trips are made. Anyone going anywhere in our area of interest is making a trip, although the definition of a trip can still vary between models. Some models only include specific types of trips, based on the agreed scope of the model, which I described in chapter 1. For example, some models don't include trips made at night; some models don't include trips shorter than a certain distance; and some will only include trips made by specific modes of transport.

If a person makes several trips, many models will store information about these trips but they will miss the fact that they were made by the same person. Only specific types of models, which we'll discuss later, associate each trip with a specific person. Usually the people who make the trips have no identity, no matter how upset this would make my auntie Tilda.

Different models vary from each other in how they represent trips that combine more than one mode of transport in the same trip. If a traveller drives to the station and takes a train from there, some models will show this as one complex trip with two **legs** (or two **stages**), while other models will store the same information as one car trip to the station and one train trip from the station. Similarly, models use different ways to deal with trips that combine a train and a bus: such trips can be modelled either as one public transport trip or as more than one.

Many models follow a convention by which a walking trip is always part of another trip. The walk from the car park to the office, or from home to a train station, don't count as separate trips, but this rule is applied only when it comes to walking. This might sound like an unfair representation of trips by foot; but wait till I discuss modelling walking trips in more detail later.

The way trips are broken down into legs (or stages) becomes critical if you need the model to provide separate information on each leg. For example, if it's important for you to have separate outputs for bus trips and train trips, then a model that combines bus and train legs into one trip might not help you.

All the trips made by all the travellers in the study area form the **travel demand** (or simply demand). Some models start with clear prior knowledge of what the travel demand is, whereas other models start without knowing the total demand, and then the demand is estimated as part of the modelling work.

There isn't a specific definition of trips and travel demand which is more correct than other definitions. If someone is developing a model for you, the important thing is to ensure you understand from the start what types of trips are in the scope of the model.

2.2 Networks

People who travel generate the travel demand, and you already know that when someone talks about "demand", soon enough they'll also talk about "supply".

The supply side in a transport model is represented by a **transport network**. Transport networks can contain streets, roads, junctions, bridges, tunnels, footpaths, cycling lanes, bus lanes, bus stops, train stations, tracks, platforms, escalators, people movers, boats, terminals, runways, and quite a few other things.

Some transport networks are shared by different modes of transport, while other networks can be used by one mode only. This complicates the definition of transport networks for modelling. For example:

- Bus lanes are for buses, but in some places they are also used by taxis and bikes.

- Many urban streets are shared by cars, taxis and vans. There's a whole range of rules in different places regarding whether or not streets can be used by bikes, trucks of different sizes, buses of different sizes, and so on.

- The network of railway tracks is normally used by trains only. But analysing the rail network alone isn't enough to understand the journey experience of railway users, because many of them travel by car, taxi, bus, bike or on foot to access the railway station, as part of the same trip.

Because of these complex overlaps between the networks, there isn't a specific way of defining a transport network which would make the modelling work easy. There are two main types of network used in a large number of transport models:

- **A road network**, also known as the "street network" or "highway network". Road networks are used for modelling the movement of private cars, vans, trucks, taxis and buses. A road network looks similar to a street map, showing the layout of streets, roads and intersections. Minor streets are often excluded since they are less important for understanding how traffic flows. The road network looks more simplified than a real street map, for example because some roads are shown for simplicity as a straight line even when in reality they aren't exactly straight. The basic unit of travel demand on a road network is one vehicle.

- **A route network**, also known as the "public transport network" or "transit network". Route networks show the itineraries of bus, train, tram and other public transport lines, including where the stops and stations are. Streets or roads where there is no public transport will often not be included, but tunnels for underground trains, for example, will be. What matters in route networks is not the road or tunnel itself but the route that passengers can take for their travel. The basic unit of travel demand on a route network is one passenger.

There are models with only a road network, and others with only a route network, and there are models that combine both. There's sometimes a need to pass information between road and route networks to keep them consistent with each other. For example, if changes are made in a street that is used by some bus routes, this will affect how the street is represented in the road network and also how the routes are represented in the route network.

Unlike the maps that people use for finding their way in the city, a network we use for modelling needs to meet some mathematical criteria. The network needs to be created so that a computer program can run vehicles and passengers through it in a logical way. This requires careful control on where exactly the streets and routes connect to each other. To allow this, networks are created using two kinds of shapes: links and nodes.

A **link** is simply a line that traffic or passengers can go through. A link often represents a road or a street; but cars or passengers cannot get into or out of a link in the middle. For this reason, a typical road would be represented in the model by a series of links and not just one. At every point where you can enter or exit a street, we end one link and start another. There will often be a junction, a bus stop or a station at the end of a link.

When a link is included in a network, we can attach various **attributes** to the link. Attributes contain useful information about the link. A typical link attribute would be the number of traffic lanes. If a road narrows down in the middle then we'll normally start a new link at the point where the number of lanes reduces, so that each link has a different number of lanes as an attribute.

Part of the
network in
the real
world. A
modelled
version is
on the
next
page.

Figure 7: coding links and nodes. Look at the real network against the modelled one (on the next page). The different nodes here represent different things. Nodes 1, 4, 6, 7 are junctions. Node 2 isn't modelled as a junction because the modeller decided not to include the small street above it, but it helps represent how the road bends. There's a bus stop at node 3. Node 5 was coded for possible future inclusion of the small streets under it.

Links are normally one-directional. A two-way street requires creating two parallel links, one in each direction. Models tend to use one-directional links so that we can have freedom to attach different attributes to each direction.

A **node** is a point where a link starts or where several links meet. Very often a node represents a junction or street intersection, although it can also represent the end of a cul-de-sac. Every link starts and ends with a node. When we use a series of links to represent one road, we need to ensure that each link starts at the same node where the adjacent link ends. If consecutive links don't meet at the same node, the model will not know that traffic or passengers can move from one to the other.

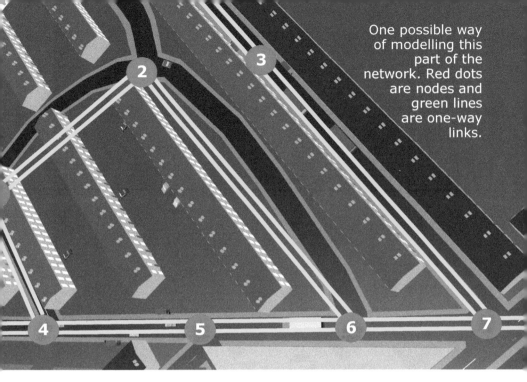

One possible way of modelling this part of the network. Red dots are nodes and green lines are one-way links.

A node where several links meet represents a junction. We usually want the model to know that some turns are not allowed in each junction. Road network models allow us to define permitted or prohibited turns.

The process of creating networks, links, attributes, nodes and turns is called **coding**. A lot of the work to develop a transport model is about laborious network coding.

2.3 Zones

Every model covers a geographical area which was agreed during the model scoping stage. When a model is developed, once it's clear what geographical area is covered, this area needs to be split into **traffic zones** (or simply zones). The zones need to cover the whole of the modelled area. The boundaries between the zones can be shown on a map.

In a typical model, each zone covers an area with a few dozens or a few hundreds of buildings. A short local street is likely to be entirely within one zone. A major street will probably cut through more than one zone. In city centres we normally use smaller

23

zones because buildings are denser. In rural areas, it's quite common to have entire communities, or even entire towns, coded within one zone.

Each zone must have one centre point, called **centroid**. The centroid doesn't have to be exactly at the centre of the zone, but it represents all travel demand to and from the zone. Centroids may look just like other nodes, since they are simply a point in a specific location, which some links are connected to. But centroids are a special kind of node because trips can start and end there, unlike a normal node, which trips just pass through. All trips in the model always start and end at a centroid somewhere.

The links that connect to the centroid are different from other links. We call them **centroid connectors**. Most links in the network represent streets or roads or railways in the real world, whereas centroid connectors are virtual links. They do represent part of the real-world network, but each connector can represent several streets.

We do this, for example, when there are many minor roads in a zone that contains a residential neighbourhood with little traffic. We often don't want to over-complicate our network with these minor roads, so we create centroid connectors that go from the centroid directly to some more important roads.

In route networks, around major rail or bus stations, it is common for the connectors to represent station exits or footpaths leading to the station. A centroid connector can represent any physical connection, be it a road, a footpath, a corridor, a lift, and so on. It simply ensures that demand in the model can travel from the centroid to the rest of the network (and vice versa).

Because centroid connectors are a simplified version of the real network, the model can be quite sensitive to the way they are coded. The fact that all passengers to a station or all traffic to a neighbourhood go through these connectors can make the model identify problems that don't exist, or ignore problems that do exist. So why do we use this concept of zones and centroids? there are three different reasons:

1. **Lack of data**. Ideally we would want every trip in the model to start at the specific address that people in the real world come from. We would want the trip in the model to end at the specific place that people really go to. But our data sources are limited, and we don't know where exactly every trip starts and ends. Even if we did a massive survey and asked all the people about all their trips, this information would only be valid for the time of the survey. The models we build also describe what the network might be like in ten or twenty years' time, when there is no way we can envisage the exact locations people will travel to and from. So by indicating the zone only, we acknowledge our limited knowledge.

2. **Computational complexity**. A model with more spatial detail, where specific locations are coded more accurately, takes longer to run because there are many more calculations to make. I'll explain later how this works.

Figure 8: zones. The first image (on the previous page) shows an urban area. The second image shows a way of splitting it into zones. The third one shows the zone centroids, which are like giant towers that all the trips go to and from. The yellow links are centroid connectors. This is how trips are actually modelled.

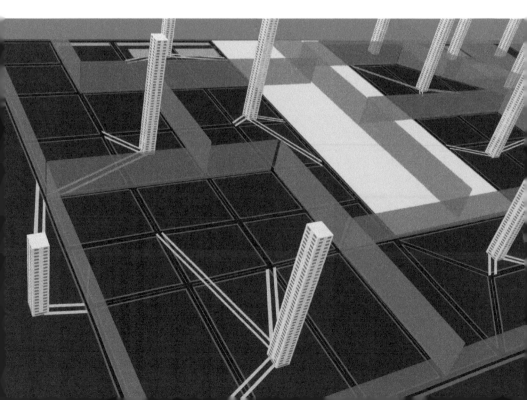

3. **Coding effort**. There are millions of homes, buildings and sites that people travel to or from. Even if we knew the details of all the trips accurately, we would have to create networks that allow trips to start or end at every house. Because of the simple way we define links and nodes, this would mean that a street with a few dozens of buildings will need to be coded as a few dozens of links. Any suspected problem with the demand will require a very laborious search for the location of the error. There will also be a higher chance that some errors are not found until the model has already been used. So by using zones instead of addresses we avoid an amount of work that we cannot resource.

So in the transport modelling language, when we talk about the **origin** and **destination** of a trip, these origin and destination are both numbers that represent zones. The model typically identifies every trip as something like "from zone 154 to zone 32". The way the model will process the trip is by assuming that it starts at the point where we located the centroid of zone 154 and ends at the point where we located the centroid of zone 32.

It's important to note that this means the model cannot analyse accurately what happens inside each zone, since it doesn't know the exact origin and destination. It also means that models may ignore **internal trips**, i.e. those where both the origin and the destination are within the same zone. When I walk to the corner shop to buy chocolate (at least twice a day), or when you drive the kid to school which is very close to home, it might be that we don't leave the zone where the trip started. Such trips are coded in the model as a trip from one point to itself. When the model checks how we might be travelling from our origin, it finds out that we already are at the destination, so it might not count the trip as part of the overall traffic in the area.

There are also some trips in the study area that travel very far, and for this reason we always include in the model a few zones to represent very remote areas. We call them **external zones**, and we model them without much detail, simply so that trips coming from (or going to) areas outside the study area can still have an origin and a destination. We don't want to lose these trips because part of the trip uses the network within the study area and mixes with local traffic.

When you develop a model, you have a lot of flexibility to decide how detailed the zones would be. You also have flexibility in deciding where the boundaries between the zones would lie. All the zones in the model, the boundaries between them and the centroid locations are part of what we call **the zoning system**. The same area can be modelled using a denser zoning system, where each zone includes a small number of buildings, or a sparser zoning system, where each zone covers a larger area. You can also make zones smaller and more detailed in specific areas only, if you have more interest in detailed analysis of these zones.

Figure 9 shows a few things we consider when deciding how many zones we need and where the border between them should be. Figure 10 summarises the key implications of your choice of zone size.

In the UK, many cities have a transport model for the city and the region that surrounds it, with the number of zones covering the area ranging between 500 and 1000. The Greater London area has a collection of models which jointly have a zoning system with about 5000 zones. Cases where such a high number of zones is needed are rare. I'll explain some other issues related to zone size later in this book.

Figure 9: considerations when designing a zoning system

	**Not too small.** We don't want a zone to cover an area that very few trips go to, because it isn't worth the additional effort and higher model runtime that come with adding more zones.
	**Not too large.** If one zone generates very high travel demand (e.g. thousands of trips during one hour) then we should probably invest in a bit more detail in the area by splitting the zone further. This way, we can later analyse travel demand in this area in sufficient detail.
	**Typical land use.** It's better if we don't mix different types of land use in one zone. This isn't always possible, because sometimes there are offices, homes and shops in the same place. But whenever possible, we should create zones so that each one has a dominant type of land use (residential, commercial, business and so on). This will allow us to do separate analysis for each type of land use.
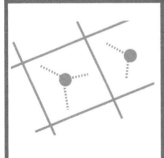	**Centroid connector capacity.** All the trips to a zone will use the link that connects the local network to the centroid. The model won't know this link doesn't really exist. So if the number of trips going to this zone is too high, the model might indicate there are congestion problems in the area even when this isn't really the case.

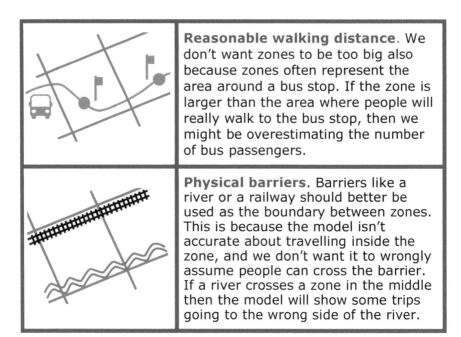

	Reasonable walking distance. We don't want zones to be too big also because zones often represent the area around a bus stop. If the zone is larger than the area where people will really walk to the bus stop, then we might be overestimating the number of bus passengers.
	Physical barriers. Barriers like a river or a railway should better be used as the boundary between zones. This is because the model isn't accurate about travelling inside the zone, and we don't want it to wrongly assume people can cross the barrier. If a river crosses a zone in the middle then the model will show some trips going to the wrong side of the river.

Figure 10: advantages of smaller or larger zones

Models with more zones (so zones are smaller)	Models with fewer zones (so zones are larger)
We can get more detail from the outputs	Shorter model runtime

Models with more zones (so zones are smaller)	Models with fewer zones (so zones are larger)
Easier to ensure that each zone has uniform land use 	There's less sensitivity to network coding detail 
Easier to ensure that zones don't straddle rivers, major roads or railways 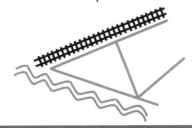	The amount of input data we have on the demand in each zone is larger, so it is more statistically robust 
Easier to produce model outputs for individual bus stops 	
Fewer problems with trips from a zone to itself 	

this space
was left empty
in order to
have enough
room for this
odd statement.

31

2.4 **Matrices**

Information about travel demand is stored in a **demand matrix** (or **trip matrix**). A matrix is a table where the rows and the columns represent the zones in your model. Each row represents one origin zone and each column represents one destination zone. Each cell in the demand matrix contains the number of trips from a specific origin to a specific destination, i.e. one **OD pair**.

Each zone can be the origin of some trips and the destination of some others. So if your model has 500 zones covering the whole study area, then the demand matrix will have 500 rows and 500 columns. If 10 trips are made from zone 65 to zone 312 then the number 10 will be stored in the **cell** located in row 65 and column 312.

A matrix with 500 rows and 500 columns has 250,000 cells. So every single calculation the model does with the matrix requires 250,000 calculations. Most models will need to perform hundreds of calculations with many different matrices, which means millions of calculations in total. This has an impact on the time it takes to run the model. If you want a more detailed model, and you double the number of zones to 1000, then each matrix will have 1,000,000 cells which is four times the original size.

So the number of zones has a critical impact on the number of calculations the model needs to make. Each zone you add will increase the computational runtime. Note that in terms of model runtime, it doesn't matter what area each zone covers, and it's also not very critical if you add links or nodes. It's the number of zones that has a significant direct impact on the computing power needed.

The majority of travellers start and finish their day at home. So no matter where they live, they will have some trips from the zone where their home is (stored in the relevant row) and some trips to this zone (stored in the relevant column). For this reason, if your demand matrix shows all the trips in a typical day, it will be quite a symmetrical matrix: the numbers is row x will be quite similar to the numbers in column x. The symmetry of the daily demand matrix isn't perfect, though:

- Not everyone returns home in the evening (e.g. if you just started a holiday today, or alternatively, if last sentence you heard in the morning was "I don't want to ever see you again").

- Not everyone starts at home in the morning (e.g. if you worked away and stayed in a hotel, or if the police found you drunk last night and you spent the night at the station).

- Some people go to other places on the way to or from home (e.g. to buy flowers for auntie Tilda, or if you're the person from the previous examples, to get legal advice).

Usually we don't put all trips over a whole day in one matrix. It is common to have separate demand matrices for each time period during the day. Much of the transport analysis is done for the time with peak traffic in the morning; the trips made during this time are stored in the morning peak demand matrix. The morning peak demand isn't symmetrical at all. It shows a clear direction of the demand from the zones where people live to the zones where people work.

When doing modelling work, some of the effort is spent developing demand matrices from other inputs. This means starting with an empty matrix, or with a matrix that we are less confident in, and gradually filling it with numbers that more confidently represent travel demand in the study area. A different kind of effort is needed if we use matrices which have already been developed. We'll return to this later.

A valuable exercise, in projects you're involved in, is to look at the demand matrices, check what they say, and think whether this matches what you know. An example of how to read a demand matrix is shown in figure 11. The matrix shows travel demand during the morning peak hour.

The format of a matrix is used for storing information about the number of trips, but it is also used for other types of information. The other common use of matrices is to store travel times calculated by a model. The rows and columns still represent the zones. In a travel time matrix, cell (45, 211) contains the travel time from zone 45 to zone 211, as calculated by the model.

Figure 11: reading a demand matrix

There are trips from zones 2 and 3 to most zones, but not many to zones 2 and 3. Since this is morning peak demand, these must be residential neighbourhoods.

Zones 4, 5 and 6 are probably a central business area. They generate very little demand (except between each other) but they are the destination of many trips from all zones.

Zone	1	2	3	4	5	6	7	8	9	10	Total
1	4	0	2	19	23	33	12	9	2	13	117
2	17	2	21	32	26	47	28	34	0	32	239
3	18	20	6	46	61	35	28	25	1	21	261
4	0	0	5	75	24	29	0	0	3	0	136
5	1	1	4	18	12	13	3	4	5	1	62
6	4	9	11	13	31	22	2	4	5	6	107
7	9	4	4	43	21	32	3	8	6	11	141
8	10	3	6	14	29	47	7	1	8	14	139
9	0	0	0	3	2	9	0	1	1	0	16
10	8	2	3	11	31	29	12	13	1	0	110
Total	71	41	62	274	260	296	95	99	32	98	1328

In each zone there is a low number of internal trips (e.g. from zone 1 to zone 1). Why is this number high in zone 4? It could be a mistake, or indicate poor design of the zones. We saw that the model might ignore these trips, so it's worth checking if boundaries can be redefined so that most trips leave their origin zone.

There is not much demand in zone 9. It might be an external zone, which isn't critical for the analysis but helps keep the total demand at the right level.

2.5 Scenarios

Transport models are often used to analyse various investment scenarios. If we consider widening a road or building a new station, there are some typical scenarios we will want to look at using our model. There are described in figure 12.

Figure 12: typical scenarios to look at

"Do nothing". This is how the transport system will be without any intervention, just as it already is when we do the analysis. It is likely to see conditions worsen over time.	
"Do minimum". This is how the transport system will be if we don't make the investment we're considering, but we do make other investments, for example those that are needed to avoid the situation getting very bad.	
"Do something". This is how the transport system will be if we make the investment we're considering.	

Using the model to only look at the scenario with the new project added ("do something") isn't enough, because some of the impacts may happen also without it. Using the model to compare "do something" to "do nothing" isn't enough either, because we rarely do absolutely nothing. Other changes and improvements happen in parallel, either because they happen naturally, or because they were agreed independently of the change we're now considering. So in most cases we need to compare "do something" to "do minimum" to understand what value the new investment would add on top of things that happen anyway.

We normally have more than one "do something" scenario, and we create different versions of our model for each. The reasons for this and the ways we do it are shown in figure 13. If the fruity metaphor in the drawings isn't clear, it reminds that some scenarios differ from each other in the main subject we model, like comparing an apple to an orange; but different scenarios are also built around the same subject, in order to see how it performs in different conditions or under different assumptions.

In addition to all these, we always define scenarios that cover different points in time. First, we should have a model for the **base year scenario**, which represents a relatively recent year for which we have enough data. The base year has the "do nothing" network and demand matrices that represent the current (or recent) patterns of travel in the study area.

Figure 13: different "do something" scenarios

Comparing alternatives. We want to select the best possible solution to the needs of our transport system. Each alternative solution forms one scenario. **Example**: if we want to build a bridge over a river, several scenarios could look at different locations, and there can also be a scenario where we build a tunnel instead.

Factors beyond our own control. Different scenarios can vary from each other in the impact of decisions which are made by other people or organisations. **Example**: imagine you test the possible expansion of an airport terminal, while a different authority considers introducing a new tax on air travel. You don't know whether and when the tax will be introduced, but it would have an impact on the number of air passengers, and this would influence the need for terminal expansion. You should define some scenarios with different assumptions about this tax.

Factors beyond anybody's control. Different scenarios can vary in the impact of factors which are uncertain. **Example**: say we test the opening of a new station in a new residential area where 3,000 new houses are planned. At the time when the decision is needed, there is uncertainty about trends in the property market; there's a risk that not all 3,000 houses are built in the end. Testing several scenarios can help us prepare for the possible cases.

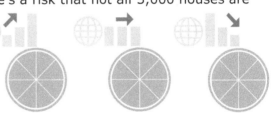

Sensitivity testing. Different tests should be defined because all models use inaccurate assumptions. We check how sensitive model outputs are to alternative assumptions. **Example**: your team makes the case for a new toll road. The estimated demand depends on a parameter that captures the proportion of drivers willing to pay the proposed price. You have limited data on the prices drivers will actually be willing to pay, so you define several tests to see how sensitive your case is to changes in this parameter.

Then we also define one or several future years, which are far enough in the future to represent a situation where our project has been successfully completed. We create future scenarios both with and without the investment; that is, both "do minimum" and "do something".

Future scenarios use networks and demand matrices which reflect how we think the transport system and the users will be at that future time. The future "do minimum" is often called the **reference case**; the benefits from the investment depend on the difference between the reference case and other future scenarios.

Agreeing on the demand and network assumptions when we define the future "do minimum" and "do something" scenarios usually requires a considerable amount of stakeholder engagement. This is because nobody knows by fact what things will be like in the far future if the investment is or isn't made. The model will help us look at the impacts of all the scenarios once we have defined them; but sadly, no model can help us define the scenarios.

2.6 **Costs**

The meaning of the word "cost" in a transport model is not the same as in the real world. Confusingly, it's not even the same as the meaning of "cost" in other parts of a project appraisal. When modellers talk about costs, it is usually an informal way of using the term **generalised costs**.

If you travel somewhere and there are different options of how you can get there, or if you might experience different travel conditions on this trip, then in each one of these the model will have a different generalised cost for the trip. The generalised cost is a number that summarises everything there is to know about each possible travel experience.

The generalised cost can include many different things about the journey quality, which influence our travel choices. Typical things which are often included in the generalised cost are shown in figure 14. You can see that part of the cost really is cost, i.e.

money we spend, but there are other things included in the generalised cost as well.

Generalised costs are defined so that the model can use them to estimate how many travellers will choose each available option, when they have a choice. So the generalised cost needs to reflect the behaviours and preferences of those travellers. Behaviours and preferences are tricky to measure. When we want to include in the generalised cost things which are hard to measure, we usually do it using **penalties** and **weights**.

Adding a **penalty** to the cost means that we make the cost higher to reflect that there's something about the journey that travellers don't like. Using a **weight** means that we take something that already is in the generalised cost and we make it a larger number, to reflect how badly travellers don't like it. Here are some common types of penalties and weights:

- **Boarding penalty**. Most public transport users prefer a route that takes them directly to their destination without having to change, but there are also travel options which aren't direct. Options that involve changing are less attractive, and we reflect this by adding a penalty to the cost each time the passenger boards a different service. The boarding penalty can be, for example, equivalent to two extra minutes of travel.

- **Waiting time weight**. Most people are more anxious when they wait for a bus in the street than when they already are on the bus. Every minute spent waiting is perceived more negatively than a minute on board, and we reflect this by using a weight of around 2, to show that the waiting time is perceived as double the actual time. Various other values between 1 and 3 are used as well in different models; the weight is usually higher if passengers have to wait in more unpleasant conditions.

- **Walking time weight**. People also generally don't like walking a long distance to a stop or a station. So every minute spent on the way to or from the stop, or walking between stops when transferring between routes, is often given a weight higher than 1, which means it adds to the generalised cost more than its actual duration in minutes.

Figure 14: components of the generalised cost. The travel time itself, by whichever mode. The walking time to/from a bus stop or train station. The time and effort to change routes. The time and pain of waiting. Time and nerves spent searching for parking. Parking fee. Fuel cost. Car maintenance cost. Tolls.

Figure 14 (continued): components of the generalised cost. Ticket cost. The pain of on-board crowding and noise. The pain of services not arriving on time. Concerns about road safety and personal security. Having an uncomfortable seat. Trudging uphill or upstairs. Having a nice view. Enjoying a walk or a ride.

- **Crowding penalty**. Most people don't like crowded travel conditions on public transport. We often add a penalty which gets higher the more crowded the train or bus is.

- **Uphill and upstairs weight**. Cycling uphill, walking upstairs inside a station, and other physically-demanding parts of the trip get a weight of up to 4 in some models.

- **Unreliability factor**. A reliable journey is one that takes the same time every day, and does not depend on unpredictable factors. Everyone prefers reliable journeys. Some travel options tend to be more reliable (for example, travelling on roads with only light traffic). Others can be unreliable (for example, using a train route which often breaks down). Measuring the level of reliability is analytically complex, so we sometimes add a simpler penalty to the generalised cost of travel by routes or roads with known reliability problems.

- **Safety and security factors**. There are places that some travellers would avoid because they feel unsafe. For example, there are specific junctions which cyclists perceive as dangerous so they prefer cycling routes that avoid those junctions. The model won't know of these perceptions unless we adjust the generalised costs, so we add some local penalties in those specific places, to represent the actual preferences in the model.

- **Ambience factor**. Some models go further and add either penalties or weights to reflect how pleasant or unpleasant the journey environment is. Such factor can also be negative: for example, some cyclists like the time spent cycling through a green park, so the model can add a negative penalty (which reduces the generalised cost) or a weight smaller than 1 (which means that the perceived cycling time counts as less than the real duration) to capture this preference.

Generalised costs can be measured in various units, but it is very common to measure them in minutes. We use different techniques to convert all the items in figure 14 to minutes, and then we add them up to get the generalised cost in minutes. The reason why minutes are a preferred unit is that they don't change their meaning over time, unlike currency units, which need various additional conversions if they are used in different years.

Adding up all the different elements of the generalised cost, so that we have one cost per travel option, is done using the **generalised cost function**. This function simply calculates the total of all these elements, including money-related elements, time-related elements, the weights attached to some of them, as well as the different penalties. Many simple models use a generalised cost function that only includes some of the time-related and money-related items I listed. More complex models may include most of the generalised cost components from figure 14.

Travel behaviour can be difficult to understand, since different people have different preferences, and they can be influenced by a whole range of factors. The generalised costs we calculate therefore represent average, typical travel behaviour, but there are many behaviours we don't capture accurately. For this reason, most models don't simply assume that people choose the option with the lowest generalised cost. They assume that an option with a lower cost will attract more people, but there will still be people choosing the other options too.

Some people refer to the generalised cost as "generalised time" or "utility". Although there are some differences in the definition, for our purposes you can consider all of them to mean the same thing.

2.7 Demand segmentation

To estimate what the transport system might be like in future scenarios, transport models need to estimate how travellers will behave. We don't consider the individual behaviour of every traveller, because this would be too complex. But it would be too simplistic to assume that there's just one average kind of behaviour which describes everyone.

Many models address this conflict through a compromise: to keep travel behaviour realistic, we do consider how behaviour varies between different types of trips, but to avoid complexity, we keep the number of different types relatively small.

This is called **demand segmentation**. Each type of trip in the model, which reflects some typical travel behaviour, is one demand segment. All segments use the same transport network: travellers from different segments drive their cars on the same road and sit next to each other on the train. But we store information on these trips in separate demand matrices. We also consider their different behaviours by having different generalised cost functions for different segments.

Introducing more segmentation in the model means splitting the travellers into more separate groups. Having more segments has upsides and downsides, as I show in figure 15.

If you create a new model, you are free to define the segmentation in any way that reflects the different behaviours that exist in your study area. For example, if you have evidence that people that own a dog have different travel preferences, you can split the demand into "dog owners" and "non-dog-owners". As a cat lover, my auntie Tilda would tell you that such segmentation doesn't sound promising. But there are other types of segmentation which are essential in almost every model. Figure 16 describes these most important segments.

It's worth remembering that we segment the trips rather than the travellers. Your income will not change between the different trips you make, but your car availability could vary during the day if you share a car with another household member, and your journey purpose will clearly change between different trips. Many transport models don't store information on whether different trips are made by the same person (although I'll mention some exceptions later).

Ideally, when you start modelling, the demand should be segmented like in figure 16 already. There are other types of essential segmentation which the model can start without, because they are created by the model itself. The main example for this is segmentation by mode of transport. To looks at traffic congestion, for example, we have to know which trips are made by car, but segmenting by mode is one of the tasks that can be performed by the model itself.

Figure 15: how much segmentation

Reasons to have more segments	Reasons to have fewer segments

Realism of outputs. Model outputs will be more credible if we considered the range of behaviours across different travellers. A person that goes to a work meeting will behave differently from a tourist, even if they travel to the same place at the same time.	**Base year data**. We need to know how many trips are made by travellers from each demand segment. This isn't easy: counting the number of cars on the road or people on the bus doesn't tell us which segment each one of them belongs to. We'll need special types of data collection.
Realism of appraisal. We use model outputs to calculate the economic benefits from transport improvements. Significant benefits can come from reducing travel times. The theory says that time saved by a businessperson is worth more than time saved by a person travelling for leisure, even if both are in fact the same person. Identifying these different trips as belonging to different segments helps us attach the right appraisal value to each trip.	**Future year data**. Even if we have good information on the number of trips in each segment, based on recent data, knowing how this will change in the future is a different challenge. The effort of adding segments won't help much if there's little evidence behind our future segmentation.

Model runtime. The trips made by people from different segments are stored in different demand matrices. Each additional matrix means that the model needs to perform millions of additional calculations. So the more demand segments, the longer the model runtime. |

Figure 16: essential segmentation

Car availability. There's a difference in travel behaviour between people that have a car available to them and people who don't. Obviously, people that don't have access to a car can't use a car. In some models, the segmentation is based on car ownership instead of car availability. People with an available car include those who own one but also those who sometimes hire a car or use somebody else's car.

Income. There's evidence that people with higher levels of income make different travel choices from those with lower income. For example, people with a higher income are more likely to use a toll road and less likely to travel by bus.

Trip purpose. People travel for a whole range of purposes: they go to work, to social meetings, to the shops, to visit family and so on. Sometimes the purpose of the journey doesn't influence how we travel. But there are two specific journey purposes that make people's travel behaviour distinct. One of these is **commuting**: people who make a similar journey to work on most days know their way very well, often travel during the rush time, and their lifestyle has a major impact on their way of commuting. Another purpose that strongly affects behaviour is travel on **business**: trips made during the traveller's work time are different because the travel decisions also reflect the preferences of the employer. Therefore, many models segment demand by three purpose only: commuting trips, business trips, and all other trips. But some models do still contain additional purposes like "leisure" and "shopping".

2.8 The value of time

The idea behind the value of time is that there's an amount of money that people are willing to pay to reduce their journey time by one minute. They'd pay half of this value to save half a minute and double this value to save two minutes. A higher value of time indicates a higher willingness to pay for reducing travel times.

We define different values of time for different demand segments. People that go to a meeting during their work time normally have the highest value of time, because they travel at their employer's expense and also because being late is less acceptable. People travelling for leisure purposes would normally not be too sensitive to changes in the travel time. The value of time will be higher for people with a higher income.

If for one of the demand segments in our model the value of time is £0.20 per minute, it means that for trips that belong to that segment, reducing travel times by 10 minutes has the same impact on travel choices as a saving of £2. The value of time could be expressed in any currency.

Before we calculate generalised costs, we take everything that has a price (fuel price, public transport fares, road tolls, parking fees) and divide it by the value of time. This converts all the prices to minutes. This way we can add together all the prices, the travel time, and other things which are also expressed in minutes (as we saw in figure 14), to have one total generalised cost. We calculate the cost this way for each origin-destination pair for each demand segment in each scenario.

When modelling work is complete, we take the final generalised costs (in minutes) and multiply them by the value of time. This gives us the model outputs in units of money again, which are more suitable for economic analysis. Doing the modelling work in time units, and converting to money later, saves us the need to complicate the model with monetary issues like inflation.

The concept of having a value of time is simplistic in many ways, as shown in figure 17. Nobody thinks that people really make their decisions based on something like a value of time, but do I have a practical method that works better than this? No, I don't. The value of time is just a simplification which makes our lives easier. It's for you to decide whether such simplification is justified in the context of your own work.

Figure 17: what's wrong with the value of time

Gain and loss. We use the same value of time for a minute saved or a minute lost. In reality people's dissatisfaction when they waste time tends to be greater than their satisfaction when they save the same amount of time.

Data reliability. No data source is very reliable when trying to estimate people's value of time, for reasons I'll explain later.

Uniform behaviour. The idea of the value of time assumes many different people make the same tradeoffs between time and money. This clearly isn't true. There are methods to reflect the variation of preferences between people, but they require much more data and modelling work.

Payment method. The value of time concept assumes that people's willingness to pay doesn't depend on how they pay (cash, card, subscription, text message, PayPal). In reality it does.

Size of the change. When using a value of time, the value per minute is the same if a project saves one minute or if it saves an hour. There's evidence that people actually dismiss small changes and attach a higher value to each minute if the overall change is big.

Chapter 3
The four-stage concept

3.1 The hierarchy in a transport model

An important concept in transport modelling is that different parts of a model form a **hierarchy**. The hierarchy is presented in a vertical way: we sometimes say that one part of the model is at the top or at the bottom of the hierarchy. Modellers can talk about whether one part is above or below another. We sometimes decide to move part of the model to a different position, higher or lower, in the hierarchy.

When you use a transport model to examine the impacts of a change in the transport system, you start at the top of the hierarchy. At this point you still don't know anything about the impact of the change. Each stage of the hierarchy adds more detail about the impacts of the change, and by the time you get to the bottom of the hierarchy, you have the most detailed estimate that this model can give you about the impact of the change.

Just because you've reached the bottom of the hierarchy, it doesn't necessarily mean that you're done. Some of the things you estimated while going down the hierarchy were based on some rough guesses. So once you're at the bottom, you may need to go up again and refine what you guessed earlier. To refine it you can use the additional detail that you now have because you've run down the full hierarchy. Applying a hierarchical model is therefore an **iterative** process, or in other words, it's a process that runs through the hierarchy several times in a loop.

This may sound very theoretical until we introduce the four-stage concept, so here it is. The most common structure of a full transport model includes a hierarchy with four stages. A common way to define the four stages is illustrated in figure 18. The names of the four stages are part of the essential terminology of transport modelling.

Figure 18: a four-stage model hierarchy

Trip generation. This is the stage of the modelling process where we estimate the total number of trips to and from each zone in the study area. We do this separately for each demand segment (i.e. trip purpose, car availability etc.).

Mode split. This is the stage where we estimate how the trips from the generation stage divide between the different modes of transport.

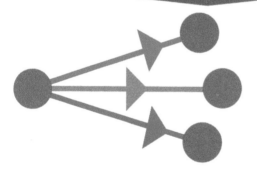

Trip distribution. At this stage we become more spatially detailed, and associate each trip to an origin and a destination. We ensure that trips from each origin are linked to destinations at a realistic distance.

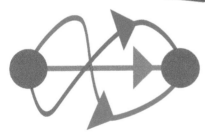

Trip assignment. Here we introduce the network and estimate the routes travellers choose from their origins to their destinations. This can give us estimates of levels of traffic on different roads and crowding on public transport routes. We say that we "assign the matrix to the network".

An important aspect of the four-stage concept is that in each stage, people make a choice. The mathematical techniques we use for these models come from the field of choice modelling. Figure 19 explains what people choose at each stage.

Some people also refer to the four-stage concept as **variable demand modelling**. This name hints that if you make changes to the road network or the public transport route network, four-stage models will show that this can lead to people changing their travel behaviour. But note that the words "variable demand" might confuse, because many four-stage models keep the total demand fixed. They allow people to change where they go to or what mode of transport they use, but they do not change the total number of trips. Some four-stage models do allow the total demand to change as well; this depends on the detail of the trip generation stage, as we'll see later. "Variable demand" therefore means that the model allows the demand to change by shifting people between the travel options that were included in the model.

Some people use the term **demand model** to refer to all the steps in the four-stage model except the assignment. This terminology implies that the assignment model deals with the supply, i.e. the transport network, whereas all other stages deal with the demand, i.e. the number of trips. This description is quite inaccurate because all stages deal with both the supply and the demand. The assignment model checks whether the network has the capacity to deal with all the demand. The generalised cost of different travel options is used in all stages of a four-stage model to describe the supply of alternative roads or transport services.

Note also that we sometimes call the whole hierarchy "a model", while sometimes we refer to each stage of the hierarchy as "a model". There aren't clear rules for what counts as a separate model and what doesn't.

Figure 19: the choices people make in each stage

Stage	What people choose
Trip generation 	Whether to travel at all. How often to travel. Where to live. Where to work. Where to shop. Where to go to school. Where to do anything, really.
Mode split 	Which mode of transport to use.
Trip distribution 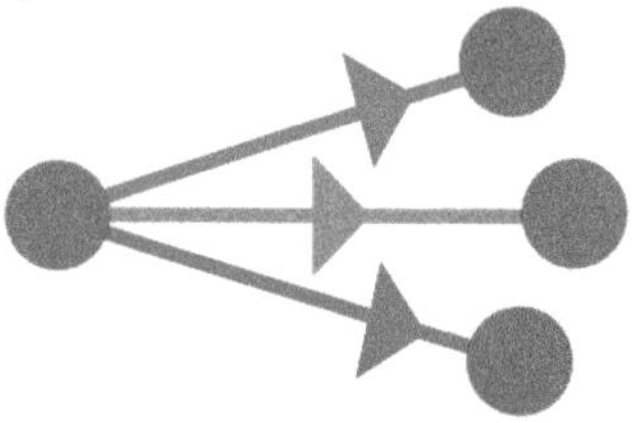	Origin and destination. The demand to and from each zone actually comes from the trip generation stage, but here we look at which trips from each zone go to every other zone.
Trip assignment 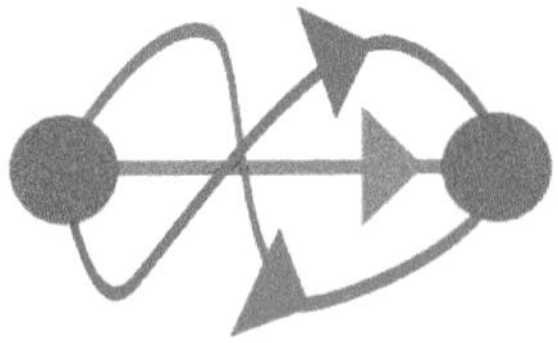	Which route to take on the road network or the route network, depending on the mode that was chosen earlier.

3.2 A matrix view of a four-stage model

The four-stage modelling process can be visualised using demand matrices. We start the process with empty demand matrices. We only know their size, since the number of rows and columns matches the number of zones we created.

At the trip generation stage, we estimate the total number of trips from each origin and the total to each destination. This gives us the total of each row and each column, but the matrix itself is still empty. We do this separately for each demand segment.

Figure 20 shows an example of where we might be at the end of the trip generation stage. Note that in this specific model, we have 12 demand segments. This is because we have:

■ Three journey purposes (commuting, business and leisure)

■ Two levels of income (high and low)

■ Two levels of car availability (with or without a car).

Each segment covers a different combination of these three segmentation criteria, and there are 12 combinations in total.

The "total" row and the "total" column in each matrix are shown in a different colour, indicating that all we know now is the number of trips from each origin and the number of trips to each destination, while all the detail in each matrix isn't there yet.

At the mode split stage, each matrix from the previous stage is further split into several matrices, one for each mode. Since mode choice in our hierarchy is above distribution in the model hierarchy, the matrices are still all empty, and we only have the row and column totals.

Figure 21 shows an example of where we might be at the end of the mode split stage. In this specific model we have three modes: car, public transport and walking. To keep things simple, I only show here the matrices for the commuting segments, but all the matrices for the other journey purposes go through a similar split.

Figure 20: an example of trip generation output matrices.
White cells are empty.

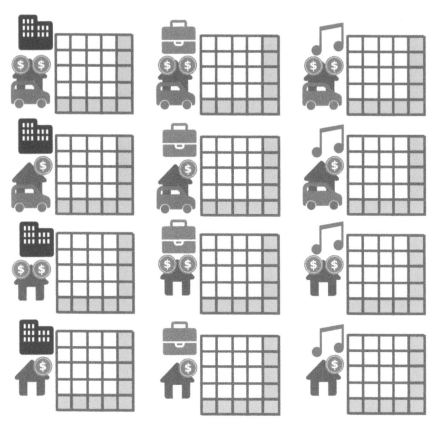

In figure 21 you may notice that this model allows people that don't have a car to travel by car. It could be, for example, that they travel as passengers with somebody that has a car. Other models may treat car passengers as a separate travel mode, and then people that have no car available can choose the "car passenger" mode but not the "car driver" mode.

At the distribution stage we fill each matrix with numbers. The number in each cell is the number of trips from one origin to one destination. We determine the numbers so that they reflect logical travel behaviour while still adding up to the row totals and column totals that we already have from earlier stages.

Figure 21: an example of mode split output matrices. White cells are empty.

Figure 22: an example of trip distribution output matrices

Figure 22 shows just a few of our many matrices, to illustrate that after the distribution stage they are full of trips from everywhere to everywhere.

So when we finally get to assign the trips to the network, we already have a set of full matrices. All the matrices for road users are assigned together since they jointly share the road network. Similarly, all the matrices for public transport users are assigned together since they share the public transport route network. If there's a cycling network model then there can be a cycling assignment, too.

Figure 23 illustrates this for the public transport assignment only. Public transport matrices from all segments are added up before the trips are assigned. A similar thing happens with other modes.

3.3 A tree view of a four-stage model

The same model can also be described as a tree diagram, i.e. showing how the different options travellers choose branch from each other. We will normally have a different tree for each demand segment. As an example, figure 24 shows a mode, destination and route choice diagram for the travellers of a single demand segment, travelling from a specific origin. The total number of these travellers has already been estimated at the trip generation stage, and the diagram shows the remaining choices.

A tree diagram, like the one in figure 24, helps realising the logic of the model hierarchy. The mode you choose determines which destinations you can go to, and your destination determines which routes you can take. Every choice depends on all the choices above it and influences all the choices below it.

In whichever project you work on, it's good practice to create such figures and discuss them in the team. You will often find that something you thought the model was doing is not done, or that the model does things you don't need. So it's an important way of setting the expectations at the right level and ensuring that the model is fit for purpose. Using silly graphics like mine isn't essential but I would strongly recommend it!

Figure 23: an example of assignment inputs

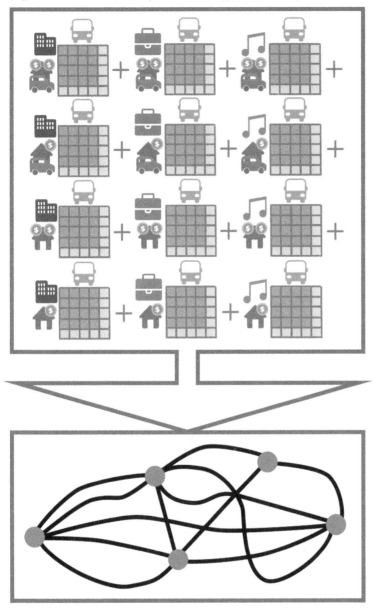

Figure 24: transport model hierarchy presented as a tree

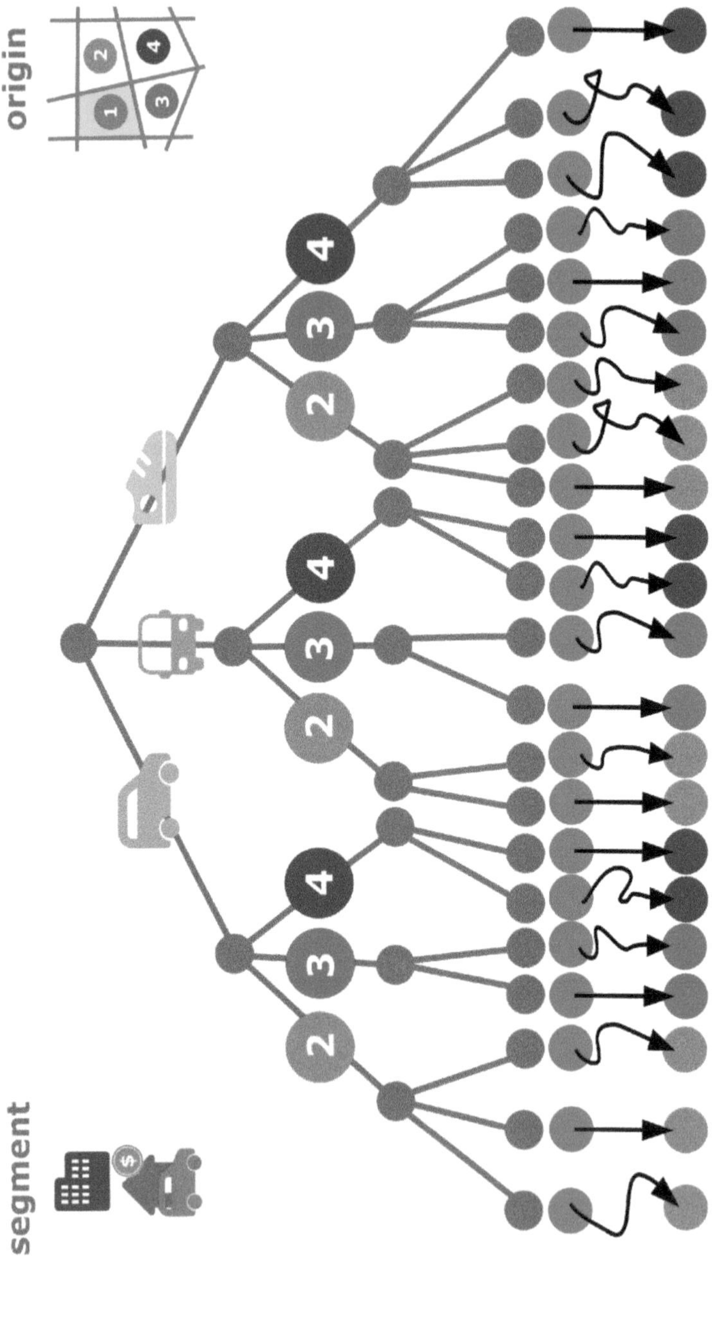
origin
segment

3.4 The composite cost

I introduced the term "generalised cost" in chapter 2. Generalised costs contain a summary of different factors that may affect people's choice between different travel options. For example, in the assignment of car trips to the road network, the route choices will be based on the generalised costs of alternative driving routes, and these costs will include travel times and other things. The model will assign more trips to routes with lower generalised costs.

In a hierarchical transport model, many option further split into sub-options, as we saw in figure 24. One option at one stage divides into several options at the stage below. In figure 24, if you choose the option of travelling by public transport to zone 4, you have two routes to choose from. If you choose the option of walking to zone 2, you have three routes to choose from. How does this affect the choice between zones 2, 3 and 4? And how does this affect the decision whether to use public transport, to drive or to walk in the first place?

The **composite cost** of one option is the generalised cost of this option, calculated based on the different sub-options that branch from it. It's called "composite" because it combines several costs into one. In figure 24 you can see that:

- The costs of the two routes going by public transport to zone 4 (calculated in the assignment) will go into the composite cost of going by public transport to zone 4. This will be used at the distribution stage to estimate how many people to go zone 4.

- In a similar way we can calculate the composite cost of going by public transport to each zone. This will be based on the costs (calculated at the assignment stage) of all the available public transport routes going to that zone.

- Once we have composite costs for all the destinations you can go to by public transport, we can calculate the composite cost of choosing public transport in the first place. You can look at it as a "composite composite cost" because first we combine the different public transport routes to each destination and then we combine the different destinations you can get to by public transport.

- In a similar way we can calculate the composite cost of using each mode. This will be used at the mode split stage to calculate how many people choose public transport, driving or walking.

The composite costs help us glue together the different parts of the model hierarchy. The costs calculated at any stage of the hierarchy are used to create composite costs one level above it. These costs are used to estimate how trips split between the different options at that level. This estimated number of trips goes to the level below, and the process of going down the branches continues in a similar way.

The calculation of composite **costs** starts at the **bottom** of the hierarchy, and then it keeps going **up**, one stage at a time.

The calculation of travel **demand**, i.e. the number of trips, starts at the **top** of the hierarchy, and then it keeps going **down**, one stage at a time.

Figure 25: up and down the model hierarchy

Composite costs, calculated from the costs of competing alternatives, go **up** the hierarchy

Trips are split between competing alternatives based on their composite costs and then go **down** the hierarchy

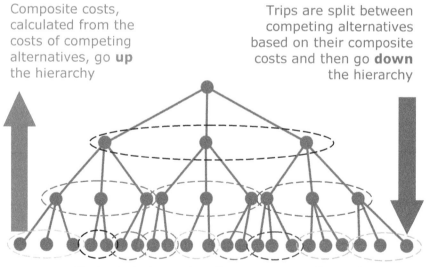

Each circled area has its own composite cost

3.5 Model hierarchy and travel behaviour

What does it mean that we model trip generation first, then mode split, then distribution and then assignment? The order of the stages has quite a tricky meaning. The simple answer would be that people choose where to live, then their mode of travel, then the destinations of their trips, and then the routes they take. The difficulty is that people make their travel choices in a whole range of ways, not necessarily in this order.

For example, a person that was offered an attractive new job with a nice company car is likely to make her travel choices in a different order. Her work location and her mode of travel are already decided when she searches for a suitable place to live. She may decide to look for a home that allows her easy parking and convenient use of her car, not only for her trips to work but also for her other trips. Having trip generation above mode choice in the model hierarchy isn't an accurate description of the travel behaviour of this person, because her home location depends on her choice of mode of transport, and not vice versa.

Another example would be a person that is a frequent visitor at the food market in the centre of the town where he lives. He rarely does his shopping anywhere else. He goes to the market by car if anyone from his neighbourhood offers him a lift to the town centre. He takes his bike if it's sunny and if he only plans light shopping, or otherwise he takes the bus. Having mode choice above trip distribution isn't a good description of his travel behaviour, because the travel mode options result from his choice of the market as his destination, and not vice versa.

If there are many travellers that behave differently from what the model hierarchy implies, you should change the hierarchy. The model hierarchy doesn't have to be the same as the one described in figure 18. The one in figure 18 is the hierarchy recommended by the Department for Transport in the UK for cases where you don't have local data to help you determine the hierarchy. It was recommended because data collected across the UK suggests that most people already have a preference for a specific mode of transport when they decide where to go. In other words, it shows that mode choice is above distribution in the model hierarchy. However, the evidence about this preference is very general, and it doesn't necessarily apply in every situation.

When the four-stage approach was first introduced in the 1960s, it included a different hierarchy, as shown in figure 26. The figure focuses on a single segment, but a similar process is run for all segments. In this hierarchy, the order of choices is **generation-distribution-split-assignment**. This hierarchy is still used in various models.

Figure 26: a model with distribution above mode split

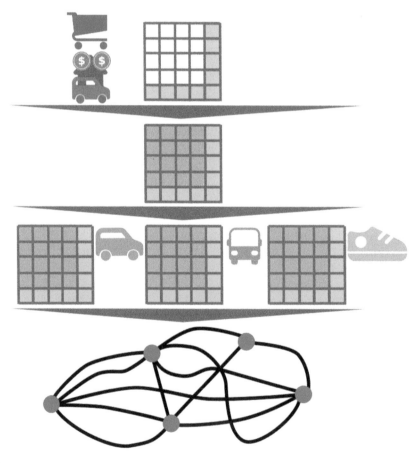

The way we handle matrices, in models with this hierarchy, is different from what I showed earlier. We fill the matrix with numbers straight after trip generation, when it still isn't split by mode. In other words, this hierarchy assumes people will choose their mode of transport based on where they go. This is the opposite of what the other hierarchy assumes.

Models built based on the traditional hierarchy will generally show more willingness of car users to sometimes take public transport, whereas models based on the UK default argue that this willingness is lower.

It is always best if the hierarchy of your model has been determined based on analysis of local data, showing the travel choices people made in a range of situations. I'll explain the data requirements in more detail later. But data of good quality is difficult and expensive to obtain. Besides, even when you choose the best hierarchy, you'll still only describe correctly the behaviour of some of the people, not all of them.

You can best reflect local behaviour if each demand segment in the model has its own hierarchy, and if you create enough segments to reflect the different preferences. If you vary the model's hierarchy by segment, then it can have very strong behavioural foundations. But the amount of work required to create such a model often makes this infeasible.

For all these reasons, it is important to remember that some model outputs are a result of the model hierarchy we've used, and not a result of a logical consideration of what would really happen. Think of a case where you use a model in which the hierarchy is **generation-split-distribution-assignment** (like the UK default). And think of a case where you use this model to look at the potential impacts of closing down one of the roads into a town centre, converting it into a pedestrian-only street. You've run the model for several scenarios, before and after the change, and you sent a map to your colleagues with model outputs.

The map from the model shows a reduction in traffic volumes throughout the town centre. Some of your colleagues will look at the map and comment on how the pedestrianisation project helps shift car users to public transport or to walking. But the truth is that your model simply isn't able to directly address the question "will the pedestrianisation lead to a shift of car users to other modes". This model was based on the assumption that traffic levels (from the assignment) are a direct result of how people choose where they travel (from the distribution stage), and not a direct result of which mode of travel they choose.

In this model, if driving to town is no longer attractive, travellers will first consider going to another destination. They may still change their mode, but since mode split isn't immediately above assignment, a change of mode cannot be an immediate response to changes in traffic arrangements.

You'll need to explain to your colleagues that the reduction shown in car trips doesn't necessarily indicate mode shift. There's a risk of confusing bad and good outcomes from the pedestrianisation project, because the outputs might be showing that people go to out-of-town destinations and this is why there's a reduction in traffic.

Figure 27: interpretation of model hierarchy

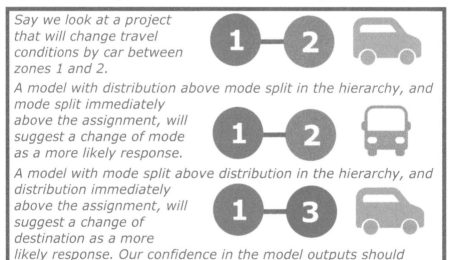

Say we look at a project that will change travel conditions by car between zones 1 and 2.

A model with distribution above mode split in the hierarchy, and mode split immediately above the assignment, will suggest a change of mode as a more likely response.

A model with mode split above distribution in the hierarchy, and distribution immediately above the assignment, will suggest a change of destination as a more likely response. Our confidence in the model outputs should depend on how we determined the hierarchy in the first place.

Unfortunately, outputs from transport models strongly depend on the hierarchy that you used from the start. There are some models that allow making fewer assumptions about the hierarchy, but they are complex to develop and their use isn't common.

3.6 Adding time choice

The four-stage concept covers the questions of where people travel to and from, by which mode and by which route. The generation stage is normally done so that it covers all the trips made over a typical 24-hour day. By contrast, the assignment stage usually focuses on the peak hours, when the number of trips in the network is the highest. Assignment models are meant to help us identify the weakest points in the transport network, and this is best done through analysis of the peak hours.

This means that at some point after trip generation, but before assignment, we need to convert 24-hour demand matrices to matrices that only contain the demand during the peak period. Using data about the amount of traffic or passengers at different hours, we can quite easily calculate the proportion of daily trips that are made during the

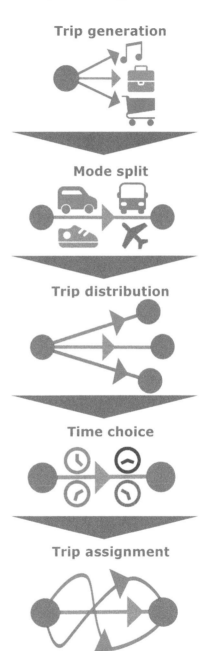

Figure 28: a five-stage model, including time choice

Trip generation

Mode split

Trip distribution

Time choice

Trip assignment

peak, and use this to convert the daily demand to peak demand. This is how matrices have been prepared for assignment traditionally.

More recently some experts observed, especially in cities with major traffic problems, that the number of people travelling in the peak sometimes needs a more sophisticated calculation. The time in the day when people travel can be a separate choice, just like mode choice or route choice. For example, if trains are so full during the peak that not everyone can get on, some people will choose to travel before or after the busiest time of the day. Similarly, some car drivers leave very early or very late to avoid heavy traffic. This can happen either in the morning or in the afternoon.

This time shift is a behavioural response which was excluded from the original four-stage approach. There are now many models that include an additional stage to the hierarchy, dealing with people's choice of the time of day when they travel. This additional stage is sometimes called a "peak spreading model", because people who shift their departure time make the peak period longer. The time choice model is normally located just above assignment in the model hierarchy, as shown in figure 28.

3.7 Tour-based models

All models are simplified in the way they describe people's real travel behaviour. Many specialists see the four-stage approach as striking a reasonable balance between the way it describes travel behaviour and the amount of work needed to develop a model. Other specialists have proposed some modifications to the traditional approach, which require additional work but may describe how people travel in a more realistic way. Whether or not the additional work is justified depends on your own preferences, and the views of your colleagues and clients.

An approach that goes beyond the traditional one is called **tour-based modelling**. To understand this approach, you first need to acknowledge that everything we've seen so far counts as **trip-based modelling**. It's trip-based because the demand matrices contained information about the number of individual trips people make, and we so far haven't bundled together trips made by the same person.

A **tour** is a chain of trips, made by one person, that start and end at the same place. This place is usually home, because there's no place like home. Tour-based models apply mode split and distribution to compete tours rather than to individual trips. When you think about it, it makes good sense: if I left the car at home in the morning and travelled to work by train, then most chances are that I'll also return by train.

A traditional, trip-based model might estimate that I return home by car even if I left it at home. That's because the demand matrices store the trips from home and to home as completely separate. So by remembering the relationship between the outbound and inbound trips, a tour-based model can reflect how people travel more truthfully.

Figure 29: trips and tours. I live at A. I work at B. If I go to work and back, a trip-based model would apply mode split and distribution separately to my "A-B" and "B-A" trips, while a tour-based model would do it jointly for the tour "A-B-A". It's trickier if I also want to visit my auntie Tilda after work. She lives at C. She'd be pleased to see me, but I'd create a challenge for a tour-based model, since it would need to know how to apply mode split and distribution to the more complex tour "A-B-C-A". Some tour-based models can do it while others only do simple "A-B-A" tours, and they treat complex tours as separate trips.

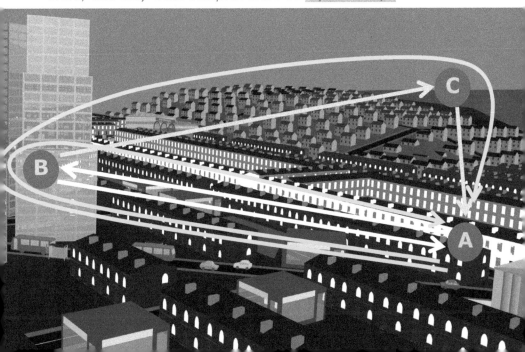

Tour-based models don't necessarily force you to use the same mode for the entire tour. For example, you can build a model that allows travellers to take a bus to the city centre and hire a bike there. The point is that a tour-based model will ensure that mode choices are feasible for the whole tour. In the distribution stage, a tour-based model will ensure that there is symmetry between the number of trips from A (home) to B (work or other places) and the number of trips from B to A.

As you could expect, the improved logic of tour-based models comes at a cost. These models are harder to set up because they need data structures that are more sophisticated than standard matrices. In addition, note that the assignment in tour-based models must remain trip-based, because traffic and route choices by their nature depend on the direction of travel. It's therefore necessary in such models to frequently convert between tours and trips.

There are different views about whether the effort to create tour-based models is justified. In Europe, tour-based models are not as common as in North America, where some of the largest cities now use them.

3.8 Other limitations of the four-stage concept

In many transport agencies and local authorities, a four-stage model is the main tool used for producing inputs into the design of transport projects and for assessing their impact. However, even when enhanced by adding a time choice model or by adopting a tour-based structure, a four-stage model will not address all the expectations that clients may have from the modelling work.

Several commonly-used types of models are not part of the four-stage process:

■ **Traffic micro-simulation models**. These models are similar to assignment models in that they examine how the network deals with the travel demand. But micro-simulation models are more focused on detailed analysis of the traffic flow within each street or junction. Estimating route choices, which is the main job of an assignment model, is just one of several concerns in micro-simulation.

- **Operational models**. These models allow more detailed representation of the decisions made by network operators, such as possible changes to signal control systems on the rail network or to traffic signal settings on the road network.

- **Uni-modal models.** Four-stage models are multi-modal, since they look at the total demand across different modes of transport and include a mode split stage. There are other types of models, which are sometimes called "uni-modal", that focus on the demand for a single mode of transport. For reasons I'll explain later, modes of transport that are sometimes analysed using uni-modal models include rail, cycling and walking.

Models which aren't part of the four-stage process still often require inputs from a four-stage model. The four-stage model outputs are taken through some further analysis. I'll describe such models later in this book.

"I'm in the 'visiting family' demand segment. Yourself?"

"Business. This model says I strictly avoid talking to strangers".

Chapter 4

Calibration, validation and application

4.1 The role of model parameters

Every transport model uses parameters. Parameters are numbers which we specify in advance and have a role in the calculations performed by the model. The number of parameters can vary from a handful to many thousands. Figure 30 explains some of the main types of parameters used by different models.

You can see in figure 30 that some parameters simply describe the world as we see it: for example, the number of seconds of green light in a junction is quite a straightforward parameter, which can be observed in the real world and then coded in the model. If all parameters were like this, we wouldn't need to do model calibration at all.

But many of the parameters aren't easy to simply go out and measure. In such cases we try to learn what their value is indirectly, by seeing how the parameter value influences a model output that we can observe in the real world. If the parameter value we chose leads to model outputs which are similar to what we see in the real transport system, then we probably chose the right value. Of course we might need to try many values before this works; model calibration is the process of searching for the right parameter values.

Model parameters are usually part of a simplified theory. The transport system is too complex for us to model within a reasonable effort, so every model offers a theory of how the system works. The parameters capture behaviours and interactions as part of this theory. Without calibration, we wouldn't be able to trust the theory: what if it doesn't describe the world correctly? The methods included in any model need to go through calibration to ensure they describe the transport system in a way we can trust.

Figure 30: types of parameters

Parameters representing sizes, durations and dimensions. To explore how traffic flows and how people move around, models often need to know road widths, number of lanes, the length of a car, the area of a station concourse, the space suitable for standing on a bus, the number of seconds of green light at a pedestrian crossing, etc.

Parameters representing individual behaviour. How far would you walk to a bus stop? When you drive a car, how close would you get to the car in front of you? When you're on a bike, how much longer would you cycle if you can do it on a nice path through the park? These and many others are behaviours which we represent in our models through parameters.

Parameters representing collective behaviour. Some behaviours are difficult to associate with a specific traveller; it's easier to see them as general statistics of all the people in our study area. For example, the average number of people in a single car ("car occupancy factor") helps us represent the chance that a traveller gets a ride with a friend or a relative.

Parameters describing the composition of traffic. We need these parameters to ensure we look at the right amount of interaction between different vehicles. For example, a "passenger car unit" for a semi-trailer is the amount of road space taken by one semi-trailer, expressed as the number of standard cars that take the same space.

Parameters describing traffic phenomena. These parameters don't always have an intuitive meaning. A model can include, for example, a function that gives the number of seconds that pass until all the traffic has gone through a signalised junction. A function 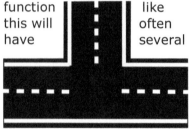 like this will often have several parameters which are all needed for the calculation of the number of seconds.

Parameters replacing missing parts of the model. Parameters can fill in gaps in the model, i.e. things that the model should ideally estimate but there's not enough time or knowledge. For example, we may want to know what part of the trips in a future scenario will be made during the afternoon peak, but our model doesn't estimate time period choices. It's common to use parameters that contain the proportion of trips made at each time of day. Unlike what we'd get from a time choice model (see section 3.6), using a fixed parameter means that this proportion will remain the same in all scenarios we test.

Segmentation factors. I spoke in chapter 2 about demand segmentation. Some  parameters store the proportion of people (or trips) that belong to each demand segment.

Weights. These are a specific type of behavioural parameters, telling the model that a unit of one thing (for example a minute spent walking) influences behaviour more than the same unit of another thing (e.g. a minute spent waiting in a passenger lounge). I gave some more examples of weights in section 2.6.

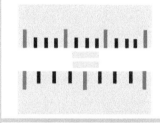

Conversion factors.

Often different parts of the model work in different units. For example, the model may generally use the number of trips per day, but when we need it to calculate annual pollutant emissions, we use an "annualisation factor".

Penalties. These are another specific type of behavioural parameters, ensuring that the model makes specific behaviours less popular than what the calculation would show otherwise. For example, if one street is quicker to drive through than a parallel street, but most drivers use the slower one since it offers nice  views, this could be corrected in the model by attaching a penalty to the quicker street. I gave more examples of penalties in section 2.6.

Scaling factors. These are used in the mode split and in any process that estimates how people make choices. A scaling factor indicates how sensitive people are to small differences. Think of a journey you can make by either boat or bus; the generalised cost of travel by boat is slightly lower, i.e. the boat has a slight advantage. A model with a very low scaling factor will estimate that everyone uses the boat because it has a lower cost. Increasing the scaling factor will give more balanced choices between the two options, emphasising the fact that the cost difference isn't large.

In the calibration process we set the values of the parameters based on observed data. For some specific parameters, such as the average length of a car, you can collect data directly and then leave the parameter out of the calibration problem. But for most parameters, data observed in the real world doesn't explicitly say what the parameter values should be, so we decide how to change these values based on more general model outputs, like traffic flows or travel times. A typical calibration process is described in stages 1 to 8 of figure 31.

If there aren't many parameters to calibrate, the process can be manual. In such cases, it takes the form of a "trial and error" experiment. Once you've collected enough data, you just run the model with different combinations of parameter values until the outputs resemble the data. If there are many parameters to calibrate, various automated techniques are used to optimise the search for the right parameter values. There are many approaches for automated calibration processes.

Sometimes we calibrate different parts of the model separately: one calibration experiment for mode split, separate processes for the traffic assignment and the public transport assignment, a different calibration of traffic micro-simulation, and so on. This is much easier than calibrating everything at the same time, because the total number of parameters in the complete model can be huge. It's easier also because we use different sources of data to calibrate different parts of the model, and combining these sources complicates things.

Still, in a hierarchical model that uses composite costs, as I showed in chapter 3, all parts of the model share their parameters. For example, the parameters used to calculate the generalised costs of different routes in the assignment become part of the composite costs which are used for trip distribution. Through the composite cost, the parameters of one stage of the model find their way into other stages. If the calibration of these different parts of a hierarchical model is not done together, we can get conflicting values for the same parameter.

Figure 31: traditional calibration and validation

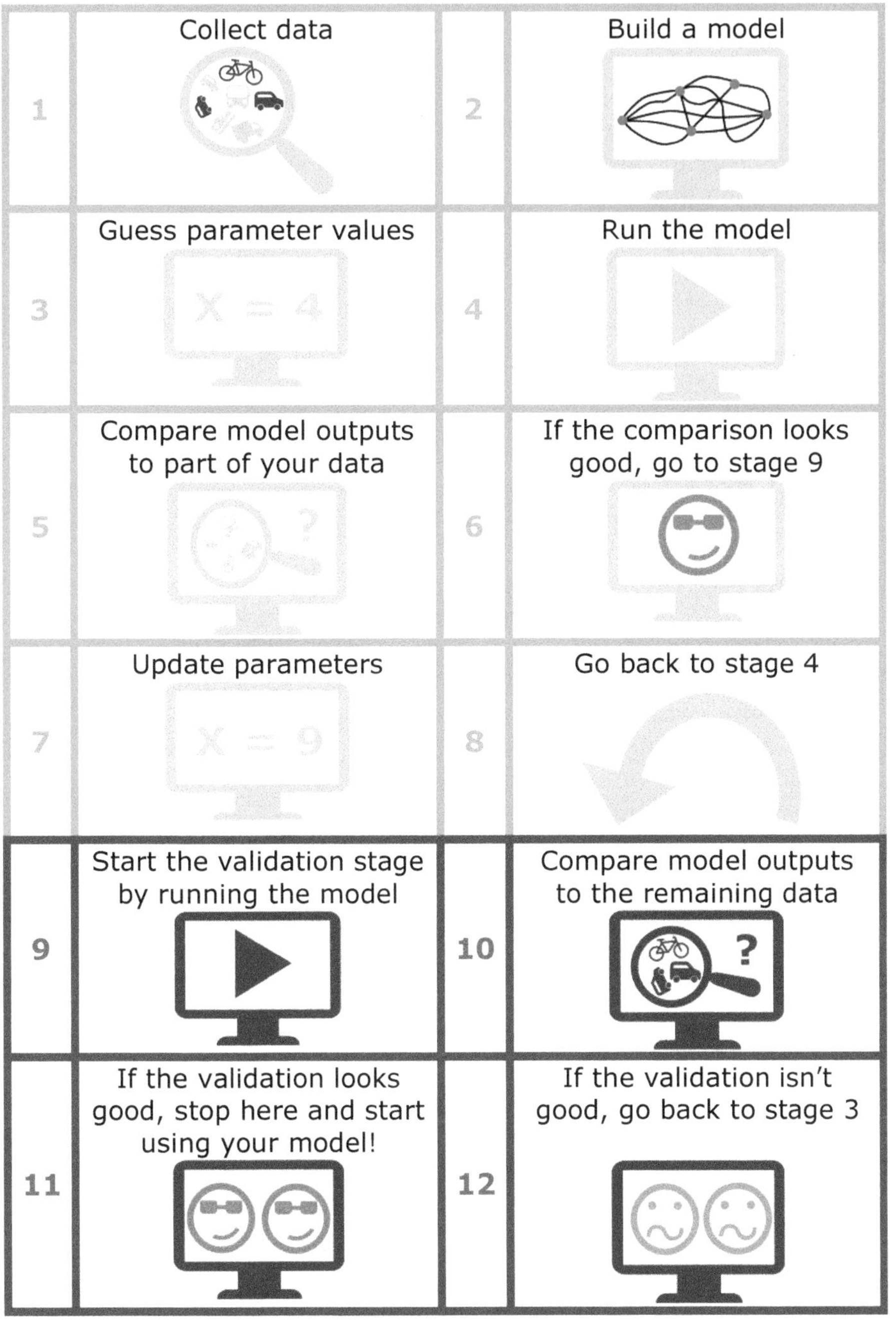

1	Collect data	2	Build a model
3	Guess parameter values	4	Run the model
5	Compare model outputs to part of your data	6	If the comparison looks good, go to stage 9
7	Update parameters	8	Go back to stage 4
9	Start the validation stage by running the model	10	Compare model outputs to the remaining data
11	If the validation looks good, stop here and start using your model!	12	If the validation isn't good, go back to stage 3

You can see that both options - simultaneous calibration of all model components or separate calibration of each one separately - involve some difficulties. These difficulties always lead to some compromises in the calibration process, since the amount of work needed for perfect calibration isn't feasible. The responsibility of modellers, colleagues and clients is to ensure that these compromises are well understood whenever the model outputs are used.

4.3 Model validation

Good calibration can be misleading. You've made changes to various parameters, and the model outputs are now really similar to what the data shows. Surely we can now apply the model in new situations to get forecasts of what would happen?

Not exactly. The confusing bit is that playing with the model parameters can always give you outputs quite similar to your calibration data. Figure 31 showed that we run the calibration process in a loop, and we keep updating the parameters so that the outputs get closer and closer to what the data shows. This is an essential thing to do, but calibration alone isn't sufficient. What if our data doesn't contain enough evidence on some of the things that we want our model to calculate?

We add the validation stage (stages 9 to 12 in figure 31) to get more confidence in our model. In the validation stage, we check if the model is able to estimate some things that we didn't check when we calibrated it. At the beginning of the whole process we split all the data we have into two parts. In the calibration stage we ensure the model can reproduce one part of the data, and in the validation stage we check if the model can estimate what's in the other part. The extra reassurance that validation gives us comes from the fact that we validate the model to an independent dataset, i.e. the part of the data that wasn't used for calibration.

The exact way we split the data between calibration and validation varies, and different modellers use different approaches. More generally, the entire validation stage is viewed

76

differently by different experts. Figure 32 gives some more detail on different approaches to validation.

I have to note that in my opinion, the role of model validation is frequently misunderstood. Of course I agree that model calibration isn't enough to give you a good model; adjusting the parameters to match the data is quite easy, and it doesn't mean we have a model that captures how our transport system works. However, I prefer to remain unsure about the capabilities of the model for a bit longer, even if it successfully passes the validation test. My reason for this is that the calibration data and validation data usually suffer from the same problems.

If some traffic phenomena or travel behaviours aren't evident in the calibration data, they'll often be missing from the validation data as well. That's because there are things that our typical data sources really don't look at, such as the way people's preferences change over time. As a result, the confidence we build in our model after validating it to an independent dataset might be too high. This point will become clearer later in this chapter, when I talk about different data sources we use, and I'll also discuss it in a lot of detail in the second part of this book.

For now, a key point to remember is that you need to agree with modellers, colleagues and clients which validation approach you'll be using. If you're not clear about this when you start the work, you might end up with some disagreement in the team about the capabilities of the model.

4.4 Goodness of fit

In figure 31, stages 5 and 10 involved comparing observed data to model outputs. In stages 6 and 11 we asked ourselves whether the comparison looks good. But how do we know whether the comparison is good looking? The kind of good looks we're talking about here isn't related to hairstyle but to goodness of fit.

When we check the difference between something we observed and its modelled equivalent, we undertake a classical statistical task of comparing datasets. Model outputs will never be identical to the real world, so we use measures of goodness of fit to decide whether they are close enough.

77

Figure 32: approaches to validation

Splitting the data randomly. About half of the data is used for calibration and the rest for validation. Both datasets are created randomly from the same source. If, for example, the data contains traffic counts from multiple days, then half the days would go to each dataset. Since the validation data isn't used for adjusting the parameters, only for testing the calibrated model, a downside of this approach is that the half of the data doesn't improve the model. So to some extent, this is a waste of data. ← ← ←

Splitting but later merging. This is the same as above, but with an additional stage. The data is split; half of it is used for calibration and half for validation; and in the end, the calibration exercise is repeated with the full dataset. The idea is that after the validation we already have confidence in the model, and the re-calibration is a just refinement that makes the most of all the data we have. → → →

Splitting by geography. This approach is common when calibrating network models. We split our data in two, but not randomly. For calibration we use more spatially detailed data, such as traffic counts and passenger counts from as many locations as possible throughout the network.

Calibration

Validation

Then for validation we specifically use data that can provide an overview of key movements. For example, the validation data can be collected in a set of locations that form a ring around the city centre. ← ← ←

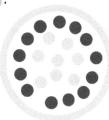

Adding realism testing. The guidance from the UK Department for Transport (DfT) says that, in addition to validation where the data is split by geography, your model should also go through an additional validation stage. The additional stage is known as "realism testing". In this stage you look at how travellers in your calibrated model respond to changes in prices and in travel times, and you compare this to evidence that DfT gathered in a review of multiple studies. The response in the model must be within the range from the DfT review, even if this means that the parameters calibrated from local data need to change again. → → →

Not doing validation. Some of us, including myself, think validation doesn't strengthen the model that much, so we sometimes just skip this stage. We do various other things instead, to ensure the model is used in a responsible way, as described throughout this book. ← ← ←

Figure 33 gives an example, assuming that model calibration is based on comparing the number of car and bus users in four locations, A to D. Let's compare how the model performs based on three alternative sets of parameters. I don't present the actual parameters here, only the model outputs obtained when each set of parameters is used. Each of these parameter sets would turn this into quite a different model.

Figure 33: a comparison of goodness of fit

Location	Observed (car/bus)	Option 1 (car/bus)	Option 2 (car/bus)	Option 3 (car/bus)
A	340 / 100	310 / 50	320 / 100	260 / 150
B	230 / 120	250 / 40	200 / 110	300 / 70
C	600 / 180	550 / 40	670 / 950	710 / 250
D	280 / 400	240 / 90	240 / 370	200 / 300

Set 1 of parameter values reproduces car demand quite well, but bus demand is consistently underestimated. Set 2 of parameter values performs reasonably well in most locations, but in location C it drastically overestimates bus demand. Parameter set 3 is less successful in estimating both car demand and bus demand, but unlike sets 1 and 2, none of the errors is systematic; there isn't any significant overestimation or underestimation of demand by any mode, at any location.

The statistical literature suggests many different measures of goodness of fit, which I don't review here. Many of them are suitable for the calibration and validation of transport models. Note that we need to have not only an agreed measure of goodness of fit, but also an agreed level of tolerance to model error. Can we accept consistent underestimation of bus demand? If we can, is the degree of underestimation by parameter set 1 within our tolerance? Alternatively, can we live with the large error in bus demand at location C when parameter set 2 is used?

Is this better or worse than the level of accuracy we get with parameter set 3?

I don't recommend here any specific measure, level of tolerance or calibration approach. In many cases, the approach to be used in your work would be dictated by the formal guidance that authorities provide in the country, city or state where you work. The point to remember is that you'll need to either follow the calibration standards set by others, or specify your own calibration standards, to judge which set of calibration results is the best.

It's also possible that no set of parameter values satisfies the calibration standards you were hoping to achieve. Figure 34 lists the options you have when this happens. You'll see that these approaches vary greatly in what they're trying to achieve.

4.5 Application of a calibrated model

Congratulations - you have achieved the standard of calibration and validation you wanted. Now that your model is calibrated and validated, what can you do with it?

The use of your model to produce various results is called model application, or informally "running the model". Once the calibration and validation process is complete, you can apply the model in a range of hypothetical scenarios, but it's important to also consider the limitations of the model.

In other parts of this book I explain the limitation caused by the modelling techniques we use. Here I'd like to stress some specific limitations which may be caused by the way we calibrate the model. Here are some examples:

- If all the data we used to calibrate the model comes from major roads and junctions, is the model a credible tool to estimate traffic on more local roads? It could be that the data we used for calibration misses some typical phenomena or behaviours that are only evident on minor streets.

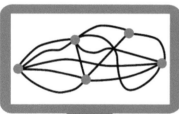

Figure 34: when calibration isn't successful

- Could it be that recent events or trends have changed people's preferences after you collected the data? For example, if you calibrate your model based on data collected last year, and since then a new railway station was opened in a nearby suburb, have the behaviours that you captured in the calibration not changed?

- Could it be that the transport investment you're testing will invalidate your calibration? Say, for example, that you're developing a model to test the transport impacts of a plan to build thousands of new luxury flats on the site of a former riverside factory. It's possible that the development will attract new types of people to live in the area. How can calibration of the model reflect the travel choices of local residents if they are very different from the current residents?

These questions don't have clear cut answers. Much depends on the specific model, the nature of the data you use, and the detailed circumstances of the study. My key point is that you have to consider these questions, and potentially debate them with colleagues and clients, to ensure that the way you use the model is justifiable.

4.6 Using a model built somewhere else

A lot of model development work is done everywhere, all the time. The efforts to build transport models in different places may seem quite similar to each other. The following are therefore some questions that I've been asked many times by clients and by consultants from other fields:

- Can we use a model developed somewhere else, to minimise our effort?

- We got a copy of an excellent model which was developed in another country. Can we do some business with it here?

- If we develop our own local model, can we use data from other places, to reduce the burden of collecting new data?

- Can we rely on data collection and model development work we did, in our study area, a decade ago?

To answer these questions, let me spell out some widely-accepted principles regarding when models, methods and data can move from one place to another. These principles are listed in figure 35.

The techniques we use are global. If a modelling technique works in one place, there's a good chance it would work somewhere else. Just don't forget that the modelling technique alone gives you nothing. The modelling technique gives you an "empty" model which needs to be built from local data.

Behaviours are local. Building the same cycle lane will have very different outcomes in Arizona and in the Swiss Alps. A model from one place will say little about impacts elsewhere because people don't behave the same. You can "import" a model from somewhere else, calibrate it to local data and make the necessary changes; but I bet building a new model is less work.

Geography plays a key role. Calibration of a model to local conditions allows us to consider not only human behaviour but also geographical features which might otherwise be missed. These include, for example, impacts of the climate in the study area and local topography.

Behaviour changes over time. Even if everything in the model was built locally, things can change over time because of cultural, social and economic trends. You can't tell whether the impact of these trends is significant until you use recent data to refresh an old model.

2005 2015 2025

It is good practice to follow these principles whenever you can. But it also has to be acknowledged that the cost of data collection, and the laborious nature of model calibration work, sometimes call for a compromised approach.

An example of a common compromise is using national defaults for some of the parameters. National values of model parameters still go through calibration, but it's done jointly for many different models, normally by government organisations. Parameters calibrated nationally probably won't reflect the behaviours and geography in your specific study area. But at least they reflect an average calculated in the same country, and that's why it's a compromise.

4.7 Aggregate and disaggregate models

For some types of models, before we do any calibration we need to decide whether we go for an aggregate or a disaggregate approach. Both approaches can be used to calibrate the same model, but they do it with different types of data.

Disaggregate calibration uses data that contains the choices of individual people. Such calibration looks at the different options that each person could choose from, and searches for parameter values that would explain why this person preferred one option over the others. Since each person is different, the process looks for parameter values that can explain the choices of as many people as possible amongst the people we have data about.

Aggregate calibration doesn't look at individual people. It usually looks together at all the people travelling from one origin to one destination. The aggregate approach analyses what proportion of these people chose each travel option, and it looks for model parameters that would get the model to produce these proportions.

If for example we calibrate a mode split model in a disaggregate way, we would typically do a survey where we ask many people about the trips they recently made. We'd use each individual trip as one piece of data. By contrast, building the same mode split model in an aggregate way would involve counting the number of people using each mode of transport. The number of people using each mode from each origin to each destination would be our basic data input. Both approaches need a sufficient amount of data to tell us how people choose their mode, but the way we collect data and analyse it would be very different.

The major advantage of disaggregate calibration is that it has stronger behavioural logic. The way people choose how to travel depends on some individual characteristics, such as the distance from their home to the nearest train station. Only a disaggregate model can include such information, because an aggregate model looks jointly at all the people in the same zone of the model, and ignores the range of distances to the station within that zone.

But using individual data for disaggregate calibration also has key disadvantages. One problem is that individual data costs more to collect. Another difficulty with disaggregate calibration is that we lose some of the behavioural insight when we apply the model. If we developed a disaggregate model and it says that mode choices depend on a people's walking distances to a station, we will need to know the walking distances of all the people in every future scenario before we can estimate mode choices for that scenario. Getting forecasts of all the inputs to the model is difficult and expensive when the data is about individual people.

In practice we rarely apply a model in a disaggregate way, despite the strengths of this approach. Even if we use individual data for the calibration, such as the walking distance from home to the nearest station, we still use the average distance across all the people in the area when we run the model. In other words, we run most models in an aggregate way even if we calibrate them in a disaggregate way.

By contrast, academic researchers do more work with disaggregate data, especially in studies where they can collect their own data from individual travellers. Such studies can deepen our insight into travel behaviour, and we can reach a wider range of conclusions from them when making transport policies. But due to the technical difficulties involved, this approach isn't seen as practical in most large-scale projects.

In this section I'll review key sources of data for model calibration and validation. There isn't a single source of perfect data, and no data source provides confidence about all the things we want to know. Therefore, most models are based on multiple data sources. We try to benefit from the strengths of each source while not letting its weaknesses compromise the model too much.

Figure 36 lists the most common data sources. With the emergence of new types of data, like those I included towards the end of this figure, one of the main challenges of the transport modelling community is data fusion. There's a serious need to agree what process for merging multiple data sources can help develop reliable demand matrices and calibrate model parameters. At the time when I write this book, there are many parallel attempts to specify data fusion approaches, but there isn't a widely-accepted approach that can be seen as the best practice.

Figure 36: data sources for transport modelling

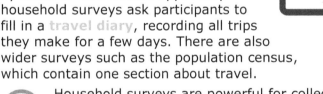

Household surveys: detailed questionnaires sent to people at home, where they are asked about their travel habits. Traditionally these were paper-based, but now they're also distributed by email or as a mobile app. Many household surveys ask participants to fill in a travel diary, recording all trips they make for a few days. There are also wider surveys such as the population census, which contain one section about travel.

 Household surveys are powerful for collecting detailed information on all the trips people make. They're a key input into most types of transport models.

 It's expensive to collect information from people at home. It's cheaper if done electronically, but the sample might be biased towards more techie people.

Roadside interviews: short questionnaires handed out to drivers by stopping them while they travel. The interview locations are usually chosen so that they give a complete picture of traffic in an area. **Cordon surveys** are based on drawing an imaginary circle around the study area, and conducting the survey on all roads that cross this circle. **Screenline surveys** are based on drawing an imaginary line that cuts through the study area, and conducting the survey on all roads that cross this line. See figure 37.

 These interviews are good for collecting information that isn't available from traffic counts, like the purpose, origin and destination of trips in the study area.

 These interviews cause disruption to traffic. They require complex coordination with bodies like the police. As a result, they are also expensive.

Traffic counts: all vehicles passing at an agreed point are being counted, and normally also classified by vehicle type, direction and time of day. Counts can be either manual (by a person that observes the traffic) or automatic. Automatic counts use different methods, including devices installed under the surface of the road, detectors installed near the road, or video footage processing. Counts are also often done along cordons and screenlines (see figure 37).

 This is one of the cheapest data collection methods, so counts are often done in many dozens of locations around the study area.

 Counts don't segment trips by purpose and don't tell us anything directly about origins and destinations. Counts collected automatically are subject to different types of errors because individual vehicles are sometimes wrongly identified. Counts collected manually can normally only cover a small number of days.

Passenger counts: public transport passengers are counted on buses and trains or at stations. These counts are normally manual.

 Passenger counts are effective when validating public transport assignment models.

 Counts don't segment passengers by their trip purpose. They may help understand where passengers board and alight, but these aren't their real origins and destinations, so it's not sufficient for building demand matrices.

Ticketing data: any data source that includes information on the purchase or use of travel tickets and cards. Some information is collected automatically by ticket barriers at stations or card readers on buses. Other information is collected through ticket sales.

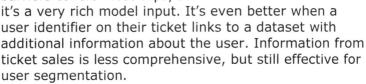

 Information from ticket barriers covers most trips, so it's a very rich model input. It's even better when a user identifier on their ticket links to a dataset with additional information about the user. Information from ticket sales is less comprehensive, but still effective for user segmentation.

 Ticketing datasets are sometimes so comprehensive that you need advanced data processing skills. There are sensitivities regarding privacy and data protection. Ticket sales data don't show actual demand - for example if you buy an annual ticket, the sales data doesn't describe the trips you make with this ticket.

On-board surveys: short questionnaires for passengers travelling by public transport. Some surveys are paper-based, with questionnaires handed out to passengers and then collected or returned by post. Other surveys are done face-to-face by an interviewer.

On-board surveys are effective for collecting information on journey purpose, origin and destination.

 There is often lower participation on crowded services, since it's difficult to fill in the questionnaire. There's also lower representation of very short trips.

Station or bus stop surveys: short passenger questionnaires. Some are paper-based, handed out to passengers at a station or a bus stop to be returned by post, and others are done face-to-face.

 These surveys help us learn about journey purpose, origin and destination.

 The low willingness of passengers to take part, if they are just about to board a bus or a train, will bias the results towards infrequent services.

Behavioural surveys: surveys where the interest is in how people may change their travel behaviour if changes are made to the transport system. These surveys take many shapes and forms. Participants can be intercepted and asked questions on the spot, or invited to a nearby venue, or handed out a postcard-shaped questionnaire to send, or it could be done by email or phone. See figures 51 to 53 later.

 These surveys are an important input to all behavioural elements of a transport model, such as the parameters in a mode split model.

 People don't necessarily behave in the same way they state they would behave in such surveys.

Mobile phone network data: following the signals transmitted by mobile phones to identify users' locations and travel habits.

 The data can cover all times of day, all modes and many locations – without any fieldwork.

Mobile cells have low geographical accuracy, so locations are subject to a large error. Complex processes are needed to identify the mode of transport and journey purpose. Also, the data needs to be purchased from the phone company. Each company has its own approach for data storage and analysis. The information does not come as a single dataset – it's split by technology (2G, 3G, 4G) and type of mobile cell. The use of phone users' data requires extreme caution in order to protect their privacy.

GPS data: following people's location using devices with a Global Positioning System. We can learn about their travel habits and collect general data about travel times. Most phones today include a GPS device, and many applications on the phone store location data. GPS is also built into vehicle navigation systems and information systems on buses.

 Data with high geographical accuracy can be collected quickly, from a large sample, without any fieldwork.

 Although the technology is widespread, data is collected separately by the different companies, depending on the application. Each app has users with specific characteristics, so the data can be biased.

Other new technology: rapidly-changing technologies provide other opportunities for collecting data on travel patterns and network performance. There are interesting applications of Bluetooth, automated analysis of video and CCTV footage, analysis of data from the accelerometer device in smartphones, and too many other examples to review here.

 There's hope that data collection will become increasingly automated, with less fieldwork and higher accuracy.

 There aren't yet agreed practices of how to use these new sources. Much depends on the creativity of those who hold the data. Some transport planners are concerned we'll become dependent on a small number of large companies who hold much data.

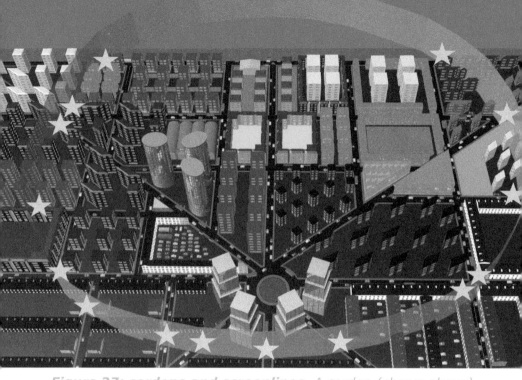

Figure 37: cordons and screenlines. A cordon (shown above) is a closed shape (e.g. a circle) we draw around an area of interest. If we collect data in every place where the cordon meets the network (the stars), we'll have a good overview of travel to and from the area. A screenline (shown below) is a line that crosses an area of interest. It doesn't have to be a straight line. If we collect data in every place where the screenline meets the network, we'll have a good overview of travel across the area.

Chapter 5

Anything from planes to bikes

5.1 Multi-modal and uni-modal models

In the transport system out there, people use cars, buses, trains, bikes, motorbikes, boats and other modes of transport. Some parts of the transport network, for example a typical urban street, are shared between different modes. Other parts of the network are used exclusively by one mode, for example a tunnel for underground trains.

When specifying transport modelling work, you need to decide whether or not you want to limit the work to specific modes only. This is sometimes a difficult decision. On one hand, it's difficult to isolate the analysis of one mode from the other modes. A project that is only concerned with bus travel times might still need to examine how these times are affected by traffic congestion, which is caused by cars and trucks. A study of strategies to encourage travel by taxi might need to understand the other modes taxi users consider as an alternative, before it can predict under what conditions more people would choose the taxi.

On the other hand, you sometimes must isolate one mode from the others, for example because there are aspects of travel behaviour which are specific to one mode only, and you need a unique type of analysis just for this mode.

In this chapter I go through individual modes of transport, and review how each mode is typically represented in transport models. An important distinction to make before I start is between multi-modal and uni-modal models. The four-stage approach, which I introduced earlier, is multi-modal. It's multi-modal because every stage of the four-stage process looks at the demand across multiple modes. Before the mode split stage, the modelling is done jointly for different modes; after the mode split stage, it is done separately for each mode. But the overall four-stage model always combines different modes.

By contrast, uni-modal models don't follow the four-stage concept, and focus entirely on the demand for a specific mode of transport, without exploring what happens to those who travel by other modes. I'll give some examples of how uni-modal models work later in this chapter, in the sections about modelling travel by rail and by bike.

I tried to cover in this chapter the main urban transport modes. There are some modes, such as boats, cable cars and hot-air balloons, which are not included. But in cases where these are used as a transport mode, the analysis actually follows similar principles to those I review here, even if they appear here under a different mode.

5.2 The feeder mode

When people travel by bus, they normally get to (or from) the bus stop on foot or dropped there by someone who drives a car. When people travel by train, they normally get to (or from) the railway station by bus, car, bike or by foot. There's also a range of "park and ride" services of different types. In all these cases, a large part of the trip is made by one mode but there are shorter parts made by another mode. A mode used for a short part of the trip is called "a feeder mode".

When developing models, there are many things we do because they make our work cheaper or easier, and not because they are correct. One example for this is that we associate most trips to a single mode of transport each. This means we often choose to ignore the feeder part of the trip in the model.

Ignoring the feeder part saves us the need to split the trip from the origin to the destination into several shorter trips with some intermediate changing points. If we wanted to model these changing points, we would need more data about travellers' decision of where and how to switch between the modes. We would also face the challenge of replacing a trip from zone A to zone B, stored in one matrix, with several trips in several matrices. For example, instead of a bus trip from A to B, we'd need a trip from zone A to the zone with the boarding stop, in the walking matrix; a trip from the boarding stop to the alighting stop, in the bus matrix; and a trip from the alighting stop to zone B, in the walking matrix again. This would be hard work.

Usually, the simplified approach has no serious consequences. There are many cases where the feeder trip is made entirely within one zone, so even if we split the trip into several stages, the feeder stage would be stored in the matrix as a trip from one point to itself. The assignment model won't do anything with such trip anyway. When the feeder journey goes from one zone to another, it will often still be a short enough trip, so it would have a minimal impact on the model outputs if it was modelled.

Still, there are also cases where ignoring the feeder has important implications. There's a risk that we won't identify a genuine need related to the point where people switch mode. For example, we might provide insufficient bicycle parking at a station, or fail to see that a bus service stops too far for people to walk to a local school.

Some models don't make the simplification described above. These models do allow for complex journeys where several modes are involved. Such models are built, for example, when there's a need to consider alternative "park and ride" services. The great advantage of these models is that they cover a more realistic range of possible journeys. Their potential disadvantages include longer development time, longer runtime, more ambitious data requirements, more ambitious error checking requirements, and reliance on more specialised modelling skills. Whether or not it's worth developing such complex models depends on your project needs; I'll talk more about these models in chapter 7.

5.3 Models for car travel

Private vehicles are the dominant mode of travel in most areas, urban or rural, in large parts of the world. The need to address traffic congestion, caused largely by thousands of private vehicles trying to simultaneously access major urban centers, is often the reason why we start the modelling work in the first place. So the analysis of car traffic is often the heart of the modelling work.

We rarely look at private cars alone, because the road network serves cars, vans, trucks, taxis and buses at the same time. In fact, the larger types of vehicles have a more critical impact than cars on levels of congestion. But we still tend to focus much attention on the demand for travel by car.

One of the reasons for our focus on car demand is that car drivers have full freedom to change their route if congestion gets better or worse, compared to buses for example, which follow a fixed route. The change of route has a direct impact on traffic volumes in different parts of the network. So focusing on the behaviour of car drivers directly helps us understand the possible impacts of projects like road improvements, road closures or developing new buildings that generate new travel demand.

Another reason for our focus on cars is that we often don't have enough data to properly analyse the travel patterns of vans and trucks. I'll return to this point in the section about modelling freight.

Figure 38 shows three common ways to model car travel. The one I've described already follows the four-stage concept; detailed analysis of travel by car is done at the assignment stage, using the road network. Matrices of car trips for the assignment come from the mode split and distribution models, so the analysis of car traffic is done within a broader multi-modal modelling framework. There is often a public transport assignment model that runs in parallel. Both assignment models, for roads and for public transport routes, help improve the estimates of travel times, and these are used to calculate new generalised costs which can feed back into distribution, mode split and trip generation. This leads to an update of the car matrices, so the traffic assignment is run again. This process is repeated in a loop until it stabilises.

Sometimes we want to understand the likely traffic impacts of a transport project but we don't think it will have major impacts on people's choice of where to travel or which mode to use. In such cases we can adopt a more uni-modal approach. We can use existing car trip matrices and use the assignment model to estimate impacts on road-based travel only. In these cases we run assignment only, without trip generation, mode split and distribution.

Figure 38: three ways to model car travel

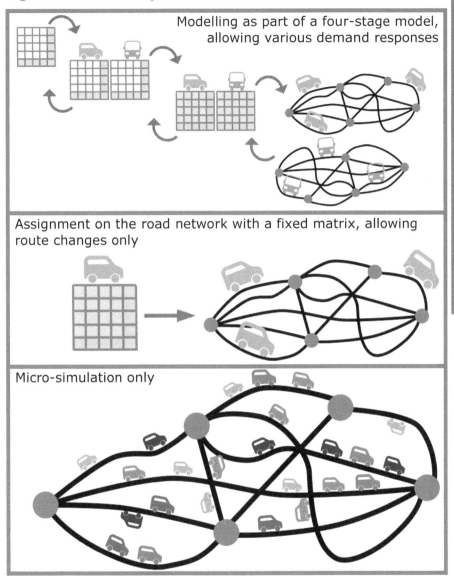

Modelling as part of a four-stage model, allowing various demand responses

Assignment on the road network with a fixed matrix, allowing route changes only

Micro-simulation only

I briefly mentioned earlier that traffic micro-simulation can be a helpful addition to the modelling work. Traffic micro-simulation is not part of the four-stage model structure because it rarely has a role in estimating travel demand. We start the micro-simulation work when we already have estimates of how many vehicles of different types are found at the place and the time of the

97

analysis. The micro-simulation model is developed to simulate the interactions between vehicles in the area in greater detail, representing every vehicle as a separate entity in the model.

Micro-simulation allows modellers to pay more attention to detailed traffic signal settings, vehicle characteristics and driving styles. Micro-simulation can have an important role in a study, either multi-modal or uni-modal, where there's interest in the detailed engineering, design and operation of the road. I'll return to this in chapter 9.

5.4 Models for freight transport

Trucks and vans form part of the general traffic that uses the road network. But they are harder to model for several reasons:

- Trips by a truck or van are made because the goods they deliver need to arrive somewhere. A generation model for freight trips would need to capture how the demand for goods transport is created. This is a complex topic, which varies between economic sectors, changes over time and requires some serious research. The transport planning community has not developed a tradition of researching this.

- There's a mode choice question for goods deliveries, which can sometimes be delivered by road, air, rail or sea. There are many studies about how the freight industry decides whether to deliver by road, but the transport planning community has not developed sufficient interest in developing a standard modelling approach.

- Freight trips involve making choices about driving routes, time of delivery, chaining of different deliveries, and destination once the delivery is complete. The driver is sometimes involved in the choice but in other cases these are fully prescribed by the business they work for. At the moment there isn't a common way of replicating these choices in a model.

- Segmentation of freight trips would be very different from segmentation of personal trips. There would be issues with the types of good they deliver, characteristics of the vehicle they drive, and characteristics of the business they work for.

For these reasons, representing the choices that affect trucks and vans is considered too complex for most transport models. We do have to take into consideration the amount of road space they take, since this has a big impact on the amount that is left for other road users. We therefore tend to capture freight movements in the model in a very simplified way, by introducing background flows.

Here's how we turn freight traffic into background flows:

- We collect data on the typical amount of freight traffic in different parts of the network.

- We consider each goods vehicle as if it was several private cars, to reflect the larger amount of road space that trucks and vans take. We use different factors for different goods vehicle types – they typically take the space of 2 to 4 cars each.

- We store this information as an attribute of each link with freight traffic. This way, before we start the assignment of car trips, there already is some background traffic on some roads. The background traffic takes some of the capacity of these links, so there's less capacity left for assigned traffic.

- Unlike most car traffic, which can choose a driving route during the assignment, the freight background flows remain where we put them and are not re-assigned.

- We apply some growth factors to the freight traffic flows when used in future scenarios, to account for the likely increase in freight movements over time.

The idea of background flows is simplistic. It gives the freight traffic limited freedom to vary its behaviour between the different scenarios we're testing. We might be missing some important impacts of our projects on freight traffic. It's important that you consider how the simplified treatment of freight might affect your own work. If you think that important impacts might be missed, it would be wise of you to introduce some bespoke analysis of these potential impacts. Such analysis can be tailored for the needs of your specific project, either as part of the modelling work or separately.

*Figure 39: **background flows**. For each link with freight traffic, we estimate the number of cars that would take the same space as the freight vehicles. We add this fixed number of cars (shown below as yellow boxes) to the relevant link before the assignment, to reflect the capacity taken.*

5.5 Modelling travel by taxi

When I say "taxi", I actually refer to any type of car that is hired for a short use. Similar to goods vehicles, taxis are part of the general traffic on the road network. Taxis are similar to trucks and vans also in the sense that they are difficult to model.

Some of the reasons why it's difficult to model taxis are similar to those I listed for goods vehicles: for example, the fact that some decisions are made by the driver while others are made by the business that employs the driver. In the case of taxis there are also some decisions made by the passenger, who isn't a driver.

There are some additional reasons why modelling taxis is hard, such as the lack of data about the time when taxis drive empty. During this time, a taxi contributes to traffic congestion but it doesn't serve any known demand. Empty trips who wait to find their next costumer won't be picked by assigning a trip matrix to the road network.

Most agencies that build transport models haven't invested in research on these topics. As a result, taxis are represented in most models as background flows, similar to trucks as I showed earlier. They take a pre-fixed amount of road space in the model, and their movements are not changed by the model.

If you work on a study where the impact on taxis could be important, there may be a need to tailor a more specific methodology for the needs of your study.

5.6 Modelling bus travel

This section is about the role of bus travel in the modelling process. Although I refer specifically to buses, the points made here may be relevant to other modes such as trams and trolleybuses. These are all public transport modes that share the road space with car traffic.

Many bus services enjoy their own segregated right of way for part of the route. Along these corridors they may have features more similar to rail services. If there is complete segregation then the route can be modelled just like a rail route, with just some adjustment of model parameters such as vehicle capacity and speed. But it's uncommon for buses, or even trams, to have their own path along the whole route. And because they share the road with car traffic, they have a role in both types of assignment models, i.e. traffic assignment on the road network and route assignment on the public transport network.

In the traffic assignment, the representation of buses is very similar to the representations of trucks, vans and taxis. Buses are added to the model as background flows, so that road space they take is taken into consideration. The traffic assignment does not look at how passengers get on and off the bus; remember that traffic assignment follows vehicles and not people.

Since bus travel times will be affected by the amount of traffic and the level of congestion, a good model will ensure that the travel times calculated in the traffic assignment are fed into the levels of bus service that is used in the public transport assignment.

In the public transport assignment, buses have a central role. They are not just a background flow, but a detailed set of routes with a detailed set of stops, which the modeller needs to specify. The passengers in the model can choose to take any route that runs along a logical path from their origin to their destination.

I discuss public transport assignment models in more detail later, but for now it's worth noting that there's more than one way to include bus routes in the public transport assignment:

- We can include buses in the model as a separate mode, so that deciding to go by bus is a mode choice, and there's a separate demand matrix for bus users. This is followed by a more specific choice of a bus route in the assignment stage.

- Alternatively, we can define all public transport as a single mode, so that deciding to go by bus is a route choice in the assignment, not a mode choice in the mode split. With this approach, bus demand is stored in the public transport demand matrix and not on its own.

Whether bus trips are stored in a bus matrix or in a combined public transport matrix, this matrix is an output from the mode split and distribution models, as part of a multi-modal modelling framework. This matrix is assigned to the route network, which is often run in parallel with the traffic assignment. When both assignments are complete, we have new estimates of travel times and other components of the generalised costs for all modes, so the mode split and distribution can be updated and fed back into a new iteration of the assignment. This process is repeated in a loop, until we get stable results.

5.7 Modelling rail travel

If you follow a multi-modal modelling approach then there are some similarities between the modelling of railway demand and the modelling of bus demand. Similar to bus services, travel by train can be defined either as a separate mode or as part of the public transport mode. If you follow the latter approach, there's no explicit rail mode with its own demand matrix; rail passengers are identified as those who choose rail routes when assigning the matrix of all public transport journeys.

In a multi-modal model, rail demand is estimated through the kind of loop we've already seen. The loop runs through generation, mode split, distribution and assignment, and all the outputs are refined several times because each stage in the model hierarchy modifies the generalised costs.

Rail services use separate infrastructure from other forms of transport. So unlike bus trips, rail trips don't need to be represented in the road network assignment.

The following point is relevant mainly to readers in the UK, because there's a UK-specific practice of rail demand modelling. Unlike the other modes I covered earlier, modelling rail demand in the UK is normally done using a uni-modal approach. The UK transport industry developed a tradition of using the multi-modal approach for all modes except rail, because four-stage models failed to produce good forecasts of rail demand.

Why did they fail? In a four-stage model, the number of rail users is calculated as a proportion of the total demand. This proportion in the real world isn't high; rail is used by a minority of travellers since only specific zones have frequent rail services. Statistically, it's much harder to be accurate when estimating a low proportion. Think for example of an area where 96% of trips are made by car and 4% by train. And let's say the best mode split model we've managed to develop estimates 97% car users and 3% train users. In relative terms, the model estimate of car demand is fairly accurate, but rail demand is seriously underestimated. The rail demand estimate misses by -25%, because 3% is 75% of 4%.

An additional reason why UK modellers weren't happy with multi-modal estimation of rail demand has to do with trip generation. There's evidence that in the last decades, socio-economic factors influenced rail demand growth more directly than the way they influenced other modes. In a multi-modal model this is difficult to represent, because demand growth for all modes is dealt with at the trip generation stage, while the split by mode is introduced later. It's difficult to tell a multi-modal model that rail demand grows faster than the demand for other modes.

A uni-modal approach helped the UK rail industry focus on the factors that directly affect the number of railway passengers. Uni-modal tools estimate the change in rail demand in a future scenario based on the current rail demand, without looking at the demand for other modes. These models use **demand elasticities**, which are parameters that capture how the number of passengers would change if and when there are other changes in the rail network. The concept of elasticity assumes, as the name implies, that demand is elastic, so the number of passengers changes if other factors change.

There are many different types of elasticities. For example, the **demand elasticity to price** is a parameter that reflect how a change in ticket prices influences the number of passengers. If you know the demand elasticity to price, the current number of passengers and the expected price change - then you can calculate the expected number of passengers after the price change.

Figure 40: how elasticities work

Calculating the elasticities: you use data about the number of passengers in situations that differed in a specific factor (like price or travel time). If that factor had a consistent impact then you can calculate the demand elasticity. You don't need to do this too often.

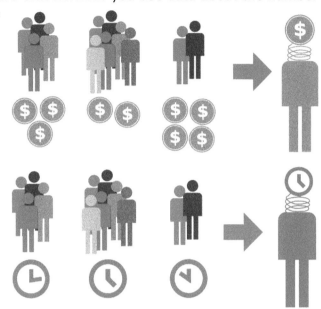

Applying the elasticities:
If you know the current demand, the current level of a factor that affects demand (like price or travel time), and the demand elasticity to this factor – then you can estimate how a change in this factor will influence demand.

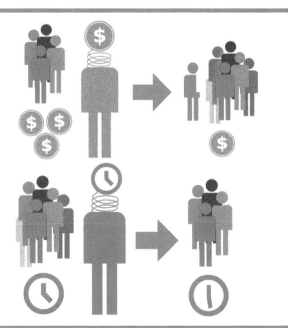

Similarly, if you know the **demand elasticity to travel time**, the current number of passengers and the expected travel time change - then you can calculate the expected number of passengers after a change in travel times.

Another example would be the elasticity of rail demand to income. If you have a source of information about this elasticity, then you can convert information about current rail demand to an estimated future demand for a scenario where people's income changes.

Estimating demand using elasticities is only valid if you have data that tells you what the elasticities are. For example: in order to derive the demand elasticity to price, you need to analyse how rail demand changed over the years as ticket prices changed, and to modify the data to remove the impact of other factors. In the UK rail sector, the Passenger Demand Forecasting Handbook (PDFH) collates a large amount of research about demand elasticities. Parameters from the PDFH are used in various software tools that do uni-modal rail demand estimation.

Figure 40 summarises how elasticities work. Figure 41 summarises some key features of uni-modal and multi-modal modelling, in the context of estimating rail demand.

The rail sector also makes extensive use of other types of models. These models don't have a role in estimating the number of rail passengers but they are critical in planning the operational side of the railway. Operation rail modellers analyse the capacity of different track sections and signalling systems to accommodate train traffic, especially around critical railway junctions. This is a specialised area of work in its own right, which some people see as a type of modelling and others see as a separate kind of engineering activity.

Figure 41: uni-modal and multi-modal models

Multi-modal model	Uni-Modal model
Demand is calculated for all modes. There's no easy way of capturing growth in rail demand only. 	Demand is calculated for rail only. 
Each calculation (generation, mode split etc.) looks at the way many factors affect one decision people make. 	Each calculation (elasticity to price, cost etc.) looks at the way one factor affects many decisions people make. 
If rail has a small share of the total demand, the relative error in estimating rail demand will be high. 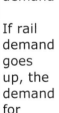	 Calculations are focused on rail demand only, they're likely to be more accurate.
If rail demand goes up, the demand for another mode goes down (and vice versa). The model can tell you what the impact on other modes would be. 	If rail demand changes, the model can't tell you whether there's any impact on other modes. 

5.8 Modelling cycling

I mentioned cycling earlier in this chapter, in the specific context when the bike is a feeder mode, for example on the way from home to a railway station. But there's more to say about the role of cycling in transport models. So here's a review of the messy relationship between cycling and modelling.

For many years it wasn't common to include cycling as a separate mode in transport models. There was no cycling demand matrix and no cycling network. In many places, giving more attention to cycling in the model wasn't considered important. Why wasn't it important? Here's some of the reasons:

- The number of cyclists was a low proportion of total demand so it didn't justify doing any extra work.

- The number of cyclists was relatively stable over time, so it didn't create much interest in forecasting.

- Cyclists didn't contribute much to traffic congestion or to any other burning problem, so there was no strong incentive to strengthen the analysis of cycling demand.

- The amount of public money spent on cycling infrastructure wasn't high enough to require detailed appraisal.

- The investment in cycling was seen as a broader social issue, and not part of a transport investment programme.

- There just wasn't a tradition of including cycling in multi-modal transport models.

In addition to questions about how important it is to model cycling, there were also issues about how difficult it is. Here are some reasons why it was sometimes considered too difficult to model cycling:

- When there were significant changes in the number of cyclists, these changes were not easily explained by changes in infrastructure or other visible factors. Without a visible relationship between a cause and an effect, there's not enough insight to base the model on.

108

- There were, and there still are, many gaps in understanding when people decide to use their bike, when they stop using their bike, and how they make their decisions if they cycle. Developing such understanding requires data collection efforts which are challenging and costly.

- Cycling in many cities is subject to significant seasonality, with much more cycling in the summer than in the winter. Introducing such seasonality to multi-modal models might require fundamental changes to the model structure.

- The traditional segmentation of demand may not be sufficient for modelling cycling. For example, there's some evidence of different behaviour of cyclists in specific age groups. But very few models include segmentation by age.

- Some cycling trips are made for leisure purposes, not necessarily in order to reach a certain point agreed in advance, but simply in order to cycle. This is difficult to fit within the rigid structure of a trip matrix, where each trip has an origin and a destination.

So the difficulty to be explicit about cycling in transport models is real. It's important to remember that many policies and investments can be justified without the use of models. Giving this mode a low priority in the modelling work doesn't mean giving it a low priority in the real transport system. I'll return to this point in the second part of this book.

Nevertheless, in the last few years, much work has been done to better incorporate cycling in many transport models. The reasons for this change include:

- There's better understanding of the health benefits from cycling, which led many authorities to promote cycling more vigorously. I actually tried convincing my auntie Tilda to cycle every now and then, and she said she'll think about it.

- Rising levels of congestion have drawn more attention to the need for alternatives to private cars.

- Social and cultural trends have created increasing pressure to invest in cycling infrastructure, and hence also pressure to develop demand forecasts that would help justify the investment.

- There's an increasing number of locations where cyclist volumes are a cause of traffic congestion, also to cars and buses.

- Media coverage of accidents which involved cyclists has created pressure, in some places, to demonstrate a more structured process of planning cycling infrastructure.

Techniques for modelling cycling are still in early stages of their evolution, so there isn't a specific approach that is considered standard. The most common practice of introducing cycling to four-stage transport models is adding "active modes", namely walking and cycling joined together, as a single mode in the mode split.

Having a single "active modes" mode is convenient because in most cities, the demand for these two modes only takes a small proportion of the total demand. Remember that we're not talking about walking or cycling as a feeder trip, e.g. to a railway station. We're also not talking about internal trips where the destination is in the same zone as the origin (I spoke about such trips in chapter 2). Once you discard these, the remaining number of trips where people walk or cycle as their main mode is usually low, compared to car and public transport. Grouping walking and cycling helps reach a slightly higher proportion, which may reduce the large relative error we get when trying to estimate a small proportion.

When walking and cycling are combined, they are sometimes later split into separate walking and cycling estimates outside the model. We know the distance from each origin zone to each destination zone in the trip matrix, so for each origin-destination pair we can assume what proportion of the "active modes" demand is likely to walk or cycle such a distance. If it's a quarter of a mile then most people would walk it. If it's five miles then it's probably mainly cyclists.

Whichever way you do it, it's important to consider walking and cycling at the mode split stage if their share isn't negligible, either together or as separate modes. It's important even if your work isn't about walking and cycling at all. It's not just because of stakeholder pressures, but also due to a more technical reason. The total demand (from the trip generation stage) may include trips by all modes, and if we simply ignore walking and cycling, these trips wouldn't just disappear; they would be wrongly allocated to public transport or car. Including the active modes in the mode split helps us eliminate walking and cycling trips from the car and public transport matrices.

Having an "active modes" combination in the mode split doesn't resolve most of the difficulties in getting a realistic estimate of the level of cycling. You may notice a similarity between these difficulties and the difficulty to estimate rail demand, which I spoke about earlier. Like with railway passengers, the factors influencing cyclists (or potential future cyclists) can be too subtle for a multi-modal model where most attention goes to the other modes. For this reason, there are some emerging examples of uni-modal models built to estimate cycling demand only. The advantages and disadvantages of uni-modal estimation of cycling demand are very similar to those I listed in figure 41.

There are also some emerging examples of assignment models for cyclists, somewhat equivalent to traffic assignment and public transport assignment models. A cycling assignment model needs to have a cycling network, i.e. a comprehensive set of links and nodes where cycling is allowed. The cycling network will be similar to the road network, but it would also include cycle paths where cars are not allowed, some paths that cut through parks, some riverside routes and so on. The cycling network would exclude major roads where cycling is not allowed.

If there is a cycling trip matrix, either from the mode split stage or from a uni-modal model, then it can be assigned to the cycling network. This would help us estimate where in the network high cycling volumes are expected. It would also allow us to calculate expected cycling times from different origins to different destinations.

Cycling might have a little role to play also in the assignment of cars to the road network, and in micro-simulation of junctions and urban corridors. I'll say more about these models in chapter 9, but I'll mention here that bikes have a role because we need to understand how much road capacity they take. Considering cycling in these road models is important only in those places where the flow of cyclists takes up considerable road space. We can calculate how much space they take and include it in the model as a background flow. The process is similar to what we do for freight vehicles, as I showed in the section on freight, except of course that one bike takes much less space than one truck.

Phew! I mentioned here a range of different roles, important and less important, that cycling can have in different types of models. I did warn you it will be a mess. A summary of all these different roles is presented in figure 42.

Figure 42: cycling in different types of models

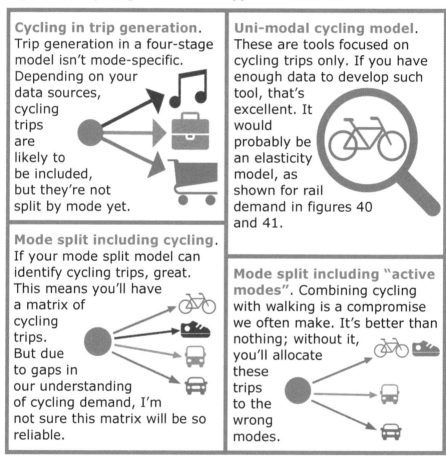

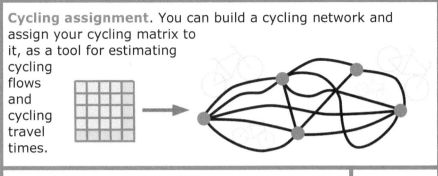

Cycling assignment. You can build a cycling network and assign your cycling matrix to it, as a tool for estimating cycling flows and cycling travel times.

Cycling in car assignment or micro-simulation. Including cycling as background flows (as I showed in the section about freight) helps us understand the impact of cyclists taking up some road space.

Not modelling cycling. Not the end of the world. Read about other sources of evidence in the second part of this book.

5.9 Modelling travel by motorcycle

The demand for using motorcycles is a matter of local culture. Like with bicycles, there are gaps in our understanding of the decision to use motorcycles in different places and the route choices motorcyclists make. We know that motorcycle use tends to be higher where there's more congestion. We also know that, similar to bicycles, traditional demand segmentation doesn't work well for motorcyclists, for example because there are more male than female users.

However, despite some similarities to bicycles, the use of motorbikes has some features very different from cycling:

- Motorcycles only use the main road network, and rarely have separate paths for their own use.

- There isn't much seasonality in the use of motorcycles.

- There aren't many investments of public money focused on this mode alone, and there's no policy to encourage it.
- The origins and destinations of motorcycle trips are similar to car trips, and there isn't a significant tendency to use them for leisure trips.

All these points suggest that in modelling terms, motorcycles are more like small cars than like big bikes. Like all road vehicles, motorcycles do contribute to levels of congestion by taking up some road space; a single motorcycle would typically take more space than a bike but less than a car.

Motorcycle trips have some unique traffic impacts in specific locations where they use their faster acceleration, or where they can fit within one lane alongside another vehicle. So it would seem sensible to develop a separate demand matrix for motorcycles and to assign it as a separate mode which shares its network with other road users. Ideally, motorcycles should be a separate mode in mode split models. But the data we have on motorcycle demand is rarely rich enough to create such a separate mode with a separate demand matrix.

Most urban areas today don't experience any significant trend of rise or fall in the use of motorcycles. Therefore, there isn't much pressure on modellers to improve the representation of this mode in their models. There are specific models developed in toll road revenue studies, which give special attention to motorcycles since they can be used as an alternative to paying the toll. But in most other situations, motorcycle traffic is handled simplistically as background flows. This is similar to the way it's done for other modes, as I showed earlier.

5.10 Modelling walking

When it comes to modelling walking, the default practice is to do as little as possible. Modellers assume that people will walk as a feeder mode to and from public transport stops. In mode split models, walking is sometimes part of an "active modes" option, which is included in order to eliminate those who walk or cycle from the car and public transport matrices.

Some of the reasons why it's a burden to model walking are similar to those I listed in the section about cycling. But in the case of walking there's an even bigger problem. The problem is that it's difficult to decide what counts as a walking trip in the first place.

With most modes of transport, it goes without saying that every trip people make is relevant to the transport planning process, so we try to store every trip in the trip matrix of the relevant demand segment. But with walking, it's less obvious what we need to define as a trip that goes to a matrix. Here are a few examples.

- There are people who live 5 kilometres from work and have a choice between taking a bus, driving, cycling or walking. Not many people commute 5 kilometres by foot, but some people do. In these cases, this definitely is a commuting trip where the chosen mode is walking.

- Then there are people who live 500 meters from a local shop. They sometimes go there to get milk and then go back home. Most people will walk to the shop and back, but there are people who would take their car, cycle or ride a bus for one stop. If we have a demand matrix for a "shopping" purpose, or a matrix that combines various non-work trips, then this trip

115

clearly belongs there. But in surveys where people are asked about all the trips they make, this type of journey is often forgotten, especially if it's done by foot. If the trip isn't recorded then it probably won't be stored in the matrix, even if it should.

- There are even shorter trips, which are almost always made on foot. If you leave the office at lunchtime to buy a sandwich at the shop next door, it does formally count as a trip, but is it very different from the trip you would make if you bought the same sandwich at the cafeteria on the ground floor, without leaving the building? Similarly, if you want to buy new shoes and you visit 5 shops on the same street, spending 15 minutes in each one before moving to the one next door, should our trip matrices store information on 5 trips between shops?

The definition of a walking trip, in reality, depends on the source of data from which you learn about those trips. Whether or not your data source is sufficient depends on the purpose of the analysis.

If your objective is to test which types of transport investments will encourage more people to walk to work, and adopt a healthier lifestyle, then the relevant trips are probably stored in your demand matrices, because they are currently made by other modes. But only very advanced models have a mode split component that will know how to identify the types of transport improvement that will make people abandon another mode in favour of walking to work.

If your objective is to estimate the number of pedestrians in the street, then you'd rarely find a satisfactory model. Many of the pedestrians may be making those very short trips that we have little knowledge of, and besides, most models lack the very high level of spatial detail needed to determine where in the street a pedestrian would be.

So if there's interest in detailed outputs that include the number of people walking, then most chances are that you'll need a bespoke methodology developed especially for your study. It's also likely that additional data collection will be needed, beyond the standard types of data that are normally used for building transport models.

A very different type of modelling, which directly relates to walking, is station modelling. Unlike the questions described above, which extend beyond the standard existing practice, modelling the flow of passengers through a public transport station is a well-established area of transport modelling. There are various commercial software packages dealing with it and providing credible insight.

Station modelling usually focuses on various areas within the building of a busy station: train platforms, concourses, ticket halls, ticket gate areas, corridors, stairs and escalators. All these are subject to high flows of people rushing in and out during busy periods, and if the design of the station building is unable to accommodate them, there are major safety risks.

Station models analyse patterns of passenger movement in the station space after they leave a train or when coming in from the street. These models explore how these passengers mix when they walk at different speeds towards different exits, platforms or other parts of the station. These models can recommend where in the building there are high risks of overcrowding.

5.11 Models for air travel

Air transport is provided by an industry which only has a partial overlap with the world of urban transport (and hence with what this book focuses on). The aviation world has its own extensive modelling practices for air traffic and for air passenger demand; I don't cover these here. However, there are three families of models concerning air passengers, which have strong links with the models I've mentioned already.

Firstly, travel by plane could be one of the alternatives in a mode split model, if the model focuses on long-distance travel. Many countries have a national transport model, which they use to assess inter-urban motorways, railway investments, economic policies and land use strategies. For some of the journeys covered by these models, the proportion of travellers choosing to fly can be considerable. Models that include an air mode can be developed, calibrated and run in a very similar way to metropolitan mode split models. However, the variables that explain passenger choices in these models, and the weights attached to these variables, will be different. That's because price, travel time, comfort, safety, security and other factors influence long-distance trips differently from urban trips.

Secondly, there are travel demand models that concentrate on **surface access** to airports. Surface access models deal with the way passengers choose their travel mode and route before or after a flight. A surface access model can often take the form of a standard four-stage model; the only unique feature is that the model concentrates on one journey purpose, that is travel to an airport. Typical demand segmentation in such a model would separate between airport employees, business travellers and tourists.

Thirdly, it's worth noting that many other decisions by air travellers can be modelled using the same techniques which we use for modelling mode choice. The choice between different airlines, the choice between holiday destinations, the choice between airports to depart from, or the choice between the different classes on the aircraft - they can all be analysed using **discrete choice modelling**, which is the same technique we use for modelling mode split. Discrete choice modelling is used in situations where people need to choose between a relatively small number of options, and each option has its own characteristics. The process of developing a model to estimate how commuters choose between car and bus is actually the same as the process of developing a model to estimate air passengers' choice between JFK airport and La Guardia airport.

5.12 Modelling self-driving vehicles

Bad news: for this topic, you'll have to wait until the last chapter of this book. That's because the modelling community has only very recently started thinking about self-driving vehicles, so I leave it for the chapter about the future of transport modelling. Of course you can go straight to the end of the book now, if you really can't wait. But please come back.

Chapter 6
More on trip generation

6.1 Trip ends and trip rates

When colleagues and clients come to a modelling expert with a request, they rarely talk about trip generation. The dialogue with clients is often limited to simple concerns, such as traffic congestion. Many clients have worked with modellers before, and are used to seeing maps showing changes in the number of vehicles or passengers in their project area. They might not be too interested in the earlier modelling work that determines what goes into these maps at a later stage.

There are cases where clients express concerns about the trips generated by a new transport investment. What they may call "generated trips" is not necessarily related to trip generation modelling:

- An increase in the number of vehicles or passengers in the study area could be a result of people changing their routes. In an informal language this is sometimes called "trip generation", but it is covered by assignment models.

- A similar change could be a result of people changing the destination of their trip. Again, some people may call this "trip generation", but this is covered by the distribution model.

- An increase in traffic can also be a result of travellers making more use of their cars on trips they previously made by public transport. Again, some people call this "trip generation", but this is explored when modelling mode split.

The key thing trip generation models deal with is the total amount of travel that different types of people make. The trip generation stage doesn't deal with how this total demand splits between modes of transport (although we do sometimes generate the demand by mode, and the mode choice model later updates this split). When we estimate the total numbers of trips to be generated in each zone, we often call them **trip ends**. We estimate the trip ends using **trip rates**.

A trip rate is the typical number of trips made by different types of people, in different types of areas, in different types of buildings, for different purposes. There's some evidence that, compared to other types of information, trip rates can be fairly consistent over time and also between different places of a similar type. This is why it's justified to see trip rates as a relatively stable piece of information, from which the modelling process starts.

In the UK, US and other countries, there are some official publications where authorities suggest which trip rates should be used. In the UK there are also formally-published trip end forecasts for different future years.

Trip rates use very detailed segmentation, i.e. more segments than those we use anywhere else in the model. Let's say our model includes demand segmentation by income, car availability and trip purpose (you can go to chapter 2 for a quick reminder). So one of the segments will include the commuting trips made by households with a medium income and one car. In the trip generation stage for this segment, we calculate the **trip ends** to and from each zone based on **trips rates** such as these:

- The number of commuting trips by households with a medium income, one car, two adults working full time, more than 2 children, living in a town centre
- The number of commuting trips by households with a medium income, one car, two adults working full time, more than 2 children, living in suburbs
- The number of commuting trips by households with a medium income, one car, two adults working full time, more than 2 children, living in a rural area

- The number of commuting trips by households with a medium income, one car, two adults of which one working full time, more than 2 children, living in a town centre

- The number of commuting trips by households with a medium income, one car, two adults of which one working full time, more than 2 children, living in suburbs

- The number of commuting trips by households with a medium income, one car, two adults of which one working full time, more than 2 children, living in a rural area

- The number of commuting trips by households with a medium income, one car, one adult, no children, living in a town centre

- And so on – the list can be very long.

We need to know the number of households of each type in each zone. We also need the total built space for different types of land use (shops, offices, hotels, restaurants, warehouses, flats, houses etc.), because some trip rates would be expressed as the number of trips per unit of built space.

To complete the calculation of trip ends for each zone, we add up trip rate information across the different types of households and different land uses in that zone. At the end of this calculation, each trip end becomes the sum of either a row or a column in our trip matrix for one demand segment, as I showed in figure 20.

If you already have a source of information on current trip ends then you have trip generation figures for your base scenario. Your trip generation model will still need to estimate, for each demand segment, whether more or less trips will be generated in other scenarios – for example if you build 5000 new houses and 20 new shops in the area.

6.2 Demand growth scenarios

If you have information on planned changes in your study area, and you turn this information into trip ends using trip rates, you might feel that now you know everything you need about future trip generation. But it's unhealthy to start your modelling process with too much confidence in a specific level of forecast growth.

It's safer to think about several **demand growth scenarios**. These scenarios vary from each other in terms of the assumed trip generation and not in the detail of your project or investment. You'll use the model to test your project under all these different demand growth scenarios, because each one of them may or may not happen.

There are no scientific methods for producing demand growth scenarios or for deciding how many trips will be generated in each scenario. But there are various considerations to have in mind when defining these scenarios, as shown in figure 43. Remember that this is the stage where you create the inputs into your entire modelling work, at the top of the model hierarchy (which I described in chapter 3). You're probably aware of the rule "garbage in - garbage out"; your entire modelling work will not be trustworthy if the assumptions behind your demand growth aren't plausible.

6.3 Production and attraction

In chapter 3 I showed a matrix view of a four-stage model. It illustrated that at the generation stage, we create a set of empty demand matrices, and we only estimate the totals of the rows and the columns. To keep things simple, I so far referred to the rows of the matrix as representing origins, and the columns as representing destinations. But there's a slight complication of this structure that I need to introduce now.

The trip generation process (that is the process of using trip rates to calculate trip ends) can be carried out in two different ways, called either **production** or **attraction**.

Figure 43: considerations when defining growth scenarios

Different trip rates. The standard trip rates are just averages calculated from data which actually varies a lot. You can define scenarios based on different rates, especially if you have local knowledge about how much people travel.

Employment growth. The number of commuting and business trips will depend on levels of employment in each zone. So you should consider different ways employment in the area may develop, the sectors that may be concerned, and whether wider economic changes are expected in adjacent zones.

Technology trends. You'll have different trip generation forecasts if you vary your assumptions about technology impacts, e.g. working from home, using apps for shared riding, and the take up of self-driving vehicles.

Population growth. Different growth scenarios can be based on different assumptions regarding people moving into or out of the area, and different plans for building new houses.

Shopping and leisure. Growth scenarios may differ in the way each zone attracts shopping and leisure trips, and you should consider the competition between retail and leisure centres when making your assumptions.

Mode-specific factors. Trip generation in a four-stage model looks at total demand, not split by mode. But the trip rates used as input may vary by mode. So we could define scenarios where an area generates more or less trips for mode-specific reasons. These could relate to car ownership, fuel prices, changes in fuel efficiency, parking policy, changes in the capacity or quality of public transport, or investment in infrastructure for walking and cycling.

Production is the same as trip generation, but only for trips people make from home or back home from somewhere else. The modelling jargon says that these trips are **produced** at home. To estimate the number of trips from or to home, we decide which trip rates to use based on various residential characteristics of the zone where the home is.

Attraction is the same as trip generation, but only for trips people make to or from places which aren't their home. Journeys to or from work are the most common example. The modelling jargon says that these trips are **attracted** to the workplace. To estimate the number of trips to or from work, we decide which trip rates to use based on characteristics of the zone where the workplace is.

Each trip is produced somewhere and attracted to somewhere. But at the trip generation stage we only estimate the total number of trips produced and attracted (in each demand segment) in each zone. The trips produced in each zone are not yet distributed between the different possible zones they can be attracted to, and the trips attracted to each zone are not yet distributed between the different possible zones they can be produced at. This is all done at the trip distribution stage.

At the trip generation stage we don't even distinguish between trips by their direction. For example, when a person lives in zone A and works in zone B, they'll usually travel from A to B and later from B back to A. But in terms of production and attraction, both trips are produced in zone A and attracted to zone B. That's because we need to know the residential characteristics of zone A and the non-residential characteristics of zone B in order to estimate the amount of commuting trips in both directions.

Trip generation is much more about processing land use information, and not so much about the direction of the trip. For this reason, we use a production/attraction format for the trip matrices at the generation stage:

- The trips in row A include both trips to zone A and from zone A, as long as they're produced there, or in other words, as long as they're based on the residential characteristics of that zone.

- The trips in column B include both trips to zone B and from zone B, as long as they're attracted to there, or in other words, as long as they're based on the non-residential characteristics of that zone.

In the trip distribution stage we will re-organise the matrix, to make sure that the direction of the trip is considered. At that stage we'll start seeing each row as an origin and each column as a destination.

The generation of trips that have no end at home (for example, from work to the gym) is a challenge. Quite often, neither of the two zones have characteristics that help estimate how many such trips will be made. The generation of trips with no end at home is often approximated using much simpler rules. For example, it can be set to be a fixed proportion (say, 30%) of the number of trips attracted to the same zone.

Figure 44: production and attraction. I live in zone 1. I work in zone 2. My trip from home to work will be stored in cell (1, 2) of the commute matrix, when it's converted to an origin-destination format. My trip back home will be stored in cell (2, 1). But at the trip generation stage we still use a production-attraction format. The information we store at this stage is that two trips (ignoring the direction) are produced in zone 1 and two trips are attracted to zone 2. Now, my auntie Tilda lives in zone 3. If I go to visit her after work, my trip there goes to cell (2, 3), no matter which format we use, because there aren't clear production-attraction rules for non-home-based trips.

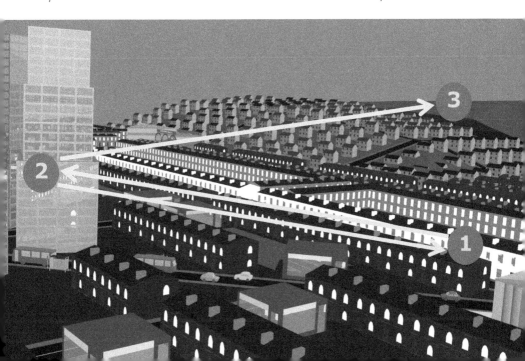

6.4 Will the total demand change?

Trip rates help us estimate the total demand from information about population and land use. If trip rates give us different demand in different scenarios then it's because we make different land use assumptions in these scenarios, not because of the transport project we're testing. But in parallel we also want to know whether or not our transport project will change the total amount of travel in the area.

A common assumption when assessing investment options is that the investment itself doesn't change land use. We can have scenarios with different land use assumptions, but for each one of them we need to run the model once with and once without our project, so that we don't confuse the impact of the project with the impact of the land use change.

If the total trip generation changes as a result of our investment, then it must be a result of changes in the generalised costs of travel. I showed in chapter 3 how we turn generalised costs into composite costs and take them one level up in the model hierarchy each time; this leads to changes in the estimated demand. So changes in trip generation should be based on the composite costs from the model that sits one level below generation in the hierarchy, which is usually mode split.

Remember (from chapter 3) that the composite costs we take from the level just below generation are by themselves a result of summarising many different costs. Therefore, when we use these costs in trip generation, what it intuitively means is that the total demand will change if there's an overall cost change across all modes, origins, destinations and routes. If the travel experience to or from a specific zone improves, across all different travel options, then there will be a reduction in the composite cost for that zone, and more trips will be produced or attracted. If travel experience gets worse, then the overall costs will rise and demand will fall.

But how exactly can we use the cost change to calculate the new number of trips generated in each zone? I showed in chapter 3

126

that in every stage of a four-stage model, the total demand comes from the level just above it in the model hierarchy. For example, in the mode split stage, the composite costs of all the modes help us split the total demand between the modes, and then the demand for each mode continues down the hierarchy. But trip generation is at the top of the hierarchy, so above it there's only blue sky!

Since trip generation doesn't have another model above it, which gives each zone a different demand if costs change, we follow a different approach in this case. I showed in chapter 5 that in some cases we calculate demand changes using **elasticities** (see figure 40). In chapter 5 this was in the context of estimating changes to rail demand in a uni-modal model. The same concept also works at the top level of the four-stage model. Here we use the elasticity of the total demand to the composite cost.

An elasticity calculation will estimate the demand in a future scenario as a function of:

■ The demand in the base scenario, i.e. before the change

■ The change in cost, taken from lower levels of the hierarchy

■ The elasticity of demand to cost changes.

We sometimes refer to these calculations as the **trip frequency** model. Trip frequency is almost the same thing as trip generation, with just a change of wording: instead of talking about how many trips are generated, we're talking about how frequently people travel. In reality these questions are equivalent, and we use the different terms just to clarify that a trip frequency model uses an elasticity-based calculation for our trip generation. There are some publications that suggest what values of the elasticities should be used to model trip frequency.

One big problem we face is that transport planners actually don't know much about how transport investment changes the overall amount of travel. Most sources of information about this have serious limitations. For example: we can't collect data that directly compares travel with the investment to travel without it. It takes a long time to build a station or a bridge, so even if we collect a lot of data, it will be about "before" and "after" rather than "with" and "without".

The opening of a new bridge or station aren't the only change that happens after we collect the "before" data and before we collect the "after" data. There are population changes, offices and shops move about, prices change, bus services are modified, and so on. This means that we only have partial answers about the question of how transport projects change the amount of travel.

There's an interesting recommendation in the transport assessment guidance from the UK government. It says that changes to trip frequency happen mainly because people use a car or public transport to make trips which they previously made locally by bike or by foot. In other words, it says that if all the trips are included in the model, including local walking and cycling trips, then the mode split stage will cover the behavioural responses which we would otherwise see as changes in trip generation. I have to say this bit of guidance is quite problematic, because we rarely have the advanced data and modelling skills needed in order to include all those very short trips people make locally.

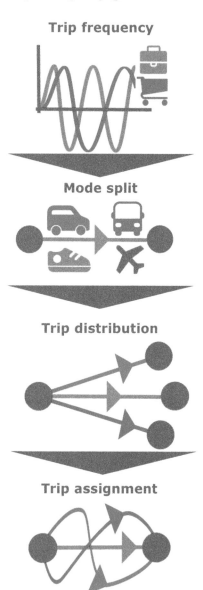

Figure 45: a four-stage model with trip frequency replacing trip generation

Trip frequency

Mode split

Trip distribution

Trip assignment

The bottom line is that you need to decide how to deal with the impact of your project on the overall amount of travel in your study area. You may accept the argument that trip frequency, i.e. changes in trip generation, won't change much because all the trips people make are already included in your trip matrices. Alternatively, you may acknowledge the limitations of your data, and do more work to improve your trip generation model. It's important that you use your own judgement to decide what's best in your circumstances, since there's no strong evidence on what is right or wrong.

6.5 Land use and transport interaction

I mentioned earlier that for the assessment of a new transport improvement, we usually assume that land use is fixed. The locations of houses, offices, factories and so on definitely do change over time, but much of the change is the same with or without your transport improvement. So we use the same land use assumptions in our scenarios with and without the project, so that our assessment of the project is fair.

The land use we "freeze" when assessing our investment includes not only the background changes, which would happen anyway, but also land use changes that would happen as a result of the investment. If we build a new station then people may find the area around it a more attractive place to live, and companies may locate there because it's convenient for goods deliveries. Similar impacts can also occur in the opposite direction, such as offices moving out of town because our project makes traffic congestion worse.

These are examples of important impacts of transport projects, and still, the tradition is to ignore them in the main modelling work. This has two reasons:

- There's a view that these possible impacts won't change the overall benefit from the investment. The property rent price near a new station may rise, for example, but all it means is that some people will pay more and others will earn more, which is overall neutral.

- Allowing for land use impacts will seriously complicate the analysis and modelling we need to do.

129

By contrast, many experts argue that it's important to understand the way transport investment leads to new property development, business re-location, and changes in people's choice of where to live. The importance of analysing these types of land use impacts is explained by the following reasons:

- Changes in where people live or work have an impact on traffic congestion and public transport crowding. So they can change the benefits from the investment.

- Changes in rent or house prices shouldn't be seen as economically neutral, even if it's just money changing hands between different people, because these changes affect some socio-demographic groups more negatively than others.

- Without considering land use impacts, models mainly show benefits from reduction in travel time. But in reality, travel time changes can make people consider moving to live or work somewhere else.

These views led to the development of a group of models which look at the impacts of transport changes outside the transport system. These models are called **Land Use and Transport Interaction (LUTI)** models. The use of LUTI models is often done not as part of the basic transport assessment but as an extension. LUTI modelling is not part of the four-stage concept, but it can complement the standard trip generation stage and give alternative estimates of trip productions and attractions.

Similar to standard four-stage models, LUTI models try to reproduce the decisions that travellers make when they travel. But unlike the standard transport models, LUTI models also try to reproduce other decisions:

- The way employees in different sectors decide where to work.

- The way employers in different sectors decide where to locate their business.

- The way developers decide where to build new houses.

- The way land or property owners decide how much rent to charge from their tenants.

130

These decisions depend on various factors, which include some transport-related factors, but not only. Many LUTI models simulate how everyone in the study area (people, companies, developers etc.) behaves over a long period of time, to show that the decisions made by one "player" in one year can affect how everyone else behaves in the following year. This is done in a loop that repeats every year. For example, the model can show that traffic congestion in the city centre causes some businesses to move to out-of-town locations, and a few years later, congestion develops in new places.

Another example is shown in figure 46. This figure shows an urban area at four different points in time, at 10-year intervals. Some of the factors that influence how the area develops are transport-related and other are not. The figure shows a possible forecast from a LUTI model, which couldn't be obtained by a standard trip generation model, because the generation model only estimates the number of trips to and from each zone.

LUTI models cover a much wider scope of behaviours and trends than standard transport models. This gives them the major advantage of helping our thinking about the broader impacts of transport investment and about wider problems in town planning. But it's also a great disadvantage, because you need a very large amount of data and a significant development effort to create a credible LUTI model. Without comprehensive research on how companies, employees and developers behave, the outputs from LUTI models will not be sound.

It's also very difficult to define consistent calibration and validation criteria for LUTI models. One key reason for this is that these models try to capture processes and trends which are very slow, like the decision of a factory to move from one location to another. Collecting information on such decisions, in a way that would then make you able to forecast when these decisions will be made in the future, is extremely ambitious.

Therefore, LUTI models provide valuable food for thought into the transport planning process, but their forecasts should always be seen as highly uncertain.

Figure 46: LUTI forecasts. The first image is the base year. The town centre is densely-built and congested. Out of town there are suburbs near an industrial area. The second image is a forecast for 10 years later. High rents and traffic in town lead to the development of new houses and shops away from the centre, and expansion of the suburb.

Figure 46: LUTI forecasts (continued). *A forecast for another 10 years later (above) shows no relief in property prices, traffic and pollution. This sees a further shift of activities out of town, where urban sprawl now surrounds the old suburbs. Another 10 years later (below), land values push the industrial area away, with high-rise development competing with the old town centre.*

6.6 The main limitations of trip generation models

To summarise this chapter about trip generation models, figure 47 contains a reminder of their key limitations. It's important to remember these limitations to ensure that you make a responsible use of trip generation outputs.

When creating models there's always a choice to make between different approaches, and this choice can have a considerable impact on model outputs. Whichever modelling approach you follow, the main limitations need to be explained to anyone who sees the outputs, even if they're not very interested in the modelling technique.

If you work on the side that creates the model, you have a responsibility to give these explanations. If you work on the side that receives model outputs, you have a responsibility to request that such explanations are given to you. If you don't follow this practice, there's a good chance that someone will think the model found some evidence about things which, in reality, the model didn't check at all.

Figure 47: limitations of generation models

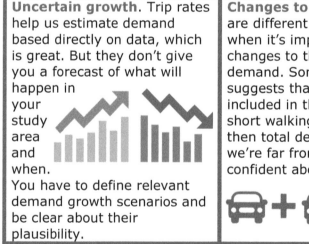

Uncertain growth. Trip rates help us estimate demand based directly on data, which is great. But they don't give you a forecast of what will happen in your study area and when. You have to define relevant demand growth scenarios and be clear about their plausibility.	**Changes to the total.** There are different views regarding when it's important to consider changes to the total travel demand. Some evidence suggests that if all trips are included in the model, including short walking and cycling trips, then total demand is fixed. But we're far from being confident about this.

What is trip generation. The definition of trip generation is not intuitive to clients. When discussing rise or fall in travel demand, it's important to be clear on whether this is modelled as trip generation or as other responses, such as people changing mode, destination or route. Otherwise, misinterpretation of model outputs is very likely.

Unclear behaviour. The generation of trips which are not from home or to home is poorly understood by many models. You should acknowledge the lower certainty about these trips, and fill in gaps using local data.

Model scope. If you don't use land use and transport interaction (LUTI) modelling as input to trip generation, you should make it clear that your work assumes nobody will change their workplace or move home because of transport issues.

Clarity of assumptions. If you model land use and transport interaction (LUTI), clients should be aware of the various assumptions made about the location decisions of employees, employers and so on. So many assumptions are needed, that they're unlikely to all be realistic.

Chapter 7

More on mode split

7.1 Mode split before or after distribution

I showed in chapter 3 that in a transport model, we can choose the order of responses people make to changes in the transport system. A different order of responses reflects a different travel behaviour. Formally we're meant to observe the behaviour in the real world and then choose the model hierarchy so that it captures the right behaviour. In reality this would require so much data collection and model calibration work, that we tend to follow what others have done before, so there's less confidence that it really reflects the correct travel behaviour.

One of the things that vary between different models is the order of mode split and trip distribution. There were times when it was common to assume that distribution comes first and mode choice follows. Now it's more common to assume that mode choice comes first and distribution follows.

The order of split and distribution isn't about what people decide first. It's about how willing they are to change their choice. A choice which sits closer to the bottom of the hierarchy is one that travellers will change more flexibly and more often. A choice that sits closer to the top is harder to change because all the choices below it will need to change as well. See figure 24 for a reminder.

So if you put mode split first, you assume that people are more attached to their mode of transport than to where they go. You do it at the trip end level (see chapter 6 if you forgot what a trip end is): you split all the demand from each origin, and also all the demand to each destination, between the different modes. When you do it you go through all origins and all destinations. So if for example your model has 500 zones, you have 1,000 calculations, because each zone is an origin and a destination.

If you model mode choice after distribution then you do it separately for each cell in the matrix, i.e. for each origin-destination pair (**OD pair**). In computational terms, applying mode split at an OD level is much more intensive: if you have 500 zones, you have 250,000 calculations (500 x 500).

Despite the difference in the computing effort, the main consideration behind the model hierarchy should be behavioural, and this is why both types of choice order are quite common. Besides, even though "split first" requires fewer calculations, you then apply trip distribution separately for each mode, which is more work. See figures 21, 22 and 26 for a reminder.

The outputs of mode choice and trip distribution, never mind in which order, usually continue to the assignment stage. It's common for clients to only ask questions about the assignment, because the geographically-detailed outputs are easier to understand. But it's important to also discuss the outputs of mode choice and distribution. Without doing this, you can't tell whether assignment results in a specific part of the network really tell you something about that location. They might be indicating something more general.

Figure 48: present the outputs from every model stage. Assignment outputs for the place shown below can tell you that your project leads to more car traffic on this street. But maybe there's more car traffic everywhere? Check this in the mode split. Or maybe the area attracts more trips by all modes? Check this in the generation and distribution outputs.

7.2 Split between public transport modes

Mode split models vary greatly in their complexity. Many of them only cover the split of demand between car and public transport. Others include walking, cycling and various other mode options. A particular aspect where models differ is in whether the choice between public transport modes is considered a question of mode choice or a question of route choice.

Figure 49 shows an example of the two approaches to splitting between public transport modes. It focuses on a single journey from home to work. The network and the available alternatives are given, but there are two different ways of representing them in the model.

Why does it matter which stage of the process distinguishes between public transport modes? It's important because each approach can give you different outputs. Each of them has upsides and downsides, which are shown in figure 50. Ideally, the choice between the approaches should be based on checking which one can best replicate observed data. But the effort of building models of both types and making the comparison isn't realistic.

Therefore, when using the outputs from a model that is based on any of these two approaches, remember that the choice of the modelling approach wasn't a scientific decision. The limitations of the selected approach, as summarised in figure 50, should be explained to clients and stakeholders together with the outputs, because sometimes they reduce the credibility of the model.

7.3 Stated Preference and Revealed Preference

The types of data we use when developing mode split models can be classified as either **Stated Preference** or **Revealed Preference**. They are often referred to as **SP** and **RP**. Figure 51 shows the key difference between SP data and RP data.

Figure 49: split between public transport modes

Stage	Public transport modes modelled as modes	Public transport modes modelled as routes
Alternatives in the mode split	■ Car ■ Bus ■ Rail	■ Car ■ Public transport
Alternatives in the route assignment	Rail users: ■ Train from Greentown to Bridgetown, with green bus as a feeder at the origin and walking as a feeder at the destination Bus users: ■ Green bus and then purple bus ■ Purple bus, with walking as a feeder at the origin	■ Green bus and then train, with walking as a feeder at the destination ■ Purple bus, with walking as a feeder at the origin ■ Green bus and then purple bus

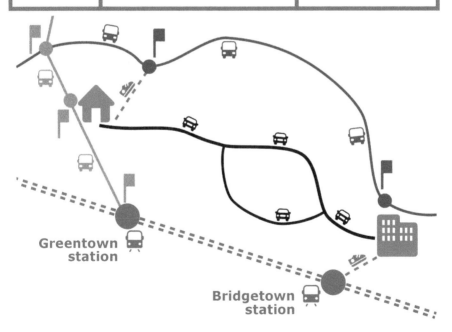

Greentown station

Bridgetown station

Figure 50: split between public transport modes

Public transport modes modelled as modes	Public transport modes modelled as routes
You can easily present mode-specific outputs and stats. Assignment is simpler, since each mode is assigned to its own network. In the mode split model we can define sub-modes, such as coach and bus, to show that they are different but related. It's easier to add new variables that affect the choice between modes, such as the type of train. Modelling trips that combine different public transport modes is very difficult. Therefore, this approach isn't suitable for big cities where people often use different modes on one journey.	Much easier to represent cases where bus, rail, metro etc. are used on the same trip. Therefore, it's the only feasible option in cities like London or NYC. Harder to present mode-specific stats. The assignment network is complex and requires a more significant effort to code and calibrate. In a route choice model it's harder to introduce special parameters that help adjust people's choice behaviour in specific places or on specific modes. It's also difficult to show that some modes split into sub-modes (e.g. bus and coach)

Figure 51: RP versus SP

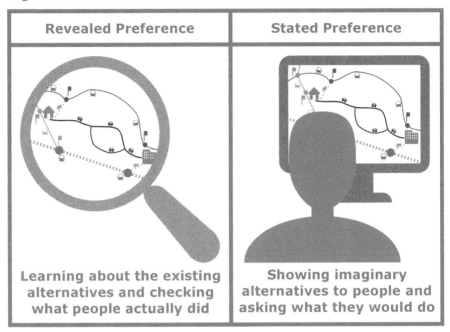

Revealed Preference	Stated Preference
Learning about the existing alternatives and checking what people actually did	Showing imaginary alternatives to people and asking what they would do

The distinction between SP and RP isn't specific to mode split, and there are other types of models where we can use SP, RP or both. But the question "SP or RP" does come up very often in the context of mode split, because it's so difficult to find good data about the way people choose their mode of transport.

The word "revealed" in RP implies that this type of data is collected by observing things that actually happened. RP is the ideal type of data, and it should be used whenever possible because it's directly based on the relevant evidence.

RP data doesn't always come in the same format. It counts as RP whenever it captures real observation, such as the amount of traffic we count on a street, or the list of journeys people tell us they made when they fill in a travel diary. Most of the data sources I listed in figure 36 give us RP data.

SP data doesn't contain information on things that actually happened. The word "stated" in SP indicates that it's about what people state they would do in a hypothetical situation, rather than what they really do. SP data always comes from an SP survey, which is a specific type of behavioural survey. In SP surveys, people are presented with imaginary situations and are asked to choose which one of them they would prefer.

There are techniques for developing SP surveys so that they seem as realistic as possible. An example of one question from an SP survey is shown in figure 52. Survey participants are usually shown a series of such questions. This survey is a computer-based one, since most SP surveys today are internet-based, although SP surveys can also be undertaken using a paper questionnaire, on the phone or face-to-face.

Why would we build a model based on things people say they'd do but they haven't actually done? We do it simply because we have no choice. In mode split modelling it's very common that RP just doesn't work, despite being our preferred type of data. Figure 53 shows the most common reasons why we use SP, together with some strengths and weaknesses to keep in mind.

Figure 52: an SP question

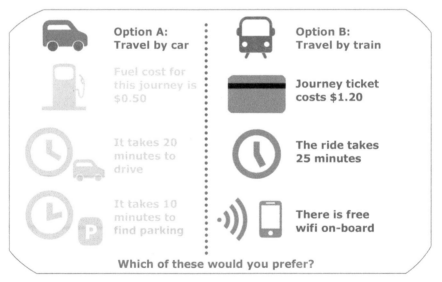

142

Figure 53: SP data as an alternative to RP

Issues with RP data	SP as an alternative
Often we simply don't have RP data. We need to look at a range of situations where people had a choice between modes. We need to know which mode they chose, and we need information on factors that may have influenced their choice, such as travel time by each mode, fare, fuel cost, and so on. RP data on all these is not always available. 	In an SP survey we can always make up any situation we want. Any choice situation is kosher in SP. SP questions are hypothetical. What participants prefer in the survey doesn't prove they'd prefer the same in reality. Sometimes respondents feel pressure to please or impress those who collect the data.
RP data is not varied enough. We need to estimate the values of model parameters (see chapter 4). This doesn't work if there isn't enough variation in the data. Each factor that may explain people's mode choice needs to be sometimes high and sometimes low; if not, we cannot identify whether the change in this factor influenced people's choice.	SP surveys are designed so that the questions cover a wide range of each factor. The variation in the SP survey is made up, so there's a risk that the model will be based on the assumptions we made rather than on the variation that exists in the real world.

Issues with RP data	SP as an alternative
One of the options doesn't exist. No matter how good our RP data is, it tells us nothing about options that don't exist yet, such as the new tram route we're testing, not to mention a hot air balloon. 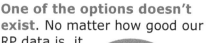	An SP survey can mix existing options with others that don't exist yet. If we present an option that doesn't exist, the resulting model might be extremely sensitive to the wording and graphics used to describe this option.
A feature of one of the options doesn't exist. Even if all the options already exist and we have good data about them, it will not allow us to test an added feature to one of those options. This is important, for example, if we consider introducing a new toll for car users in an area that hasn't so far had tolls. 	An SP survey can mix features that already exist with new ones. Sometimes respondents want to influence the results of the survey. They tend to say they are willing to pay a high price for something they want, but in reality they might not pay it.

7.4   The mode constant

Mode split models try to use the values of different variables to explain how demand splits between modes. These variables often include travel times by the different modes; the price you need to pay for your ticket, fuel or parking; and various aspects of the quality of the journey, like the level of crowding on the bus. A generalised cost function is used to calculate one cost that consists of all these. See figure 14 for a reminder.

When the mode split model is part of a four-stage model, the generalised cost is calculated from outputs of the distribution and/or assignment models. The generalised costs for all destinations and/or routes that can be taken by one mode are combined into the composite cost of that mode. I explained all these in more detail in earlier chapters.

Still, it's rare that any combination of variables from the distribution and assignment models is enough to explain how people really choose their mode of travel. In many areas around the world, most people travel by car even if public transport is quicker and cheaper. There's plenty of evidence that people have pre-fixed attitudes, which are not easy to explain, towards travelling by different modes. The actual mode choice is a result of a mix of straightforward considerations (like travelling quicker or paying less) and these more blurred ones.

Mode constants are special parameters that we make up in order to reflect this pre-fixed preference people have for some modes, as illustrated in figure 54. During model calibration, we decide what value to give to these constants so that the number of trips using each mode in the model is similar to what our data shows.

It's easiest to think about mode constants in units of time. A mode constant of 20 minutes for the bus option means that the model will split the demand between the modes as if travelling by bus took 20 minutes more than it actually takes. We use this to reduce the bus demand in the model, if the model otherwise shows too much bus demand.

Mode constants are very powerful, on one hand, but they're a source of trouble on the other hand. During model calibration, you can add constants to any mode and set their values so that you get an excellent match between your data and the outputs. It's very tempting, and also very common, to achieve a good match and then brag about your perfect calibration. The problem is that constants are really constant: their values will remain the same in every future scenario you use the model for, whether or not this makes sense.

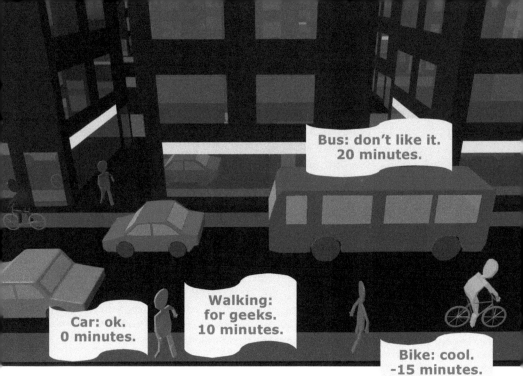

Figure 54: an example of mode constants.
What they capture isn't what each mode is really
like, but what the typical attitude towards it is like in the study
area. In this example, the bus is perceived most negatively
whereas the bike is perceived positively (the negative constant
indicates that a 60-minute bike ride is perceived as 45 minutes).

In the data that was used to calibrate your model, people's chosen mode depends on many things that were relevant when the data was collected. These things may include travel times, prices, people's pre-fixed attitudes, the weather on that specific day, a football match that took place in town, and an accident that happened nearby. Some of these are things you don't even know about – but they still influenced how people behaved at the time when your data was collected.

If you calibrate mode constants so that people split between modes exactly as the data shows, then you now have constants that contain the impact of the pre-fixed attitudes (which is what you wanted) but they also contain all the other temporary impacts: the weather, the football match and the accident.

That's a very bad thing. If you now use your model for testing future scenarios then all kinds of unknown factors, which were only relevant temporarily when the data was collected, will influence your results in the wrong way, as if the football match and the accident continue forever. The model will think they were part of people's attitude towards a specific mode.

The problem of trying too hard to make the model match the data during calibration is called **over-fitting**. A typical symptom of an over-fitted mode split model is that the mode constant is very large compared to the other elements of the generalised cost. When using such a model, the number of people choosing this mode will depend primarily on the constant. Models which have been over-fitted demonstrate better fit to the calibration data, but they have lower sensitivity to the different variables in the generalised cost.

Over-fitting is a very serious issue in modelling because clients are often impressed by good calibration results. It's sometimes difficult for the modelling team to explain that they preferred to compromise how well the model replicates real data in order to avoid over-fitting. It's easier to show that the model reached perfect calibration by over-fitting the mode constants.

The idea of adding a constant to one option to ensure that it calibrates properly is a standard practice not only in mode split models. Constants that are used in order to fix the demand are generally called **alternative-specific constants** (ASCs). Different ASCs can also be added to specific origins and destinations in the distribution model or to different routes in the assignment model. A risk of over-fitting exists in all these cases.

Figure 55 shows a more general description of the over-fitting problem. There are no fixed rules for what's right or wrong when dealing with this problem. Since over-fitting can reduce the sensitivity of the model to things that might change in the future, the most important question is how sensitive the model should really be. A large mode constant could be the right thing for your model if people in your area rarely shift between modes. But the large constant is a problem if you simply didn't have data on situations where they do shift between modes. You might become a bit too sure that you have good forecasts, when the model actually misinterpreted people's true behaviour.

147

It's important that you compare model result to other sources of evidence about people's willingness to shift mode. This can help become more confident that your mode constants (or other ASCs) make sense.

Figure 55: over-fitting

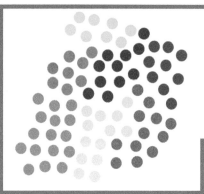

← The different colours indicate the different choices that people in your study area make – for example between modes. There's a wide range of behaviours, varying between people, locations, seasons etc.

When we collect data, it's → hard to cover all relevant behaviours. Things that happened recently or nearby lead people to making specific choices. So the data only gives a partial view of what the model should really capture.

← Over-fitting occurs when we calibrate the model to closely match the data despite its limitations. This might make us over-confident in the model's ability to forecast how people will behave. Large mode constants are prone to this risk.

7.5 Models allowing trips by more than one mode

Trips where the traveller uses more than one mode complicate the modelling process. There are several common ways people combine different modes during their trip. I already mentioned some of them, and figure 56 contains a more comprehensive list.

Figure 56 also shows how we model these different combinations of modes. You'll see that it's sometimes difficult to allow people in the model to travel the way they do in the real world. Deciding whether to make this effort is a dilemma.

On one hand, the model is meant to replicate the real world, so isn't it obvious we should include all realistic travel options? Ignoring some options will lead to allocating some demand to the wrong mode, and we might miss some important insight. On the other hand, the technical difficulties involved in capturing complex trips, and lack of data in some cases, mean that we might not be able to have much confidence in the outputs even if we make the extra modelling effort.

It's always important, early enough in your project, to consider what would be the implications of either modelling or not modelling behaviours which are technically difficult. In some cases it's better to leave gaps in the model. We can compensate for the simplification by finding evidence from other sources and by spending more time discussing what's the best way to interpret the model outputs given the gaps in the methodology. I'll discuss this in more detail in the second part of the book.

Figure 56: modelling trips that combine different modes

Walk to/from public transport. Most public transport trips involve walking to stops and stations, so mode split models take it for granted. All route assignment models consider walking as a feeder mode which is used between the public transport stop and the trip origin or destination.

Combine public transport modes. Many public transport  trips involve changes between routes, either of the same mode (e.g. two buses) or of different modes (e.g. bus and train). I dedicated  section 7.2 and figures 49-50 to the way this can be modelled.

Walk to/from a car. You walk to/from a car because your   parking is far, or because you're picked by someone else. Adding this to the mode split model isn't hard. But then we need the assignment to allow part of a car trip to be made by foot, or we need to change the car demand matrix so that you get by car somewhere which isn't the  origin or destination of your full trip. Since data on where people park is limited, and since this combination of modes isn't a high priority for policy makers, the modelling effort is considered too difficult to justify.

Taxi to/from public transport. I explained in chapter 5 that   very few transport models have a good understanding of taxi demand. There's limited shared knowledge across the modelling community about anything to do with taxi travel. This might become an issue with the recent rise of taxi and car sharing alternatives like Uber. So if this combination of modes matters in your work, you'll need to develop a bespoke methodology to suit your own objectives.

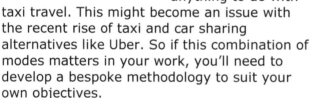

"Park and ride". Adding "park and ride" as a separate mode  in the mode split model isn't challenging. But since the relative number of "park and ride" users often remains a low proportion of the total demand, model outputs are subject to high uncertainty. Furthermore, matrix development becomes hard work, because a "park and ride" trip from zone A to zone B includes a change of mode in zone C. The model needs to identify the zone C where a traveller wishes to change between car and public transport. The model then  needs to create a trip from A to C in the car matrix and a trip from C to B in the public transport matrix. This is feasible and there are models who do it. But it requires more data, longer model development time, more advanced modelling skills and longer model runtime.

"Kiss and ride" (i.e. get a ride in somebody  else's car and then take public transport). The challenges and common  techniques are the same as with "park and ride".

"Bike and ride" (i.e. cycle and then take public transport).   Most models consider the cycling part as a feeder, which isn't assigned to any network. In such cases, only the public transport leg of the journey is modelled. If cycling is modelled more explicitly, the challenges and common techniques become the same as with  "park and ride". There might be additional challenges if there's interest in the capacity of bike parking at the station, or interest in the volume of passengers who take their bike with them on the public transport part of the trip.

7.6   The main limitations of mode split models

To summarise this chapter about mode split models, figure 57 includes some reminders about their key limitations. Understanding these limitations, and checking how critical they are in the context of your own work, will help you make wiser use of model outputs even if they are limited.

As with any type of model, it's important that those who see and use the outputs understand where the model is weak. This remains important even if these stakeholders don't ask for a discussion of the technical aspects. Without clarity about the gaps in the modelling approach, the risk is that clients think you're showing some new insight even when you actually don't.

Figure 57: limitations of mode split models

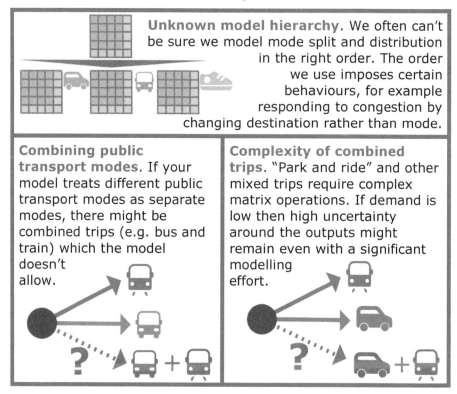

Unknown model hierarchy. We often can't be sure we model mode split and distribution in the right order. The order we use imposes certain behaviours, for example responding to congestion by changing destination rather than mode.

Combining public transport modes. If your model treats different public transport modes as separate modes, there might be combined trips (e.g. bus and train) which the model doesn't allow.

Complexity of combined trips. "Park and ride" and other mixed trips require complex matrix operations. If demand is low then high uncertainty around the outputs might remain even with a significant modelling effort.

Modes modelled as routes. If your model treats different public transport modes as separate routes, there might be factors that affect people's choice which the model can't take into account, because assignment models are primarily based on travel times.

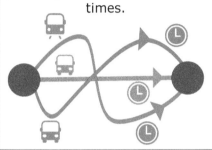

Limitations of RP data. If your model was created using RP data, there's a risk that the data did not include a wide enough range of the variables in the model. You won't be able to look at modes that still don't exist or at features

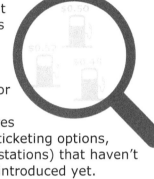

(e.g. ticketing options, nicer stations) that haven't been introduced yet.

Limitations of SP data. If your model was created using SP data, the outputs might be compromised by the hypothetical nature of SP questions. They might also be sensitive to how different options were explained or presented in the SP survey.

Risk of over-fitting. Mode constants help represent people's pre-fixed attitudes towards specific modes, but they might reduce the responsiveness of the model to future changes because of over-fitting.

Timing of mode shift. Even if we were confident about an expected shift between modes, models give us little confidence about how quickly this change in people's behaviour would occur.

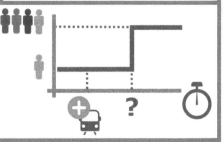

Chapter 8
More on matrix development

8.1 Distribution or destination choice

Trip distribution is the stage where we estimate the number of trips from each origin to each destination, i.e. for each **OD pair**. We start the distribution stage with some estimates of the total trip ends in each zone (see chapter 6 for a reminder). If we model mode split before distribution, we already have the trip ends split by mode. If we model distribution before mode split, we have the total trip ends for all modes together. But the way we model trip distribution is very much the same in both cases.

The output from the distribution stage is a full trip matrix. We often do trip distribution separately for each demand segment, for each year and for each scenario we include in our model. See chapter 2 if you need a reminder about any of these. As I showed in chapter 3, it's easier to explain things if we say that the trip matrix was there before the distribution stage, but it was an empty matrix waiting to be filled with numbers. Now is the stage where we decide what numbers to fill it with.

For journey purposes like "home to work", we tend to be confident in both our **production** trip ends and our **attraction** trip ends. We estimated them in the trip generation stage. As we saw in chapter 6, the "home to work" productions for each zone are based on its residential characteristics, and the attractions are based on employment figures. We use some factors to convert from a production-attraction format to an origin-destination format. So we start the actual distribution process knowing what the sum of each row and each column of the matrix should be. Our challenge is to come up with a set of numbers that can fill in all the cells of the matrix, in a way that adds up to the right totals in every row and every column.

Naturally, things like the level of traffic on different roads or the frequency of public transport routes play a role in trip distribution. They take the form of generalised costs, which come from the assignment models. But for "home to work" trips, the productions and attractions from the generation stage are the main input, while the generalised costs are a secondary one. Trip distribution for "home to work" trips simply isn't the right time to give these costs a bigger role: if congestion or poor service continue for a long time, this should affect trip generation, mode split or route choices, but we're not dealing with these here.

This is all different for journey purposes like "home to shopping", "home to leisure", or the more generic "home to other". Trip **productions** for each zone are still an important input into trip distribution; they are calculated in the generation stage from trip rates that describe how many shopping or leisure trips people make. But for these journey purposes, which aren't work-related, we attach lower importance to the total **attractions** from the trip generation stage.

When looking at these non-work-related trips, we feel less constrained by the attractions because people can change the destination of these trips all the time. When going to the theatre or the supermarket, changes to the generalised cost of travel can easily make people decide to travel somewhere else. So for these trip purposes, the most important inputs are the trip productions and the generalised costs, whereas trip attractions become a secondary input.

This means that the trip distribution for the journey purposes which aren't work-related starts with fixed totals of the rows of the matrix, but not the columns. Our challenge is the same as with trips to work, i.e. to come up with a set of numbers that can fill in all the cells in the matrix. But this time, these numbers need to add up to the right totals only in the rows. The distribution process has freedom to move trips between the columns if the generalised costs suggest that it's more attractive to go from the origin to a different destination.

For trips to work, when the totals of the rows and columns are fixed, we're not really modelling a choice. The distribution model in these cases is just a mathematical process of filling the matrix. For other trips, where only the attractions are set, the distribution stage selects which columns should have more trips, so there's a more intuitive choice process. This is sometimes called **destination choice** modelling.

155

Figure 58: distribution for different trip purposes

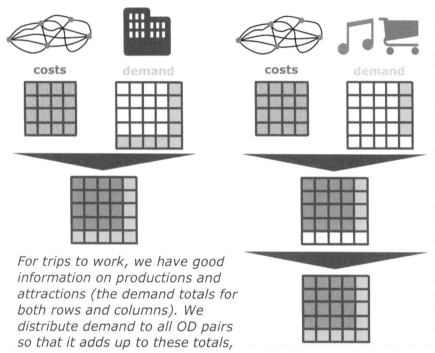

costs   demand   costs   demand

For trips to work, we have good information on productions and attractions (the demand totals for both rows and columns). We distribute demand to all OD pairs so that it adds up to these totals, with a bit of help from the generalised costs from the assignment. For other trips, we know more about productions than about attractions. So we use the generalised costs to distribute the demand between the columns in each row, and then we sum up each column to get the attractions.

Sometimes people use the term "destination choice" for any trip distribution model, even where the destinations have already been fixed at the trip generation stage. It's good practice to always discuss explicitly how the choice of people's trip destinations is determined for each demand segment.

When the distribution process is free to decide which destination each trip goes to, you should check whether it has sufficient inputs to do it properly. In the distribution of the "home to other" matrix, the process will allocate more trips to columns where the generalised cost is lower. But in reality people go to the places where their friends live or where there are shops and concerts. Ideally, the generalised costs you use for destination choice modelling should include additional variables which describe the things that make a zone attract more trips.

In any case, trip distribution is dominated by arithmetic computations, which aren't always too meaningful. Remember that in a model with 500 zones, we need to distribute trips across 250,000 OD pairs in each demand matrix. We can remain quite intuitive when splitting demand between modes, since there are only a few modes, and each one has recognizable features. But when distributing demand across so many OD pairs, the modelling work tends to focus on the automation of this heavy number crunching. This comes at the expense of our focus on the behaviour aspects.

8.2 Balancing a demand matrix

You can probably imagine that the process described in the previous section and in figure 58 also has a heavy mathematical side. Mathematically, this process follows a technique called **gravity modelling**, which ensures that more trips are allocated to OD pairs with a lower generalised cost.

Sometimes we can't do trip distribution using gravity modelling. This could be, for example, because we don't know any generalised costs yet. These costs come from the assignment model, but before we have a demand matrix, there's nothing to assign. So in the very first time we fill the matrix with numbers, we need to do it without costs.

There are also cases where we do have a matrix with the generalised costs of travel from each zone to each zone, but we're not sure we should use them since they come from sources we don't trust. This can happen if some early attempts to use these costs have led to strange results.

For these cases, there are simpler mathematical processes (sometimes known as the **Fratar** or **Furness** techniques) where we take the total productions and attractions and fill the matrix with numbers without knowing the costs. What these processes do is simply **balancing** the matrix, i.e. finding a way of filling it with numbers which add up correctly to the known totals.

We also sometimes do matrix **re-balancing**. We do this if we already have a trip matrix from earlier work, and we have new figures of the total demand; we need a new matrix, where the rows and the columns add up to the new total productions and attractions. In the re-balancing process, we follow the new totals but we still use the old matrix to learn which OD pairs are likely to have more trips than others. Figure 59 illustrates balancing and re-balancing procedures; you can compare it to figure 58.

Figure 59: matrix balancing (left) *and re-balancing* (right)

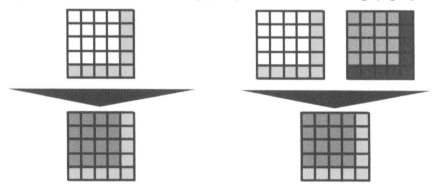

8.3 Matrix conversions

Once we have a full matrix from a distribution process like in figure 58, we need it to be in a format that can go into our assignment model. But as I explained in chapter 6, the distribution matrices are in a production-attraction format whereas assignment models need matrices in an origin-destination format.

We prefer the production-attraction format for most of the demand modelling work, because it gives stronger explanations to people's travel behaviour. It puts people's trip back home in the same cell as their trip from home, so similar choices apply to both trips. The assignment model can't accept such format because the route people take depends on their direction of travel. The route must start at the origin of each trip and end at the destination; travel conditions on the opposite direction of the same route might be completely different.

158

So we need to convert our matrices from a production-attraction format to an origin-destination format just before the assignment. Luckily this conversion isn't a big deal: we take the trips that go towards people's home zone and reverse them, i.e. store them in the cell that reflects the real travel direction. Still, you already know that each operation we perform on a matrix involves millions of little calculations, so these matrix conversions increase model runtime. They also are an invitation to make various errors, since they require a lot of attention to detail, and the modeller who designs them is only human.

There are models that don't use a production-attraction format; they model everything by origin and destination. This saves the hassle of these conversions, and also makes things somewhat more intuitive, because each trip is in the right direction throughout the modelling process. But models with this simpler format have weaker behavioural foundations, because they don't ensure that the trips from home and back home follow consistent choices. So this approach is suitable mainly for models where trip generation was based on poor data in the first place.

You may remember from figure 23 that before the assignment we add together matrices from different demand segments, since they all share the same network. This is another form of matrix conversion, which can be done at the same point in the modelling process where we convert the matrices to an origin-destination format.

Before the assignment we also need to create separate matrices for different periods of the day. Trip generation, mode split and distribution usually cover the full 24-hour demand on a typical weekday, but the analysis of traffic levels and passenger numbers in the assignment is always done separately for each part of the day.

In theory we could have a time-of-day choice model, which would determine how the 24-hour demand splits between the morning peak, afternoon peak and other periods. But it's much more common to do this conversion using a fixed set of factors that we apply to the 24-hour trip matrix after the distribution stage. These factors can be obtained from any data source that tells us what proportion of travel is made at each time of the day.

159

The idea that these factors can be fixed shouldn't be taken for granted. It's based on the assumption that the scenarios you're testing won't make people change the time of day when they travel. Before creating the assignment matrices from the outputs of trip distribution, you should consider whether or not this assumption is reasonable for your project.

8.4 Conflicts between the matrix and observed traffic

Let's say you've completed the development of your demand matrices after a process of trip generation, split and distribution modelling. You also created a network for your assignment model. You can finally assign your demand to the network, but when you compare the assignment outputs to observed traffic data, you find large differences. In other words, the base year assignment doesn't pass your validation criteria.

All the work we've done in the generation, split and distribution stages, which gave us a shiny set of matrices, doesn't guarantee reasonable outputs when the matrices are assigned; disappointment when we first assign our matrices is very common. It can result from various gaps in our data and methodology, which I review throughout this book. The basic cause is that it's the first time we compare the model visually to simple data such as the amount of traffic on different roads.

You may want to go to chapter 4 for a reminder about validation. Figure 34 is particularly relevant here: it showed some common things we do when validation fails. If we try the improvements listed in figure 34, and then the assigned matrices give us a reasonable picture of network conditions, we can go to Auntie Tilda's and eat cake. But it's not unheard of that the assignment of our best demand matrices still gives results we can't accept.

Not accepting the assignment results means that we give a higher priority to these outputs than to the whole process that preceded the assignment. I'll comment later in the book about whether such priorities are right or wrong, but the fact is that assignment outputs are more visible and intuitive than the outputs of the earlier modelling stages. Therefore, when we don't like the assignment outputs, we often decide to introduce some serious corrections to the work we did at the generation, split and distribution stages.

This changes the role of the demand matrices. Their consistency with known trip rates and land use becomes less important, while the ability to reproduce congestion in the right places becomes critical. There are matrix development processes that follow this mindset. They are mainly used to modify car demand matrices to match traffic counts from the road network. A common matrix development process of this nature is described in figure 60.

The **matrix estimation** procedure, which is the final step of the matrix development process shown in figure 60, makes comprehensive use of traffic data. This has great advantages and also great disadvantages. The process is very effective in removing conflicts between the demand matrix and observed data, so we can usually use it to demonstrate a better standard of model calibration. But there's also a high risk that we've gone too far from our original trip generation and mode split, which were based on sound behavioural evidence.

Traffic data suffers from various errors, and even without any errors, it only represents the time when it was collected. We never know whether traffic was counted at a time that truly represents typical demand. And it could be that, just by chance, we undertook roadside interviews and traffic counts on days where demand was particularly low, or particularly high, or heavily influenced by temporary factors. When this happens, it would be a classic case of **over-fitting.** I showed a different case of over-fitting in figure 55, although the nature of the problem is the same.

The matrix we get after **matrix estimation**, in step 4 of figure 60, is sometimes extremely different from the **synthetic matrix**, i.e. the matrix developed with a traditional distribution model. The matrix estimation process runs by an automated program, which makes thousands of adjustments to thousands of OD pairs, so it's impractical to check each adjustment. Matrix development processes which are directly based on traffic data are therefore somewhat controversial. There are no fixed rules for deciding whether and when their overall contribution is positive; you are the best judge, in the context of your own work.

Figure 60: building matrices directly from traffic data

Step 1: synthetic matrix. We follow the classical distribution process, as I described earlier (figure 58 for example). The matrix we get is called "synthetic" because it has not been adjusted yet to match observed traffic.

Step 2: partial matrix. For specific OD pairs, demand has been observed directly if we conducted roadside interviews (explained in figure 36). We can create a matrix with the demand from the interviews shown for these OD pairs. The rest of the matrix remains empty. This matrix is "partial" because we never have enough roadside interviews to cover all OD pairs.

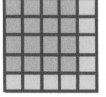

Step 3: prior matrix. Now we create a matrix that has the observed values from the partial matrix where they're available, and values from the synthetic matrix in all other OD pairs. We call this a "prior" matrix because it's the input into the procedure in step 4.

Step 4: matrix estimation. This is an automated procedure which adjusts the prior matrix and then assigns it to the network. The assignment outputs are compared to traffic counts, especially along cordons and screenlines (explained in figures 36 and 37). The process is repeated in a loop, making more matrix adjustments, until the assignment outputs are close enough to the counts data.

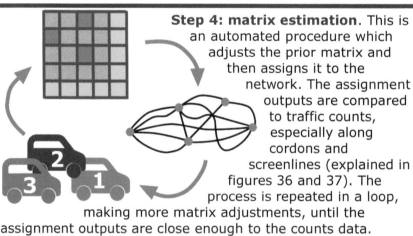

8.5 Trips inside a zone

I showed in chapter 2 that many trips never leave the zone where they started. These include your trip to the corner shop to buy milk; a short bus ride to see an exhibition at a community centre nearby; and also the trip to work of many teachers, shopkeepers, artists, priests and others who work in the same neighbourhood where they live. Figure 11 in chapter 2 showed where in a matrix we find the internal trips.

If the origin and the destination of a trip are in the same zone, then the trip is ignored in the assignment. That's because all trips are assumed to go from the centroid of the origin zone to the centroid of the destination zone, and an internal trip has already reached the destination centroid before the assignment started.

Nevertheless, it might be important to include these trips in the demand matrix in your project. Internal trips are potentially important because their origins or destinations could change as a response to changes in the transport system. For example, people who currently travel inside their origin zone might decide to use the new bridge you're building and get a job on the other side of the river, which is no longer in the same zone. So you need to consider what such re-distribution might mean for your project.

"I said at home I won't leave the zone, but this side of the bus should be fine."

Zone 22

Zone 23

A key challenge in handling internal trips is estimating their generalised costs. Since these trips aren't assigned, the assignment model doesn't estimate their costs. We normally address this in a very simplified way. For example, we assume that for every internal trip, the generalised cost is 70% of the cost of travelling from the same zone to the nearest one. This is based on the assumption that travelling within a zone will always be quicker and cheaper than travelling to any other zone.

8.6   Understanding the demand matrix

We fill our demand matrices with numbers which will directly influence any output from our model. I showed in figure 11 how we can read these numbers in order to ensure they make sense. But we can't check the entire matrix by simply reading the numbers in it, because there are millions of OD pairs. The fact that so many important numbers are calculated through an automated process should be a source of concern.

Since it's too difficult to look at the entire contents of a demand matrix, we assess how logical the matrix is by looking at it from various perspectives, one at a time. The following paragraphs review a few techniques for describing the trips in a matrix. These techniques can help you get an intuitive feeling of the story that all these numbers are telling. It's important to use more than just one of these techniques, because each one of them only shows part of the picture.

A very important technique is the analysis of the **trip length distribution**. The trip length distribution is a graph (like the one in figure 61) that shows what proportion of the trips in the entire matrix fall into various trip length categories. The length can be measured either as the distance from the origin to the destination, which we can calculate from a map, or as the journey time, which we could estimate if we already have an initial assignment model.

The trip length distribution looks at the matrix as a whole, and doesn't check the demand for specific OD pairs, so there are many problems it won't detect. But it's a critical check because

164

this is the quickest way to spot major problems in your matrix. From your various data sources, and from your own previous knowledge, you must have a feeling as to what lengths of trips people make in your study area. You should be able to comment on whether it's logical that 20% of the people travel less than ten minutes or more than two hours. If these don't make sense, or if they have changed too much from a matrix you saw previously, then there might be issues to fix in the model.

Figure 61: trip length distribution

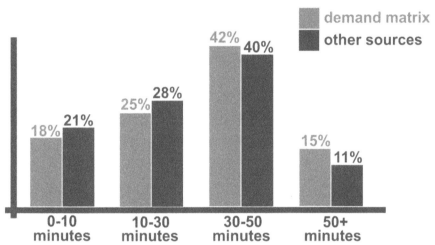

If the matrix you're looking at is from one of your "do something" scenarios, and the trip length distribution has changed from the "do minimum" scenario (see figure 12 for a reminder of these terms), then there are additional questions to ask. You should think whether it makes sense that the transport project you're testing causes people to make longer or shorter trips, compared to the way they travelled before.

We can plot a summary of trips from all origins to all destinations if we group the zones in our model into a small number of large areas. Showing the number of trips from each group of zones to each group of zones isn't ideal, because we won't see the travel demand inside each area; but it does give a good summary of the estimated travel demand between these areas. If the number of areas isn't too high then a very effective way of visualising the total demand is using a **chord diagram**, as shown in figure 62.

165

Figure 62: visualising the full matrix with a chord diagram

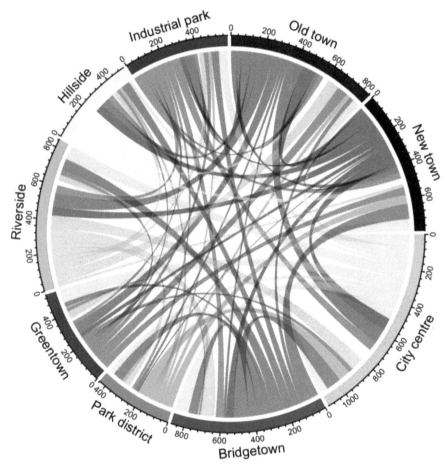

If many people travel from one area to another, then the "chord" that connects these areas in the chord diagram is thicker. The total number of trips is shown near each area, but the diagram is effective even if you ignore these numbers, and you can simply consider whether the relative demand across different areas is as you would expect. Each area is both an origin and a destination, so in the chord diagram we can either use the total of both directions (as I did in figure 62) or draw a different chord for each direction.

If the demand between two areas in the matrix is unusually high, this type of diagram will show it easily, since the very thick chord will attract your attention. The downside of this type of plot is that it becomes too messy if you group your zones into more than 10 areas, more or less.

We can visualise the demand matrix with some good old maps, with different colours indicating different levels of demand. When using a traditional map, we don't need to group the zones, and each one of our zones can be shown with its own demand, even if there are hundreds of zones. Traditional maps are therefore the primary way of showing the contents of the matrix in full geographical detail.

The problem is that in a standard map we can only give one colour to each zone. In the matrix, each zone has some demand that goes there from every other origin, and demand that goes from there to every other destination. So we need to decide which of the following our map will present:

■ The total demand from each zone

■ The total demand to each zone

■ The demand from each zone to a specific destination of interest

■ The demand from a specific origin of interest to each zone.

Figure 63 shows a map of the number of trips from different zones in a matrix to all other zones in the area. Similar maps can also cover a much larger area, with many more zones. A single map can't tell the full story behind the matrix; but a series of maps, which also look at trips to and from several key locations of interest, can be highly informative.

In figure 62 we saw the option of grouping the zones into areas. In figure 63 we saw the option of showing the number of trips to/from specific zones or all zones combined. It's worth mentioning that we can also combine these two things in one figure, i.e. show the number of trips from one group of zones to all other groups, or from all groups to one. Such figure would be a high-level summary, which doesn't summarise the full matrix (unlike figure 62) and doesn't show demand by zone (unlike figure 63). But it's still worth presenting because of the reason I already mentioned: the demand matrix is a complex thing, so we need to look at it in many different ways in order to make it easier to understand. Without making the matrix more catchy, you'll never be able to spot errors or suspicious behaviours.

To illustrate this, figure 64 shows an example of how we can visualise the demand from all groups of zones into a specific group. This time I used the format of a **word cloud**. The figure shows the relative number of trips from different areas in or out of Greater London into the City of London. In a word cloud, the name of each area is shown in a larger font if there are more trips from that area. Smaller print indicates that there are fewer trips from the relevant area to the City (the colours or layout don't matter). The format of a word cloud can also be used to show trips in the opposite direction (from one area to all others), or simply the total demand to/from each area.

Figure 63: mapping all trips from one zone

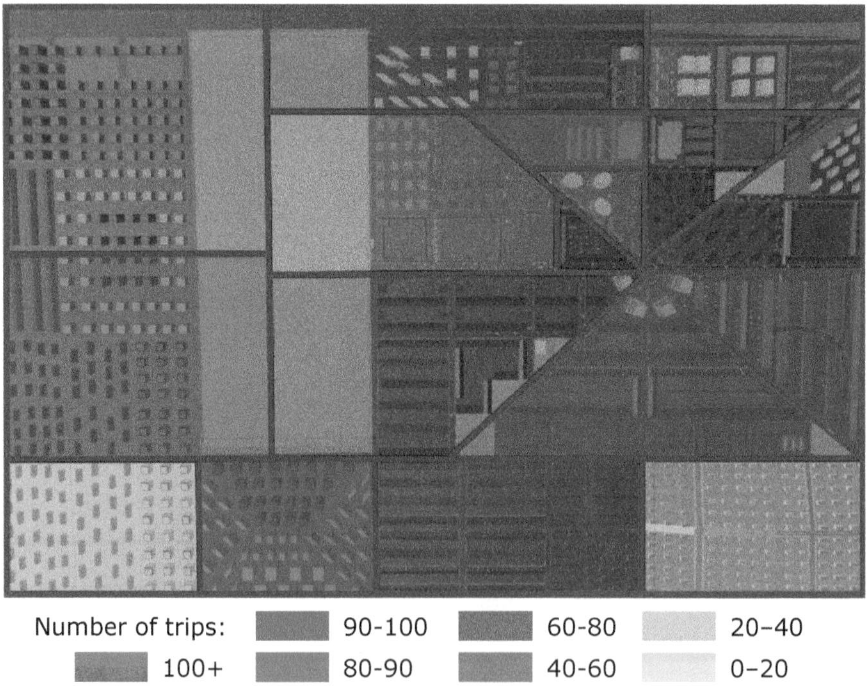

Number of trips: ▮ 90-100   ▮ 60-80   ▯ 20–40
▮ 100+   ▮ 80-90   ▮ 40-60   ▯ 0–20

Figure 64: a word cloud visualising demand to one area

World clouds are clearly not a traditional way of showing travel demand, and I know some people who dislike this presentation style. It's for you to decide how helpful such visualisation might be in your project. My own experience suggests that word clouds can be effective when working with "numerophobic" colleagues, i.e. those who turn off whenever any numbers are shown; a word cloud describes quantitative information without presenting any numbers.

8.7   The main limitations of matrix building processes

I reviewed in this chapter key topics related to the development of demand matrices, either through traditional trip distribution or using processes which make more direct use of traffic data.

Some of the key limitations of the way we build matrices are listed in figure 65. As with any other modelling work, it's important to consider these limitations before, during and after the work is done. This can help us keep it simpler, more focused and more insightful.

169

Figure 65: limitations of the matrix development process

A "black box" process. Filling a matrix with numbers involves a lot of number crunching, which is mostly automated, and based on inputs of compromised quality. There will always be some OD pairs where the demand we estimate is just nonsense.

The devil in the detail. The amount of detail in a demand matrix is so large that it's difficult to sense-check. It's important to visualise and scrutinise the demand in the matrix in different ways, as shown in section 8.6.

Behavioural consistency. Traditional trip distribution often gives us matrices which don't work well in the assignment; the assignment outputs don't match traffic data. It's common to use a process that mixes distribution and traffic data from the start. But this process might break the consistency across the four-stage hierarchy, so the behavioural explanation for how people behave is weaker. This makes our model less reliable when we use it to estimate future behaviour.

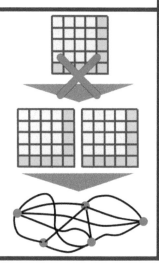

170

Factors explaining destination choice. When we model destination choice, we distribute trips between destinations based on the generalised cost of travel from the origin. It's important that this cost includes not only transport-related factors, because people consider other things too when deciding where to go.

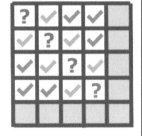

Internal trips. The generalised costs for trips within a zone are calculated in a very simplified way. This reduces the credibility of the number of trips identified as internal trips. The number of trips to adjacent zones may suffer from this too, because there's often some re-distribution of internal trips to other zones nearby.

Neo knew how to handle a matrix when he saw one.

Chapter 9
More on network models

9.1 **Road networks and route networks**

We saw that some models produce outputs which aren't easy to visualise. Trip generation, mode split and distribution models give us outputs at the zone level, which is not the most intuitive. By contrast, when a model includes a detailed representation of a transport network, the outputs can be shown on a street map. Clients and colleagues can then easily associate the results with specific places they know.

Models with a detailed network include assignment models, micro-simulation models and junction analysis tools. Since network models produce simpler outputs, much of the communication between modellers and their clients tends to focus on models of these types. In this chapter I'll talk about assignment modelling first, and then move to other models with a detailed network.

I dedicated chapter 3 to the **hierarchy** of a typical model. Network models are always at the bottom of the hierarchy; they are the last thing we update, so that their visual outputs reflect everything the model has estimated. If you run a full model for two scenarios and there are differences between them, you might spot the differences only when looking at the assignment outputs, even if the main change is in trip distribution. This means you always need to look back at the outputs from different stages of the modelling work, even if you identified the change in the assignment outputs. Of course you also need to examine different OD pairs and different parts of the network.

In Figure 38 earlier I showed that in many projects, the team decides to only use a network model, without running a full four-stage model. This can save much effort in cases where the only impacts you want to test are at the network level. If you can justify why you don't expect changes to trip generation, split, distribution and time choice, then there's no problem with only

172

running assignment. But remember that clients who only spend a minute looking at the assignment outputs will not know what modelling process you followed before the assignment (unless you tell them). The fact that you didn't run a mode split model won't necessarily stop them from interpreting the assignment outputs as evidence on people's mode choice.

As you already know, a transport model that deals with the overall demand for transport will normally have more than one network:

- A network of roads, which serves the traffic of cars, trucks, vans, taxis, buses and bikes. Some of these modes have their demand stored in a matrix that we can assign to the network. For some other modes we don't have a demand matrix, and they are treated as **background flows** or not included at all. See chapter 5 for a reminder about these.
- A network that consists of all public transport routes mixed together, if the choice between public transport modes is to be done in the assignment. See section 7.2 for a reminder.
- A separate route network for each public transport mode, if the choice between public transport modes is dealt with at the mode split stage.
- A separate network for cycling, if we developed one and we have a matrix of cycling trips.

There are some tricky relationships between the networks. For example:

- Buses take some of the capacity of the road network, so we need to consider whether the time they spend at bus stops delays traffic. But when dealing with the road network we don't know how many passengers are on these buses or where they go. Bus passengers are allocated to bus routes separately, in the public transport assignment.
- Bicycles in the car assignment are only there to take some space on the road, if we think they are worth adding. If we have a cycling assignment model, we can take bicycle flows from its outputs and convert them into background flows in the car assignment. If we don't have a cycling assignment, we can add bicycle background flows to the car assignment based on where we found bikes in traffic counts.

The way trips are assigned to a road network is different from the way they're assigned to a public transport route network. A trip by car from zone 1 to zone 4 needs to find a series of **links** that form a complete route from the origin to the destination (see chapter 2 for a reminder about links). If there's such a series of links, the model assigns car traffic to all of them in a sequence, because all of them are needed in order to get from zone 1 to 4.

A public transport trip from zone 1 to zone 4 doesn't have the freedom to choose any series of links. It can only use combinations of links that have a public transport route along them, and it needs to have stops or stations close to both the origin and the destination (see figure 49 for a reminder). The route also needs to have departures at the time of day when the trip is made. If there are public transport routes with some departures and stops at the relevant times and places, the trips from the origin to the destination follow the links along the itinerary of these routes.

Figure 66: car assignment and public transport assignment

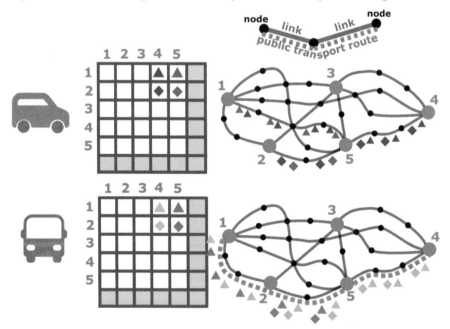

Figure 66 illustrates the assignment of demand from a small number of OD pairs. Car demand can be assigned to any sequence of links from the origin to the destination, while public transport demand is assigned to links that are served by public transport routes (there's only one route in figure 66). In both types of assignment, we see on each link a mix of the demand from various OD pairs.

9.2 From the matrix to the network

Before the assignment starts, the trips we estimated for each OD pair sit in the matrix and wait. The zones, centroids, centroid connectors, links and nodes sit in the network and wait, too (I explained all these terms in chapter 2, in case you need a reminder). At this stage we haven't yet assigned any demand, but the network already contains some background flows in different places. We added them in advance to represent the road space taken by trips which aren't in our demand matrix.

When the assignment starts, it searches for possible routes from each origin to each destination. A typical route in the assignment of car trips would always look like this:

Every route starts at the origin centroid, followed by a centroid connector. It always ends at the destination centroid, preceded by a centroid connector. The number of links and nodes between the origin and the destination will vary between routes.

A typical route in the assignment of public transport trips would look like this:

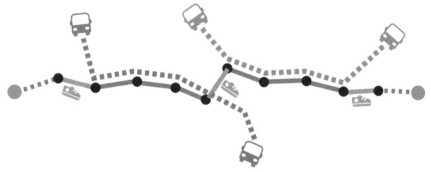

The route from each origin to each destination always uses a centroid connector near each end of the journey, and short walks to and from the stop or station. Between these two ends of the route, the trip may be assigned to one public transport route or more.

There are normally several possible routes between the origin and the destination. In a complex network of a big city, there can be hundreds of possible routes for each OD pair. Since there are usually millions of OD pairs, identifying all the possible routes is a task that cannot be undertaken by a human being. Some assignment models start with a stage that automatically identifies all possible routes and then assigns demand to the most reasonable ones. Other models skip the stage of identifying all routes, and try to find only reasonable routes from the start.

The difficult question is, though, what counts as a reasonable route? Let's say I'm travelling from home to my Auntie Tilda's house. She wants me to get there quickly because my tea is getting cold, so I won't choose a route that is too long. But this doesn't yet answer the question, because…:

- Auntie Tilda is very impatient.
- Some routes are shorter in distance but take longer to travel. Travellers may or may not be aware of this.
- Some routes are longer but travel conditions are more pleasant, for example because there are more available seats on the train or because there's a nice view.
- Some routes are faster but cost extra money, for example when using a toll road or a high-speed train.
- Some routes are shorter but steeper, which is a consideration if you walk or cycle.
- These considerations vary between people based on personal circumstances and tastes. That's the case even if they travel from the same origin to the same destination at the same time and using the same mode.

Putting the same thing in a more formal way, every route has its own generalised cost, and we've already seen that many different things can affect the generalised cost. See figure 14 for a reminder.

Travellers will find routes with a lower generalised cost more reasonable. The assignment model is expected to replicate the way people think when they make these route choices, i.e. to assign the demand from each origin to each destination to routes with low generalised costs. But as you've figured out already, this is a complex problem. It's complicated by the high number of OD pairs; the high number of possible routes for each OD pair; the overlaps between similar routes serving different OD pairs; the different considerations I've just listed which determine which routes people prefer; and also the limited data we have about which routes people really take in the real world.

Since the problem is so complex, many solutions have been suggested. The question of how to assign the demand from the matrix to the network has been the subject of hundreds of research studies, and different models follow different approaches. Figure 67 reviews some of the most common methods for identifying the most reasonable routes and dividing the demand between them. It also reviews the main strengths and weaknesses of these methods.

Figure 67: ways to split the demand between routes

"All or nothing". For each OD pair, all the demand is assigned to the route with the lowest generalised cost.

It's very simplistic to assume that everyone takes the same route from A to B. Demand will be assigned to main corridors only, and it might not show the variation in route choices in reality.

There are so many OD pairs, that we'll get a good spread of demand across the network anyway, even if only one route is used for each OD pair.

"All or nothing" by segment. I spoke about demand segmentation in section 2.7. This approach still assigns all the demand to the route with the lowest cost, but this route might be different in each demand segment.

 It's still a simplistic assumption, that everyone in a large group of people makes the same choice.

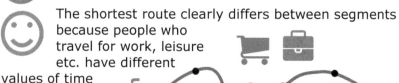 The shortest route clearly differs between segments because people who travel for work, leisure etc. have different

values of time (explained in section 2.8). The difference in the value of time makes this approach more realistic.

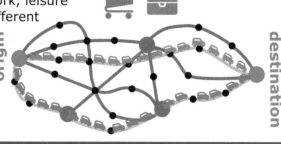

"User equilibrium". This is the most common approach. Demand for each OD pair is divided between possible routes based on the principles of "network equilibrium". This means that trips are assigned in a way that nobody could reduce their generalised cost by choosing a different route.

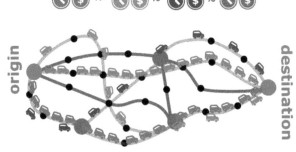

 Network equilibrium is quite a theoretical idea. It doesn't reflect the complexity of people's behaviour in the real world.

 This approach simply splits the demand between routes so that they all have more or less the same generalised cost. In many cases this makes good sense.

"User equilibrium" with more variation. This approach is similar to the previous one, but it allows more variation in the generalised costs between routes. Some routes with a slightly higher cost can still be used.

 The process of adding this variation is mathematically complex, and the resulting route choices can be harder to explain.

 This is more realistic. Some people don't know 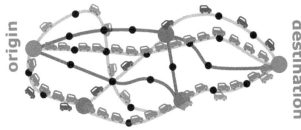 the network very well, so they aren't able to choose a route that reduces their generalised cost.

Dynamic assignment. This approach is based on running several assignments for short periods of time. For example, instead of running an assignment for the morning peak hour between 08:00 to 09:00, this approach could run four models for each 15-minute "sub-period" within the peak hour. The assignment for each sub-period uses the outputs from the earlier sub-period. In each sub-period, travellers may choose different routes.

 Dynamic assignment has higher computational complexity, so the model takes longer to run. Calibration of such models is more ambitious.

 It's more realistic. This approach shows how the network gradually becomes busier 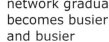 and busier during the peak time, and how this changes the routes people choose.

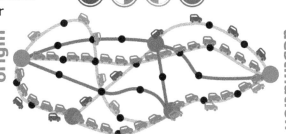

9.3   Route choice for public transport users

Figure 67 showed different mechanisms for modelling the choice between routes, whichever mode of transport is used. More specifically, when looking at the choice between public transport routes, there are some additional issues to address, which different models approach in different ways. Figure 68 summarises various problems that need a solution when we build a model to represent the public transport network.

Figure 68: public transport assignment challenges

Calculating generalised costs. In most public transport assignment models, the generalised cost of each route includes the time to get to from the origin to the boarding point; the travel time while you're on board; the time to get from the alighting point to the destination; time spent changing between routes; waiting time for each service you use; and the fare you pay.

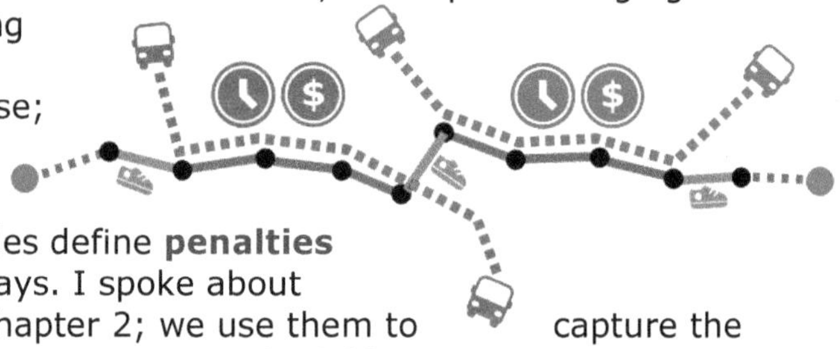

Different modes define **penalties** in different ways. I spoke about penalties in chapter 2; we use them to capture the impact of things passengers don't like. Penalties are sometimes pre-fixed; for example, each transfer between routes adds 3 minutes over and above the time it really takes. Sometimes they come as a higher weight on an existing part of the cost; for example, every minute spent on a very busy train counts as 2 minutes.

Calculating travel times. Sometimes travel times between stops don't need to be calculated, because they are fixed in the service timetable. Many models use these preset times as the default when calculating the generalised costs. The public transport model itself doesn't deal with congestion.

This becomes a problem if, for example, buses get delayed by general traffic. Ideally there should be a linkage between all assignment models, so that general delays on the road influence the calculation of bus travel times. Some models include this feature and others don't.

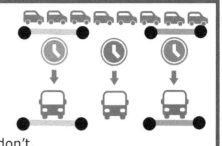

Coding bus routes. If we code the road network so that there's a node at every bus stop, it makes the coding of bus routes in the public transport network simpler. It also allows us to locate every bus stop in the model in its exact real-world location. But it also adds more detail to the network, which isn't always a good thing. The alternative is not to worry so much about the exact match between bus stops in the model and in the real world, because this apparent accuracy is offset by many other inaccuracies in the model. I'll talk more later about network detail and accuracy.

Coding timetables. There are models where the whole timetable of each bus, tram or train route is coded in detail. When the model assigns passengers to routes, it knows that there are departures at 07:45, 08:02 and 08:19. This is used to calculate waiting times and the overall capacity of the service, and these influence the generalised costs.

Sometimes we don't have such a detailed timetable. There are also cases where departures are so frequent that it's not worth making such fine calculations. In these cases, the model includes a parameter for each route to indicate its frequency (e.g. "every five minutes"). This is used instead of the timetable, to calculate average waiting times, capacities and generalised costs.

Representing crowding. Most models identify very crowded route sections. The physical capacity of trains and buses is a parameter in the model, so crowding can be shown wherever the number of passengers is close to this capacity.

Showing crowding is easy; letting it change people's route choices is hard. The model needs to take passengers off the crowded sections, move them to other routes, and then run again. Some models do this and others don't.

In some places, trains get so crowded that passengers can't get on. They need to wait for another train, and this increases the generalised cost of the journey. Many models don't have a feature to prevent passengers from boarding the first service that arrives. We sometimes address this in a simplified way by manually setting a higher waiting time. But then the model can't tell us whether the capacity problem is solved if we improve the public transport network, because waiting times are a manual input and not an output.

Representing fares. You'd expect the ticket cost to be part of the generalised cost when modelling bus or train travel, wouldn't you. Well, it's not so simple.

In the model we assign single trips, but we often don't know how much people pay for a single trip. People use day tickets, hourly tickets, season tickets, travelcards, senior citizen cards, student tickets, or cards with daily capping. With most of these, the price of one trip depends on how many trips you make during a period that is longer than the modelled period. So that model doesn't know how much you really pay.

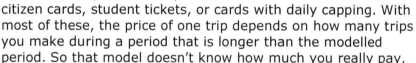

In addition, we can't update the model every time fares change. Furthermore, people have different values of time (see figure 17 for a reminder of all the problems this creates).

So calculating the real price paid per journey is a genuine challenge. We usually make some assumptions so that the model only knows a "typical" fare. The "typical" fare is decided outside the model, so the model can't be used to assess the impact of changing fares or introducing new tickets.

Since the use of fares in the model is so simplified, it's often best to simply not model the impact of fares at all.

9.4 Route choice for road users

Nothing occupies the world of transport modelling more than the question of how to represent traffic congestion. Many people have spent their entire careers exploring different ways to improve the modelling of traffic jams. It's relatively simple to model how vehicles interact with each other when there's enough space on the road for everyone. But when traffic isn't running smoothly, it becomes difficult to estimate traffic volumes, speeds and travel times in different scenarios.

You already know that when we assign the car trip matrix to the network, we estimate which routes drivers would choose on each trip. This requires estimating travel times on the different routes they could choose from. Some routes are congested, so we need a method for calculating the delays that vehicles experience in congested conditions.

There are different approaches to estimating traffic delays. Some models focus on the way queues build up. Other models focus on the way junctions get gradually blocked when the number of vehicles in the area rises. Other traffic theories concentrate on the levels of congestion along entire road corridors.

Figure 69 reviews the key types of methods we use for assigning road trips. Getting your head around these methods can be quite confusing, because we use them for calculating delays, and also for estimating travel times, and also for splitting trips between different possible routes. These challenges are so closely related to each other, that we address them as one big problem.

To make it even more confusing, the approaches shown in figure 69 mix traffic assignment with **micro-simulation**. When I introduced these types of modelling in chapter 3, I presented them as separate things: I said that assignment is part of the traditional four-stage concept, while micro-simulation is an add-on which zooms further into the network for a more detailed analysis. I wasn't lying, honestly, but over the years, different variants were introduced which mix both types of models.

Figure 69: approaches to road traffic assignment

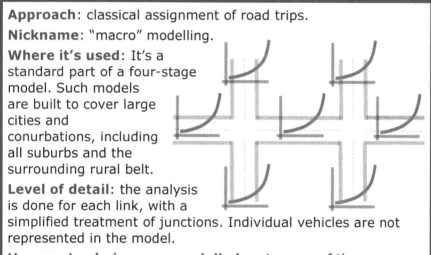

Approach: classical assignment of road trips.

Nickname: "macro" modelling.

Where it's used: It's a standard part of a four-stage model. Such models are built to cover large cities and conurbations, including all suburbs and the surrounding rural belt.

Level of detail: the analysis is done for each link, with a simplified treatment of junctions. Individual vehicles are not represented in the model.

How route choices are modelled: using one of the approaches from figure 67.

How delays are calculated: using a speed/flow function, that estimates the speed on each link for a given number of vehicles. Junction delay is considered part of the delay on the links near the junction.

Approach: classical traffic micro-simulation.

Nickname: "micro" modelling.

Where it's used: it's often used to study a small number of junctions or streets in a lot of detail. Occasionally it's also used for larger areas.

Level of detail: the model follows every vehicle in the network and the way it interacts with every other vehicle.

How route choices are modelled: they aren't. Traffic flows are taken from an assignment model, and the routes people chose are kept unchanged.

How delays are calculated: the full movement of every vehicle is simulated, so that the travel time can be measured.

Approach: assignment with junction simulation.

Nickname: "meso" modelling.

Where it's used: it's considered mandatory in the UK and Ireland. It's less common elsewhere. It is used in models for large cities and surrounding areas, just like "macro" models. Junctions in urban centres are micro-simulated, while other parts of the network are treated like in a classical assignment. Both approaches are combined into a single model.

Level of detail: at junctions in busy areas, the model follows every vehicle. This is based on the idea that junction blocking is the main cause of most delays. Along links and in quieter areas, the analysis is done at the link level, without representing individual vehicles.

How route choices are modelled: using one of the approaches from figure 67.

How delays are calculated: the travel time for each vehicle is the time it spends on "macro" links (calculated using a speed/flow function) plus the time it spends crossing "micro" junctions (which is measured through simulation).

Approach: various newer approaches.

Where it's used: newer mixes of micro and macro are increasingly common. They're being adopted by different software packages and applied in many projects. But they're not yet standardised, and do not follow a widely-agreed set of modelling principles.

How route choices are modelled: there are now micro-simulation models that allow changes in route-choice without running a separate assignment model first. In such models, assignment and micro-simulation fully merge into a single model.

How delays are calculated: using various combinations of "micro" and "macro", which the user has more freedom to specify based on their project needs.

9.5 The level of network detail

When coding a road network, we need to decide how detailed it is going to be. I spoke about the level of detail in chapter 2, in the context of the number of zones in the model. But network detail is also about whether we code every minor street, junction, lane or turn. Deciding on the level of network detail relates to whether we expect the model to help us answer questions of a very local nature.

A high level of detail in our network coding means that we try to include many of the following in the model:

- Minor junctions and side streets.
- The settings of traffic signals, including the amount of green light they give to different parts of the traffic.
- The correct split of lanes between the different turns in each arm of each junction.
- Bans on specific vehicles, such as bikes or trucks, on some lanes and turns.
- The exact shape of each traffic roundabout.
- The exact location of each bus stop.

- The exact layout of bus lanes (possibly coded as separate links).
- The exact locations where the number of lanes changes on a street.
- The accurate width of each lane, including places where it is wider or narrower.

A network that is coded in less detail may include some of these things too. But the focus in a less detailed model is on having a decent representation of the main roads, without attempting to make the modelled network look very similar to a full street map.

Figure 70 presents some important advantages and disadvantages of coding the network in more detail. There's no specific level of detail that is always the best. When we code a network in a model, we need to use our judgement and consider what amount of detail would best meet our modelling objectives. I'll show some more examples of where we need to use our judgement in chapter 11.

There are also many network coding dilemmas where the level of detail is just one consideration amongst others. Put another way, sometimes there simply are different ways of coding the same thing, and they all have various upsides and downsides.

Figure 71 shows four examples of locations which could be coded in more than one way. The choice between the options may seem like a tiny thing, but these choices do influence the model outputs. In a road network for a large city, such local dilemmas exist in hundreds of places, and their cumulative effect on the model outputs might be large.

It's good practice to experiment different ways of coding, and check their impact on the level of model calibration and validation. We wouldn't want the model to be sensitive to arbitrary coding decisions. Having said this, in reality we rarely have the time to ensure that every coding decision is fully justified. This means that most network models are indeed sensitive to arbitrary coding decisions, and this has to be borne in mind when you examine their outputs.

Figure 70: upsides and downsides of more network detail

More network detail	Less network detail
We add detail because we want to know more about the expected level of traffic everywhere, for example the number of people turning right or left in a junction.	A less detailed model has fewer calculations to make, and will normally take less time to run. This can be critical because we need to run the model many times in a loop.
Sometimes the model cannot show that a problem exists without sufficient detail.	Checking the network for coding errors is a more reasonable effort when there's less detail to check.
A more detailed model has more calculations to perform and will take longer to run.	Examining the outputs to identify clear patterns is easier when the network is less detailed.
Spending effort on detail leaves less time for ensuring similar things are coded consistently across the network. This can cause problems later.	In a less detailed network, it's less of a problem that we have no information on future scenarios where the network has not been designed yet.
The more detailed the model, the less time we have to scrutinize the outputs in detail to find errors or issues.	Clients can be unhappy to hear that the model can't answer their most detailed questions.
If the base year model is very detailed, we'll need to assume how each detail will change in the future, and this makes our outputs sensitive to more assumptions.	Some network details are essential for the model to be able to replicate important traffic phenomena.

Figure 71: different ways of coding the same thing

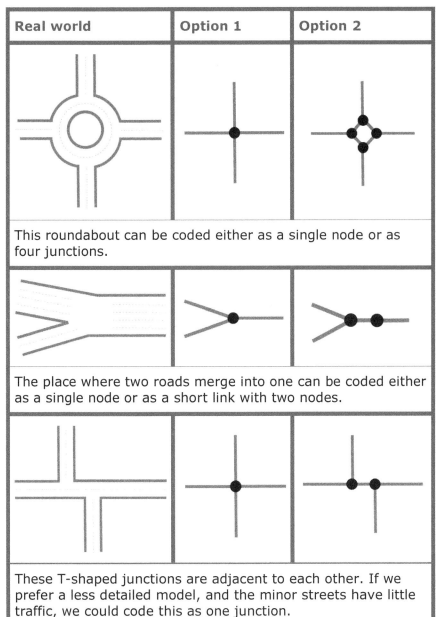

Real world	Option 1	Option 2

This roundabout can be coded either as a single node or as four junctions.

The place where two roads merge into one can be coded either as a single node or as a short link with two nodes.

These T-shaped junctions are adjacent to each other. If we prefer a less detailed model, and the minor streets have little traffic, we could code this as one junction.

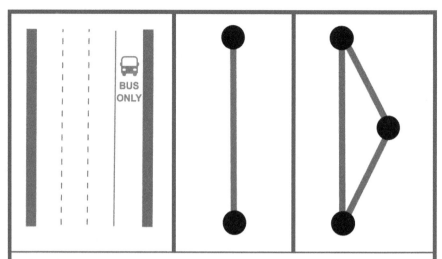

A bus lane is sometimes represented in the model by changing some link parameters, without coding it as a separate link. Alternatively, we could code the bus lane as a separate link, parallel to the link used by other traffic. Most models don't allow having two different links connecting the same pair of nodes, so we'll need some kind of workaround, such as adding a node in the middle of the bus lane.

9.6 Junction modelling

Transport networks are full of conflicts between vehicles, people or both. Junctions are where these conflicts are the most serious. Traffic conflicts in a junction are so serious, that they need resolution by experts. Traffic engineers design junctions in an attempt to balance between the needs of road users who go in different directions.

For traffic engineers, a single junction can be a whole universe. There's a lot of detail in every crossroads, which needs careful design if we want to optimise its capacity, improve travel times or increase safety. The design can be assisted by forecasts of how well it would work. Therefore, over the years many software tools have been introduced, that specialise in junction modelling.

Traditional junction modelling tools didn't involve traffic assignment or any other assessment of how the junction design affects demand. In a traditional junction model, a given demand from each side to each side of the junction is an input to the model, either directly from collected traffic data or from an assignment model. Then the model looks at how the junction performs when it serves this demand, and how this may change if the junction is designed differently.

Today, the boundaries between junction models, assignment models and micro-simulation models are less fixed. There are many methodologies that offer different combinations of these by performing junction modelling as part of a wider modelling process. It's common now to model all the detail of multiple junctions together, and it's also common to re-assign traffic as part of the modelling of junctions. This means that assignment models can examine the performance of each junction as a factor that affects routes choices across the network. It also means that the junction design work can consider the impacts of the design on other places, away from the junction.

In signalised junctions, i.e. junctions with traffic lights, a lot of attention in the modelling work is given to the number of seconds of green light that each side of the junction gets. Each signalised junction has its signal plan, which defines when green light is allocated to whom. In some cases, the signal plan is a preset input, and the model estimates how it affects the queues of vehicles waiting to enter the different sides of the junction. In other cases, the model itself optimises the signal plan. It tests various plans and suggests one that leads to shorter queues or reduces the total amount of time it takes everyone to cross the junction.

The modelling of signalised junctions has to work differently when the signal plan is traffic-operated. Many junctions have sensors installed under or beside the road. The sensors detect which sides of the junction have more vehicles waiting for their green light, and they change the signal plan in real time, to give more green light to the sides with more traffic. In such junctions, what the model needs to capture isn't the signal plan itself but the method used to decide which direction gets priority. If the model captures this then it can change the signal plan while it runs, so that it simulates the real time traffic-operated plan.

191

There are many cases where the signal planning is done together for all the junctions along a major road. If signals along the road are coordinated, the green light in a junction can be designed to start exactly when the first vehicle from the adjacent junction arrives, so that less time is wasted on green light that nobody uses.

Modelling junctions without traffic lights puts more emphasis on driver behaviour. Our objectives when we model these junctions remain the same: to reduce congestion, delay and accident risks. But without traffic signals, a lot depends on how road users choose to interact with each other. Every junction has some defined priorities, with traffic signs telling vehicles that come from certain sides that they need to give way to others. There's a lot of variation between different road users in how they interpret these rules, and some models reflect this variation in their estimates of travel times and queue lengths.

Many considerations are shared by models for junctions with or without traffic lights:

- The delays caused to cars by pedestrians, and to pedestrians by cars. We mainly model this where there's a pedestrian crossing, but some models also try to reflect the impact of pedestrian activity where there isn't a crossing, or the impact of pedestrians crossing when they have a red light.
- The delays caused to cars by bicycles, and to bicycles by cars. There are many factors to consider either when there's a cycle route crossing the junction or when there isn't.
- The interactions between the general traffic and public transport vehicles crossing the junction (buses or trams). These interactions vary between cases where there are bus lanes or tram tracks across the junction and cases where there aren't.

Junction models give much attention to small detail. This makes them powerful as inputs into the design of transport infrastructure in or near the junction. Clients and colleagues are often very interested in the detail, and they will have a lot to say when the detail in the model doesn't resemble their own experience. But as I explained just a few pages ago, a high level of detail has a price.

Having to provide all the inputs to the model is challenging even when you model the network the way it is now; the information we have on levels of traffic and on travel behaviour is limited and full of gaps. Our data is even weaker when modelling future scenarios. It may be very tempting to use detailed junction modelling as part of our analysis of traffic conditions in future scenarios. But think about those calculations that involve the number of seconds of green light for a specific left turn on a specific street, 10 years from now; does the reliance on something so particular make your analysis stronger or weaker?

In my work I've also come across some local authorities where junction modelling is the only type of travel demand analysis ever done. This happens for understandable reasons: junction modelling deals with intuitive and visible problems, free from the abstract discussion that you need when modelling trip distribution, for example. But the significant risk, when focusing on junction modelling only, is that you ignore likely changes in the demand that enters the junction in the first place.

9.7 Traffic micro-simulation

Traffic micro-simulation is sometimes done for the whole network, and sometimes for specific roads or junctions. In the UK, it is usually done for most junctions in the main part of the study area, as part of the assignment. But micro-simulation is also done without assignment at all, i.e. with fixed traffic flows that come from a separate assignment model. See the "micro" and "meso" options in figure 69 for a reminder.

The common thing to all kinds of micro-simulation is that the model creates individual vehicles and gets them to interact with each other, unlike models which aren't micro, where similar trips or similar vehicles are analysed together.

The main thing we micro-simulate is the behaviour of each driver and the location of each vehicle. The model looks at expected changes in behaviour and location at very frequent time intervals, typically every second. The same process is repeated every second within a pre-defined simulation period, e.g. the morning peak hour. The expected behaviour of each driver and the location of each vehicle are based on where they were and what they did in the previous second. The result is a continuous analysis of how locations, behaviours and traffic conditions evolve throughout the simulation period.

A traffic micro-simulation model is a collection of several sub-models. We need these sub-models to cover different behavioural aspects which jointly explain how traffic flows. The sub-models vary between different micro-simulation software packages, but some themes are used in most of them. These are shown in figure 72. The types of behaviour presented are usually estimated every second for every vehicle.

Because micro-simulation models look at individual vehicles, one of their attractive features is the ability to visualise traffic in the network. Even the most traditional micro-simulation tools usually allowed users to follow a two-dimensional visualisation of the network from above, showing where every vehicle is at every second and how they accelerate, change lanes, enter a junction and so on. Today many micro-simulation tools can produce a three-dimensional video, showing a movie that follows vehicles as they travel on different routes, allowing you to experience the levels of traffic they go through.

These three-dimensional visualisations of micro-simulation outputs have become very popular, and they're very effective in impressing clients and colleagues. They also have a major downside, though. The visualisation can seem so realistic, that it makes us forget our responsibility to be skeptical about model outputs. The ability to see in these videos what exactly happens on the street gives some people a feeling of certainty around the expected impacts of a project. This certainty is misguided, because the results still depend on a large number of assumptions, simplifications and data sources with many gaps. In fact, traffic figures which are visualised in full detail depend on even more assumptions and simplifications than outputs with more modest visualisation.

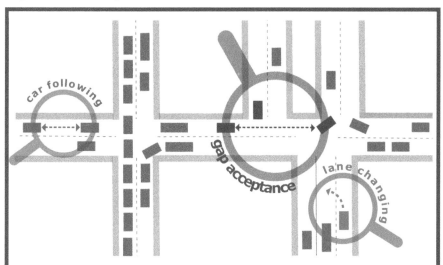

Car following. When you drive a vehicle, you are often just behind another vehicle. The car following model estimates how close you want to be to the vehicle ahead of you. The car following distance of each vehicle affects whether they decide to speed up, slow down or remain at a fixed speed. Looking at these distances across all vehicles, the micro-simulation model will determine how much traffic can fit into each road.

Lane changing. Every driver sometimes has to move to another lane, either for overtaking another vehicle or in order to get to a lane from which they can turn right or left. Each driver is different in how cautious they are when changing lanes. The lane changing model estimates for each vehicle when they will start their lane change, how long this would take them, and how they will interact with other vehicles while changing.

Gap acceptance. When entering a junction with no traffic lights from a side road, you need to wait until the gap between vehicles on the main road is large enough for you to go through. Some drivers will wait longer, while others will try to sneak between cars that are relatively close to each other. The gap acceptance model decides, for every driver across the network, what gap in the opposing traffic they'll accept. This will have an impact on how much traffic each road can accommodate.

It's worth noting that the trip matrices or assignment outputs which go into the micro-simulation bring all their limitations with them. On top of these, there are the weaknesses of the micro-simulation tool itself, such as:

- Aspects of people's behaviour which are too difficult to model.
- The impact of pedestrians and cyclists which are only partially represented in the model.
- Traffic incidents that cannot be forecast.
- The impact of unpredictable weather conditions.

Therefore, as with any other modelling capability, micro-simulation isn't a technique that tells you what's really going to happen. It has its upsides and downsides, and is powerful mainly in giving you some good food for thought as one of the inputs into your work.

9.8 Dealing with parking

One of the weakest spots of transport models is the way we represent car parking. The availability of parking is a critical consideration for car users, but capturing this in the model involves so many challenges, that we usually consider parking in an extremely simplified manner. Parking issues are relevant to all stages in a full transport model, and not only to the assignment.

The difficulty to deal with parking in transport models is, naturally, a big problem when testing changes in parking policy. But it's an equally big problem also when using the model for any other purpose. Since people have a choice between using car and public transport, and between destinations that have different levels of parking supply, our understanding of their behaviour can be seriously compromised by not knowing how parking affect them. This remains an issue even if the project we test has little to do with parking.

Figure 73 lists the reasons why parking is such a major modelling challenge, together with some solutions, even if some of them are difficult to implement.

Figure 73: challenges in representing parking in a model

Challenge: any handling of parking in a model requires knowing where parking is actually available, whether it costs to park there, and how much it costs.

Possible solution: we generally have good information on the number of parking spaces on the street, in residential buildings and in organised off-street car parks.

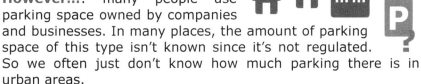

However...: many people use parking space owned by companies and businesses. In many places, the amount of parking space of this type isn't known since it's not regulated. So we often just don't know how much parking there is in urban areas.

Challenge: sometimes people park away from their trip destination, where parking is available, so the modelled car trip goes to the wrong place.

Possible solution: the car trip in the trip matrix should go to the parking zone, with a separate trip (by foot or another mode) from the parking place to the real destination.

However...: building the trip matrix this way is challenging and requires more data. Most models just assume that parking is in the same zone as the destination.

Challenge: we use traffic counts to calibrate our assignment models. Part of the traffic seen in these counts is drivers searching for parking, or driving to their parking place, not to their real destination. These parking-related trips are not in the trip matrix, so the model calibration process might misinterpret them.

Possible solution: advanced models store some information on where people park, which makes the comparison to counts easier.

However...: storing separate information on where exactly people park is ambitious. Most models don't do it.

Challenge: the availability of parking influences people's mode choice. Short supply of parking near the destination encourages people to use public transport.

Possible solution: the availability of parking can be part of the generalised cost used in the mode split model.

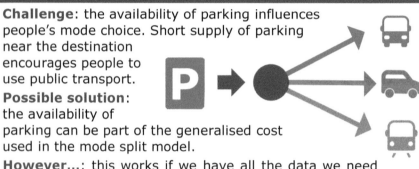

However...: this works if we have all the data we need on parking availability. Quite often we don't.

Challenge: the availability of parking influences people's destination choice. If car is their preferred mode, they'll only go to places with parking.

Possible solution: the availability of parking can be part of the generalised cost used at the destination choice stage.

However...: this works if we have all the data we need on parking. Quite often we don't.

Challenge: to represent parking availability in a specific place, the model needs to consider the amount of parking there at the start of the day and how it then gradually fills up. It shouldn't allow car users to end a trip in a zone where all parking spaces have already been filled.

Possible solution: advanced models calculate changes to parking occupancy in each zone throughout the day. The amount of parking space at any time depends on the overall parking capacity and on the arrival and departure times of vehicles that parked there already.

However...: adding such a detailed parking mechanism seriously complicates the modelling process. Developing this model would be costly, with demanding calibration and validation needs, as well as higher model runtimes. Such models are not in common use.

Challenge: the availability and price of parking at the destination of one trip also has an impact on whether people will use their car when they travel onwards from there.

Possible solution: this is straightforward to address if the model is tour-based. When people do a chain of trips, a tour-based model looks at the whole chain together.

However...: modelling tours has upsides and downsides - see section 3.7.

Challenge: people's willingness to pay for parking depends on their income. It also depends on whether they travel for their own purposes or for business, since the cost of parking may be covered by their employer.

Possible solution: this is addressed when using segmentation by trip purpose and income.

However...: segmentation is a fundamental requirement, but having separate trip matrices for people with different income levels is challenging, because the data we have on people's income is often of limited quality.

9.9 The monetary cost of car travel

I mentioned earlier the complications involved when we want to include public transport fares in the generalised cost. For example, the use of ticket types that are valid for multiple trips means that we don't know how much people pay per trip. The way we mix money and time together, using an artificial **value of time** (see section 2.8 for a reminder), has its limitations too.

Similar challenges also exist if we want our model to capture the fact that travel by car costs money. It might sound surprising, but people's travel behaviour isn't directly influenced by the money they really pay. It's much more directly influenced by the money they think they pay, i.e. by the **perceived cost** of travel.

A fundamental question is, therefore, what expenses people perceive as the cost of their car journey. Some people consider the price they pay for fuel as the cost of their car trip. Other people don't associate more car travel with a higher cost of fuel, because on most trips they don't need to refill their tanks, so most of the time they pay nothing.

Car maintenance costs are complex as well, because they are not part of the cost of any specific journey. An analytical person would spread their annual car maintenance costs over all the car journeys they make, to figure out how it affects the cost of each journey. But many car owners see the need to pay for maintenance as a separate issue, which isn't a consideration when deciding how to make a specific trip.

Even if everyone considered how much the cost of car maintenance contributes to the cost of each trip, this calculation is difficult to replicate in a model. It depends on factors which vary greatly, even between people who make exactly the same trip. The cost per trip would vary, for example, based on the total amount of travel you make with your car; whether you are the only person using the car; and whether you are the only person contributing to its maintenance costs.

When building transport models, we normally bypass all these challenges by including a general "price per mile" or "price per kilometre" in the generalised cost of travel by car. If your trip is 10 miles long then this adds 10 times the price per mile to the generalised cost. The price per mile isn't a way of telling the model that people prefer a shorter journey; this is already included in the value of time, and we don't want to count the same thing twice. The price per mile is whatever monetary cost we think people take into account when considering travel by car. It's a simplified way of implicitly including all fuel costs and car maintenance costs together.

This may all sound confusing, but the hardest part is yet to come. The toughest thing to model, when it comes to the money you pay for using your car, is **road user charging**. Road user charging may include any type of toll that applies to the users of specific roads or specific urban areas.

There are many projects around the world that involve building new toll roads or applying tolls to existing roads, so there is great interest in using transport models to examine tolling options. A scenario where a road or an area cost money to use will definitely change people's route choices, but there's no wide agreement on what's the best way to represent tolls in models, and especially in assignment models.

Figure 74 offers you a glimpse of the challenge of representing a toll in a network model. It shows several approaches for representing the toll in the model. Most of these approaches use common network modelling techniques, like those described in figures 67 and 69, but some changes are made to help us assess how traffic splits between tolled and toll-free roads.

Figure 74: different ways of modelling tolls

Adding the toll to the generalised cost in the assignment. To reflect the fact that some links are tolled, we add the toll to the generalised cost of the tolled links. Since the generalised cost is usually expressed in minutes (see section 2.6 for a reminder), we use the value of time to convert the toll into some extra minutes. So the toll is coded in the model simply by making the tolled links physically longer than they really are.

 This is the simplest approach. The coding effort is minimal.

 It can work even if the toll applies to a whole area (like the Congestion Charging zone in London) and not to specific links. We just need to add the toll to the roads that enter the tolled area.

 It's difficult to represent cases where paying the toll once allows you to use the tolled road several times within one day. The model will add the extra time every time you use that road.

 This approach is heavily reliant on the value of time, even if there's a lot of uncertainty around this value.

Creating a separate "toll payers" segment. In this approach we don't add the toll to the network but use additional segmentation instead (see section 2.7 for a reminder about segmentation). This means that we create separate demand matrices not only to reflect differences like the journey purpose, but also to reflect which travellers are willing to pay tolls and which ones aren't. In the assignment, the "toll payers" matrix is assigned to routes that include the toll road, and the "non-payers" matrix is assigned to other routes.

 This approach avoids the artificial conversion of the toll to additional travel time. It also avoids the problem of drivers being charged multiple times in cases where you're actually only charged once.

The big question is how we create the separate "toll payers" and "non-payers" matrices. A Stated Preference survey is a common solution, but it has many downsides (see section 7.3 for a reminder). Alternatively, we can assume that people with a higher income will pay the toll, although this is quite simplistic.

 Using this approach means that people's decision whether or not to use the toll road is analysed outside the model. So the model itself doesn't help us estimate how the toll we charge, or the level of traffic congestion, affect the number of toll payers.

Adding a toll choice model to the model hierarchy. In this approach, we create a special model to split people into "toll payers" and "non-payers". This model is added to our model hierarchy, just above the assignment. The model creates a "toll payers" matrix which we then assign to routes using the toll road, and a "non-payers" matrix which we then assign to routes that avoid the toll.

 This approach is similar to the previous one which created a "toll payers" segment. But segments remain the same across all scenarios we test, whereas here the model may identify different toll payers in different scenarios. This means that changes in traffic conditions, or different pricing policies, can change the number of toll payers. This is more realistic.

 To build the model that estimates who pays the toll, we need some strong evidence regarding the factors that affect this choice. This remains a challenge, just like with the previous approach.

Using toll elasticities in the assignment. In this approach we run a normal assignment, ignoring the toll. From the assignment outputs, we take the number of users on the toll road and apply a "toll elasticity" to it (see figure 40 for a reminder of how elasticities work). This gives us a corrected number of users, which also considers the toll. We also correct the number of users on all other roads, so that the total demand remains as in the trip matrix.

☺ As I explained in chapters 5 and 6, elasticities allow us to convert the level of demand before a certain change to an estimated level after the change. So an elasticity-based approach can fit very well if we are considering applying a new toll to existing roads.

☹ We need to have a source of information on toll elasticities. This could be, for example, some evidence on the impact that tolls had on the demand in places where they were already introduced. We can't use this approach without knowing what the toll elasticity might be.

☹ Even if we can calculate a toll elasticity based on the way people behave on a different toll road, will people respond to the one we're now testing in a similar way? The toll elasticity may have been calculated at a different place and a different time, and we need to consider how comparable these were to our situation.

Building a separate model in a spreadsheet. In this approach we don't use our existing model at all. Instead, we build a new model in a spreadsheet, with a much simpler network and matrix. The new model focuses only on the area around the toll road, and only on the people's choice between the toll road and competing routes.

☺ It's good to keep things simple. This approach stays away from the complexity of our full network, and only asks questions relevant to our project.

☹ The key question remains where we can find sufficient insight on people's considerations when they choose whether to use a toll road. We need such insight even if our model is compact.

☹ Simplifying the problem can prove very effective, but there might be traffic phenomena that the simplified tool can't capture. For example, to identify the levels of traffic when long queues start to develop, we sometimes need a fully detailed network model.

9.10 Model convergence and iteration

One thing that is in common to most types of models mentioned in this book is that you can't run them just once. By the time you've done one round of all the calculations, they already contradict each other. The generalised costs you used in the mode, route or destination choice models helped you estimate choices people make. But now that you have these estimates, they would change your generalised costs. For example, if you estimated that more cars would use a specific street because of its low cost, now it attracts more cars and this will increase journey times, which are part of the cost. The costs depend on the demand and the demand depends on the costs.

This is what triggers the process I spoke about in figure 25. We go down the model hierarchy from top to bottom using some guess of the costs, until we have a first estimate of the demand for all modes, destinations, routes and so on. The assignment models give us updated costs and we now take these costs up the model hierarchy to re-calculate the demand. This gives us yet another update of the costs and we can re-calculate the demand again. Each run of the model before we update the costs is called an **iteration**. This loop is an **iterative** process.

The purpose of the iterative process is to keep refining the demand and the generalised costs until they stabilise, i.e. until they no longer change much from one iteration to the next. This gradual refinement of the model outputs is called **convergence**. The level of convergence is good if the model meets all the following:

- The number of iterations we've run isn't too high (less than 10 iterations is a common rule of thumb).
- The outputs make good sense.
- In the final iteration, the outputs are no longer very different from the previous iteration.

Reaching this kind of stability indicates that the estimated demand and the generalised costs are now consistent with each other, so we can now do with these outputs whatever we planned to do with them.

In addition to the need for convergence of the full model, there's also a need for convergence within the assignment. We assign the demand to different routes based on their generalised costs, and then we have new volumes of traffic or passengers in different places, which we can use to update the generalised costs, so that we can re-assign the demand and so forth. We run several iterations of the assignment within each single iteration of the full model.

In some projects we run an assignment model only; the assignment needs to reach internal convergence even if it's not part of a four-stage model, because otherwise the costs and the demand contradict each other. In some projects we create a bespoke model structure, which isn't consistent with the four-stage concept. The kind of convergence such a model would need depends on how it works, but if the model uses demand and generalised costs, then it's very likely that it needs to run in a loop, just like a full four-stage model.

Figure 75: an iterative modelling process

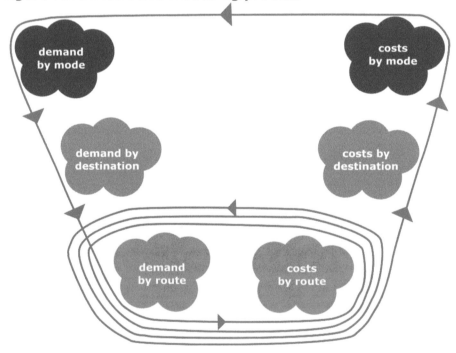

A sketch of how we run transport models in an iterative loop is shown in figure 75. The figure shows a simplified version of the real process, for example because it doesn't show where exactly it starts and where it ends. It's also just an example, since the loop can be set up in a slightly different way in each model. The important thing to note in figure 75 is that we have a loop within a loop:

- The outer loop runs the whole model several times, until anything that has some demand (e.g. every destination and every mode) has a generalised cost that is consistent with this demand.
- The inner loop runs through the assignment only. It runs several times in each run of the outer loop, until the demand and the cost of each route in the network are consistent with each other.

The fact that we run the model several times means, naturally, that it takes longer to run. The time it takes to iterate through the model should be considered when we design the model and plan any scenario testing work. Anything that complicates the model, such as having more detailed zones, increases runtime not just once but repeatedly, in every iteration. This isn't a problem in models that only take a few minutes to run; but there are complex models, where the assignment alone can take hours to reach convergence, so a complete model run can take several days for every single scenario.

The iterative process sometimes fails and doesn't converge. When this happens, the difference in the model outputs between consecutive iterations get larger all the time, instead of getting smaller. Lack of convergence means that we've been unsuccessful in building a model that gives stable outputs. In such case, we need to consider changes to the network, or to various model parameters, or even to the entire structure and scope of the model.

It's worth saying here that model convergence is purely a mathematical thing. When we loop through the model, we're not representing people's process of adapting to varying travel conditions. We need the iterations simply because we start with just a guess of the demand for each mode, destination and route; the iterations gradually improve this guess. On the other hand, remember that convergence itself isn't a sufficient indication that the model gives us good forecasts. It only means that the outputs are stable and won't change if we run the model once more.

9.11 Short-term prediction

When talking about different types of modelling work, most of the examples I gave so far are about assessing how the transport system may operate in the long term. I spoke about how we use models to test projects (like a new railway station), scenarios (like a shift of businesses to out-of-town locations) or policies (like a new tax on car use).

But transport models, and network models in particular, also have an alternative use, which focuses on the much shorter term. We use models to test the possible impacts of much smaller interventions, which don't involve heavy infrastructure. Such interventions are being introduced all the time and people often don't even notice. The modelling of such changes looks at their potential impacts next year, next week, tomorrow or even in real time, when we consider changes to apply immediately.

The most common type of short-term intervention we assess with network models is the update of traffic signal settings. This includes fine-tuning the allocation of green light to the different sides of a junction, and optimising this allocation across all junctions in a larger area. This kind of optimisation can help minimise the overall delays, emissions and accidents. Such use of models is typically done in a traffic control centre, or in a team that is responsible for the ongoing operations of streets and highways.

Since such use of models is done on a continuous basis, we can't spend time on network coding, calibration and validation before each use. On the other hand, surely we shouldn't use a model which hasn't been calibrated and hasn't proven to be a reliable tool. An effective approach is by using an existing model as our starting point, and preparing in advance a large collection of modelled scenarios which are suitable for use in real time.

208

Ideally, we should have a library of modelled scenarios that cover many different combinations of all the following:

- Different traffic control settings.
- Different levels of traffic.
- Different weather conditions.
- Some scenarios just before or after major events.
- Some scenarios during road closures.
- Some scenarios after major accidents.

For each scenario we should ideally have the model outputs, which include information on travel times and network performance in this scenario. If we had such a comprehensive library of modelled scenarios, then whatever the condition of the transport system, we can always browse through our library and find the control settings that optimise network performance. When an unexpected problem (such a major accident) occurs, we don't need to prepare a new scenario and run the model, only to identify similar scenarios, and choose from them the control settings that lead to best network performance.

In reality, our scenario library may not be that comprehensive, but the ongoing nature of such model use means that we can continue enriching this library gradually. This process is most effective if our network is equipped with cameras and sensors that allow us to continuously collect traffic data. With such automated data collection capability, every time we face network conditions we don't have a stored scenario for, we can collect the relevant data and develop the missing scenario. If we follow this practice then over time we'll have a highly effective library which we can use in large number of situations.

In my opinion, the use of network models to help us make short-term decisions is the most important application of any type of transport model. Figure 76 shows my reasons for saying this. There are indeed some serious challenges I'll talk about in chapters 10 and 11; my point here is that when doing short-term prediction, these challenges are a bit smaller. Of course these are very general points, and you'll know best whether they apply in your own work environment.

Figure 76: why short-term modelling is more powerful

Less uncertainty. When our focus is on how the transport system would perform tomorrow or next week, we are free from many of the challenges of long-term forecasting. Many things are still uncertain, even when predicting what will happen in five minutes; but the list of uncertain things is much shorter than when looking into the further future. For example, in short-term prediction we don't need to speculate whether some offices will move to other locations; we know how many residents live in each neighbourhood; and we know exactly what transport infrastructure is in place.

Strong link to data. The scenario library approach I described on the previous page balances the use of the model with the use of data. We can add a scenario to our library only if it has been calibrated to recent data. This approach encourages continuous data collection, so that the scenario library can be updated and expanded. This focus on the data side is important given all the limitations of the model itself.

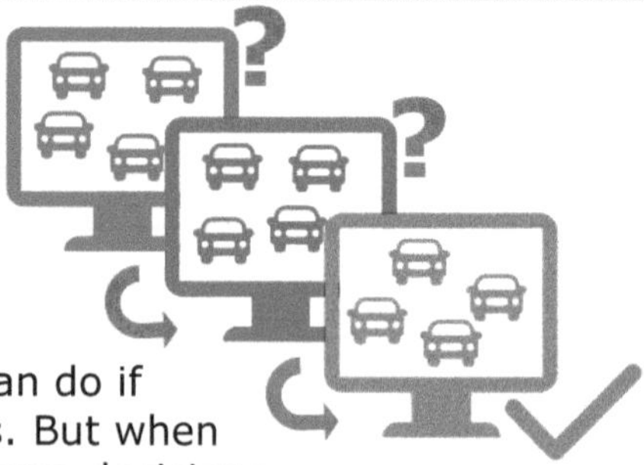

Trial and error. When using models to support long-term decisions, we need to complete all the modelling and appraisal work, and only then work can start. By the time our long-term transport project is implemented, there's little we can do if it was based on wrong forecasts. But when using models to support short-term decisions, we continuously monitor the impact of our decisions. There will always be cases where the decision doesn't lead to satisfactory results. In such cases, we can immediately change our decision. We can also update our scenario library with any lessons we have learnt.

Less stakeholder pressure. The modelling work that we do when testing large, long-term infrastructure projects is often interrupted by pressures from stakeholders, and is influenced by these pressures. The types of decisions we make using short-term prediction tools are sometimes more technical and microscopic. Therefore, they tend to be of less interest to senior decision makers, who sometimes simply let us get on with the work, and improve the performance of the network!

Scenario selection process. The scenarios in the library will not have a perfect match with the current state of the network. This encourages us, over time, to develop more scenarios, also when the differences between them are subtle. Then we need to continuously select the most relevant modelled scenarios from the library, and this is an excellent opportunity to discuss these subtle differences while using our judgement and logic. Such selection process is healthier than what often happens in long-term projects, where each scenario is a completely different situation, and we tend to dismiss the importance of subtle things that are difficult to model.

9.12 The outputs from network models

Assignment models and other network models are the direct source of information we use in the appraisal and design of transport improvements. The outputs from the network model are often seen as the outputs from the entire four-stage model, because the detailed network modelling is the final stage in the modelling process.

The most common types of outputs we take from network models are listed in figure 77. The following are the meanings of the symbols used in figure 77:

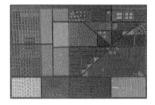

- Outputs where I show this symbol can be presented as a **map by zone**, summarising information across all trips to/from that zone. For these outputs you can also use any other type of presentation that breaks things down by zone, such as a bar chart or a word cloud (see figure 64).

- Outputs with this symbol can be presented as a **matrix**. For each **OD pair**, information is summarised across all routes from this origin to this destination. Matrices can also be visualised as chord diagrams (see figure 62).

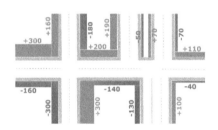

- These outputs can be presented as a **map by link**. Links have a direction, so you need a mapping tool that can show two different numbers on one link, and it should be clear which one represents each direction.

- Outputs with this symbol can be presented as a **map by node**. The nodes represent junctions, bus stops or stations.

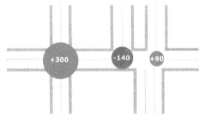

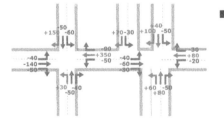

- These outputs can be presented **for each turn** in a junction. But be careful when presenting outputs at such level of detail. Many models aren't reliable when looking at such fine-grained outputs.

212

- These outputs can be presented **by public transport line**.

City line	1,200
Circle line	1,500
Central line	2,900
Cucumber line	2,000

- Outputs with this sybmbol can be visualised using a **video**.

Figure 77: typical outputs from network models

Volumes of traffic. This information can feed into our analysis of the traffic impacts of proposed projects and the differences between scenarios.

Queue lengths. Ditto.

Speeds. Ditto.

Generalised costs. The generalised cost matrices, for scenarios representing policy or investment options, are the main model output that feeds into the appraisal of these options.

213

Passenger volumes (on-board, boarding or alighting). This information can feed into our analysis of possible changes in passenger demand between scenarios in specific places.

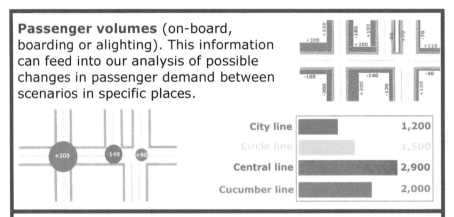

City line		1,200
Circle line		1,500
Central line		2,900
Cucumber line		2,000

Travel times. This information feeds into our analysis of traffic impacts, and is used in the appraisal.

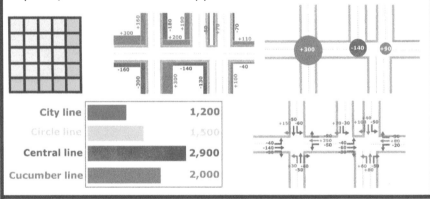

City line		1,200
Circle line		1,500
Central line		2,900
Cucumber line		2,000

Tolls paid. This output can help us understand the impact of tolls on different people (although the representation of tolls in the model might be very limited,

so look again at the points made in section 9.9, and be cautious about using model outputs to estimate toll revenue).

Fares paid. This output can help us understand the impact of fares on different people (but note again that fares are included in the model in a very simplified  way, so check again my earlier comments about this, and be cautious about using model outputs to estimate fare revenue).

Travel distances. This can help us check if the estimated change in travel behaviour is consistent with other data sources. Change in the travelled mileage are important for any discussion about the impacts of projects and policies.

9.13   The main limitations of network models

This long chapter covered a whole range of topics related to network models. I include in this category assignment models for different modes, junction models and micro-simulation. I see them all as one family because the boundaries between the different network modelling techniques are blurred, and many packages today perform various combinations of these.

There's a big appetite for using network models to understand the impacts of projects and policies, because clients often find their outputs visual and intuitive. But I'm worried by how often these outputs are presented without emphasising their limitations. Figure 78 contains a summary of some key limitations. This figure also closes the first part of this book.

Figure 78: limitations of network models

Theoretical route choices. Route choices in the model are sometimes based on theoretical assumptions, such as "user equilibrium", which might not match how people really choose their routes.

Quality of demand inputs. Network models don't estimate demand but get it as an input. Demand information may come from a distribution or mode split model, or directly from data collected in the area, or it might even be made up. Network model outputs tell us nothing about the quality of the inputs; outputs based on unreliable sources can look exactly the same as reliable ones. You need to understand the demand modelling process that fed into the network model, and remember the rule "garbage in – garbage out".

Behavioural realism. The generalised costs of different routes reflect things that we can measure and model, but they don't necessarily include everything that influences people's real route choice.

Modelling parking. We only have partial ability to represent car parking in the model. We have limited information on the locations where people park and on the trip from the parking to the destination. Modelling the availability of parking at different

times of day is complex, and it's also difficult for the model to reasonably reflect the willingness to pay for parking.

Modelling over-crowding. On busy public transport routes, it's sometimes not possible to board the first service arriving. Some public transport assignment models can't reflect this.

Modelling monetary costs and tolls. We model anything that costs money in a very simplified way. This has particular relevance when looking at people's choice between routes with fare or toll differences. We convert all types of payment to time units in the same way, so we might be distorting people's real preferences. You should understand your model's technique for handling fares and tolls, and consider whether this approach is acceptable in your project.

Level of detail. More detail in the coding of the network, or in the micro-simulation modelling process, is sometimes critical for understanding traffic phenomena. The detail also helps answer questions that clients and colleagues often have. But more detail also means higher runtimes; higher risks of inconsistent coding; higher occurrence of coding errors; greater effort when interpreting results; and greater sensitivity of the outputs to inputs we don't have. You must resist the temptation to zoom in too much.

Part II:
the culture of
transport modelling

Chapter 10
Why we really use transport models

10.1   The political and organisational context

Who would have thought it? I've managed to write over 200 pages about the principles of transport modelling. It took me 9 chapters and 78 silly figures to review the things that models try to estimate. I also spoke quite a lot about the limitations of the models we commonly use. But I've so far said very little about the organisations, teams and individuals involved.

I'd like to talk more about the people who decide to do modelling, the people who do the modelling, and the organisations where they work. The organisational background is important to understand because it doesn't stay in the background. The working culture of modellers, colleagues and clients gets inside every model and influences the outputs.

At the very beginning of this book, I said that a key reason why we use models is to produce inputs to the appraisal of transport investments. I'd like now to highlight the difference between several types of appraisal. Figure 79 shows four typical situations where transport models are used. These four types cover almost everything we use models for. "Valuation" situations happen mainly in the private sector, while the others are mainly in the public sector. Consultants work in all these types of situations.

I'm classifying these situations here because the organisational attitude towards modelling is different in each type. A key difference is in terms of whether there are sufficient opportunities to discuss the limitations of the model. I focus on the limitations rather than the strengths, because I've not seen cases where model strengths are underplayed. I clearly have seen cases of reluctance to face the weaknesses; the way we handle the limitations is what determines the quality of any modelling work.

In figure 80 I therefore describe the role of models and the ability to discuss their downsides in the four mentioned types of situations. This is not based on any theory, but purely on my experience of being a participant in dozens of such situations.

Figure 79: organisational situations where we use models

Arbitration. These are situations where models are used to help set the 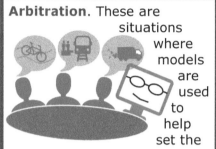 priorities within a group of partners, who promote different infrastructure improvements. Typically, this would happen in a local or regional authority, where there's no sufficient funding for all the transport projects that stakeholders want, so the model helps resolve disputes about precedence.

Valuation. These are situations where a private sector investor uses a transport model to help them decide whether or not to participate in a commercial activity. This could include, for example, a decision on whether to participate in a bid to operate a toll road or a railway.

Vindication. In these situations, modelling work is done because decisions that authorities have already made are challenged by the public or by other stakeholders. Model outputs are shown in order to demonstrate that the decision has a solid justification.

Competition. These are situations where there's a formal funding competition between different projects, and models help decide which ones get funded. Unlike an "arbitration" situation, here there's no partnership between bidders. A central government body usually acts as the judge. The competitors do the modelling work for their own projects, and they need to present it in their bid.

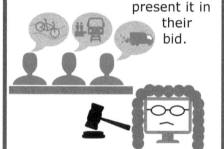

Figure 80: the role of the model in different situations

Arbitration. Models often have a critical role in political disputes about local funding allocation. Since the model and the modellers are not a party in the debate, the outputs are seen as the most factual evidence. There are cases where the political discussion

gets into model capabilities: when some projects have benefits which are difficult to model, the promoters of these projects will highlight this. But the coordinating body, which is responsible for the modelling work, often has interest in establishing its own role as a "fair broker" that knows all the answers. Limited technical skills amongst stakeholders, and the desire to reach a decision and move on, often lead partners to avoid a discussion about model weaknesses.

Valuation. When investors start a serious assessment of a project to put their money on, they have strong appetite for it already. Without such appetite, the project would rarely get to the stage of commissioning modelling work. Investors expect model outputs to confirm a deal that already is in early drafting stages, although concerns about low profitability will still be taken very seriously. Investors have great interest in risk and uncertainty, and therefore they welcome a discussion about model weaknesses. But if the modeller is unable to give a clear "yes or no" conclusion, the client will often get angry. There will be real pressure on the modellers to present a concise set of numbers that summarise the entire story in one slide with no caveats.

Vindication. If a decision is challenged when the project is already at an advanced stage, the authority who made that decision already knows what they want. Any new modelling result that suggests otherwise is seen as a distraction. Those who challenge the decision often attempt to undermine the modelling work, although they might not have the expertise and resources this requires, while the authority does. So the authority isn't too interested in discussing model limitations, but once they've been raised, the authority can usually get away with them quite easily.

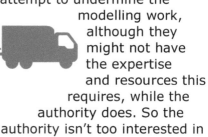

Competition. To win funding through a competition, bidders need to meet various criteria. Some strategic criteria are harder to demonstrate using model outputs, so the weight attached to model results varies between funds; but technical model-based assessment criteria remain critical in most funds. The bidders usually do the modelling for their own projects. They have a strong incentive to highlight the strengths of the model and tone down the weaknesses, in order to present the case for their project as free from doubt. The central body that acts as a judge scrutinises the modelling work, but seldom has enough resources to do this thoroughly. In addition, the central body has its own reasons to present the modelling work as the robust basis for funding allocation, and play down the limitations: if the funding allocation accepts how subjective the evidence from models can be, it would attract more criticism.

It's worth noting what type of situation isn't represented in figures 79 and 80: we don't do much modelling at the early optioneering stages, when there's a wide range of ideas to look at. One reason for this is that modelling all the options, before any short-listing, would be a lot of work, and we might struggle to resource it. Another reason is that some of the options at this stage aren't well-defined, so it's not clear yet what to model.

Now that you've read figures 79 and 80, it's time to refine something I said in chapter 1. I said that models help us choose between project options, but in reality it's not uncommon that we start developing a model after the choice between the options has already been made. This might sound outrageous, but it can happen in quite a natural way. Let me explain how it works.

Modelling work is time-consuming and costly, so the decision to start this work is usually made by senior people when they see in the horizon a need to justify a project. What makes them sense that this is coming is pressure from stakeholders, who push for transport improvements which they find necessary. For understandable reasons, these stakeholders don't care too much about modelling. Think of newly-elected politicians, local businesses, charities or community representatives who make the case for transport improvements: it's not their job to know the formal procedures for prioritising investments. Many of them have not even heard of transport models. My auntie Tilda, for instance, never heard of these models until I told her everything she needs to know.

When political or public pressures lead us to start modelling and appraisal work, we try to catch up with the pace of the political discussions. Sometimes this is successful, and we're able to develop a model and provide some valid evidence to present in discussions with stakeholders. In such cases, the political and analytical processes can merge, and the decision at the end of the process is really based on both. It's fantastic when this happens.

But there are also many cases where the modelling and appraisal work fails to meet the timescales that are dictated by political and organisational processes. In such cases, decisions which were meant to be assisted by models are made before the final model outputs are available. The role of the model is then limited

223

to providing some material to be used when the decision is documented and communicated later. The role of the model is further reduced in cases where the modelling work doesn't show what clients wanted it to show. In such cases, much of the modelling work might be archived without being used.

What all this means is that, if you work on a transport model, you'll spend much time without being sure what's your exact contribution to the broader project. Tensions between your technical expertise and your duties as a project team member might arise. Some clients will see your entire contribution merely as a formality, which is only meant to approve decisions already made. If you don't simply give the anticipated answer, their response might be hostile. And if you need to highlight the limitations of the evidence you can reliably provide, some colleagues will not understand why you're being so difficult.

Of course there are many examples of projects where modelling work is delivered successfully and the contribution of modellers is celebrated. I'm highlighting the more negative cases here because they are an integral part of the culture of transport modelling, which this part of the book is all about. Most of the remaining part of this book looks at different aspects of this culture.

10.2 The practical side of model scoping

Back in chapter 1, I listed various considerations that we take into account when deciding the scope of our model and our modelling work. I recommend that you have a quick look at chapter 1, and figure 2 in particular, as a reminder before you read on.

Chapter 1 was too early in the book to elaborate on considerations related to the organisational and political environment. Figure 81 tries to fill in this gap by listing some additional model scoping considerations. Each row in the table covers a question that is asked when the need for new modelling work arises.

Figure 81: model scoping practicalities

1	**What model already exists?** The big majority of projects rely on an existing model. New features are introduced in some projects, but the default is to accept the existing capabilities of the model.
2	**Will the model itself be viewed by others, or just the outputs**? In some situations, there's a chance that the model will be audited by an external reviewer. In some funding bids there's even a formal requirement to submit the model itself. But in other situations, the modelling work is internal to a company, and can be kept confidential. The choice of modelling techniques may depend on who might see the model.
3	**Is there a tradition of modelling such projects in a certain way?** Some things are modelled differently in different places simply because this is the local modelling tradition. Figures 38, 41 and 71 include some examples of different ways to model the same thing.
4	**Who is the client for the modelling work?** The identity of the client will often affect the scope of the model. For example, an investor will want the model to be able to produce outputs which a public transport agency will not require, even if both cases relate to the same project.
5	**Who funds the project we model?** The sources of potential funding for the transport intervention can have a major impact on the modelling approach. When requesting government funding, there's a need to follow their modelling guidance. Other sources of funding may or may not define their own rules.
6	**Who funds the modelling work?** Sometimes there are different options for who would pay for the model: the local authority, a property developer, a railway operator and so on. Those who pay will usually want more control over the model specification.

7	**Is the budget sufficient for meeting the expectations?** There's often no match between the list of questions the model is expected to answer and the modelling budget. Getting more insight from the model normally requires doing more work.
8	**What modelling expertise is available?** Some questions with high relevance to a project require specific expertise, which might not be available in the modelling team. The modelling of land use and transport interaction, for example, is frequently given a low priority simply because there's nobody around who knows how to do it. There's also the opposite case, where a low-priority question is given too much attention since the relevant expertise exists in the team.
9	**What data is available?** In figure 36 I reviewed the different data sources we use when developing models. The behaviours and phenomena that the model can describe should match the behaviours and phenomena that are captured in the data. If there's no such match, we should either collect more data or reduce the scope of the model.
10	**How much time do we have for modelling?** Even in the rare situation where budget, data and skills are sufficient to develop the model of our dreams, we seldom have the time! Modelling is usually done under significant time pressure. Doing modelling activities in parallel isn't common; I will comment on this point in chapter 12.

The scope of every model is compromised from the start; there's no perfect balance between all the constraints. The practicalities listed in figure 81 tend to have a more notable impact on the scope of the model than those listed in figure 2. For example, we often re-use similar modelling solutions in a large number of projects, even if they are far from ideal for the project.

I once mentioned, in an article I wrote, a list of considerations to have in mind when scoping your model. I got some positive responses from readers, but also a couple of angry responses who said that my purist approach had no room in the practical world. Of course this was a misunderstanding, since I'd never advise anyone to put more time, effort and money into modelling than what they can afford. I'm listing these model scoping considerations so that you try to find the best compromise in your own work environment. Even more importantly, I'm listing them so that you acknowledge the drawbacks of your model, and make a responsible use of its limited capabilities.

10.3 Abuse and misuse of transport models

If you state that a model gives stronger insight on the transport system than it really does, you are misusing the model. It is a matter of professional ethics to give an honest description of the capabilities and limitations of the technical tools you use. Without such honesty, you'd be exploiting the fact that your audience may be less knowledgeable than you are.

The misuse of transport models is a common problem in all fours types of modelling situations I described in figures 79 and 80. In all these situations, there's no feasible way of developing models that address all the needs and answer all the questions. Many of the model limitations I reviewed earlier (in figures 47, 57, 65 and 78) will not be addressed even if you spend years improving your model. So the only practical way of dealing with these limitations is to acknowledge that model outputs give very partial answers to the questions we want them to answer.

I dedicate figure 82 to twelve common cases of bad use of models. Each item in figure 82 describes one problematic behaviour related to the use of a model, as well as an example. Then, in figure 83, I present my understanding of why and when models are misused. This figure contains a list of ten possible reasons that may explain the behaviours in figure 82.

I don't claim to know the full psychological, organisational and cultural background to model misuse. The reasons described in figure 83 simply seem to me the most logical ones. The drawings from figure 79 are re-used in figure 83 to show the situations where the different issues arise. The drawings from figure 82 are also re-used, to show what types of model misuse might result from each issue.

Figure 82: how transport models are misused

1	**Referring to model outputs in a discussion about impacts which weren't modelled.** Example: a team develops a model to test traffic changes on a main road. They review the outputs, see a reduction in traffic, and present this as evidence of drivers shifting to public transport. But the model hierarchy has trip distribution just above the assignment, so the model doesn't allow drivers to simply shift to public transport. In the model, the reduction in traffic is probably due to drivers going by car to other destinations. 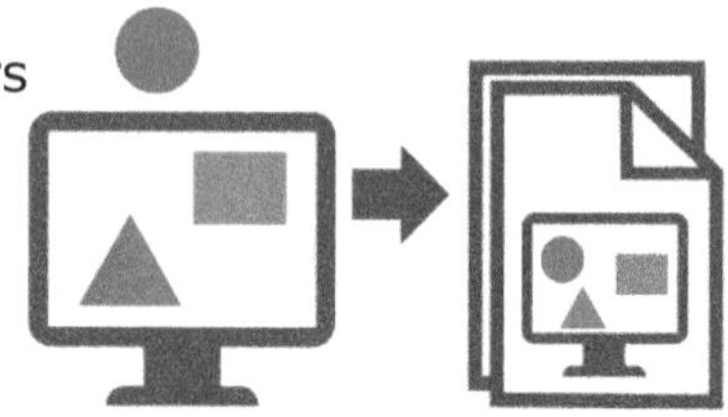
2	**Presenting the modellers' assumptions as if they were forecasts.** Example: a micro-simulation model is used to look at the traffic impacts of increased cycling flows. The modelling software used doesn't consider bikes separately, so the team codes each bike as a vehicle that is 25% the size of a car. The results are used to report the expected impact on road space, but in fact the outputs simply show what the team assumed. 
3	**Blurring the caveats provided by the modellers when presenting a summary of model outputs.** Example: to assess the impacts of a new cycling lane, it is assumed that 10% of the people travelling less than 2 miles will start cycling. The technical report explains that the presented impacts are based on this assumption. But a two-page executive summary simply says that the project will increase cycling demand. 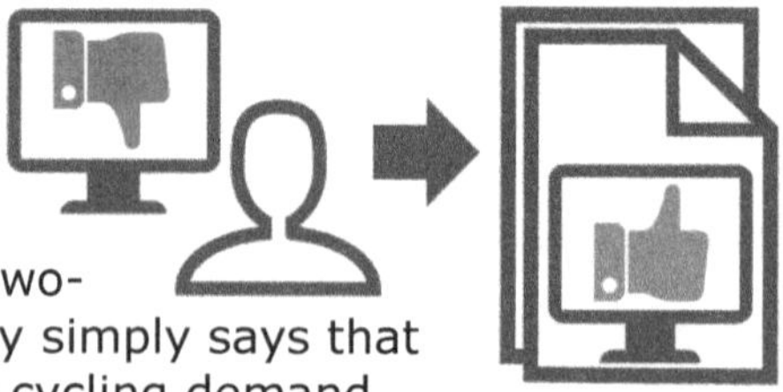

4	**Reporting model outputs at a level of detail which doesn't match the capabilities of the model.** Example: a road network assignment model for a dense urban area is built from screenline counts (see figure 37 for a reminder). Then it is used to examine the amount of traffic turning left in a junction just outside a main development site. 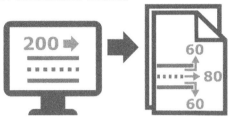
5	**Presenting precise outputs without explaining their low accuracy.** Example: a model estimates an increase in the demand for a local train line, from 100 to 103 passengers per hour. The increase is used to estimate economic impacts. 
6	**Developing many modelled scenarios, with no time to interpret the results properly**. Example: four locations are considered for a new bridge. The plan is to build either one or two bridges, so there are 10 combined network scenarios. There are 3 demand growth scenarios and 3 model years. 90 Model runs are planned (10 x 3 x 3) which must be completed in 6 months. Each run takes one day, and there's only one license for the modelling software. The team plans to spend two days per scenario – one for running the model and one for analysis, so 90 x 2 = 180 days in total. In reality, it's questionable whether the team can absorb the huge amount of expected model outputs. 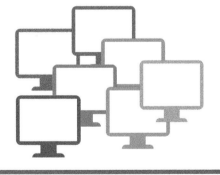

7	**Letting our audience believe that we know the future pace of social and economic trends**. Example: a transport strategy for a suburban county boasts advanced handling of land use dynamics through the use of a LUTI model (see figure 46 for a reminder). But the LUTI model doesn't consider a recent wave of asylum seekers joining a local community of former immigrants, and the range of possible outcomes from this wave. 
8	**Testing the sensitivity of the results to some inputs, and then using the model to test the impact of other inputs**. Example: a new model is developed, and the modellers show that the demand responds as expected to changes in public transport fares and travel times. The new model is used to examine the demand impacts of new policy scenarios, including reduced standing density on crowded trains and better bus punctuality. However, the ability of the model to estimate the response to such scenarios has not been tested.
9	**Discussing uncertainty around the scale of estimated impacts, ignoring possible impacts of a very different nature**. Example: a city-wide transport strategy is prepared. Due to the uncertainty around future levels of economic growth, hundreds of factors affecting potential growth are combined to create "high growth", "standard growth" and "low growth" scenarios. All spatial policies are assessed against these 3 scenarios, and this is presented as addressing the uncertainty issue.

10	**Trusting the capabilities of a "black box" model because it has been used before.** Example: all demand forecasts for a city are made using a model created in the 1990s. The model has been updated regularly since, but not all parts are always updated, and some parts were developed by people who have all left. The current model owners know that it performs an "incremental trip distribution", and sometimes they tell clients that the incremental distribution explains the results, although none of them understands the detail of the script that runs this process.
11	**Using a model to forecast trends that weren't observed in the base year.** Example: a model calibrated in 2013 is used to examine 2014, 2024 and 2034 scenarios. The study area is dominated by shopping trips. Current travel trends to shopping areas have limited representation in the 2013 data, because internet shopping has caused a significant change since then. 
12	**Comparing similar metrics calculated using different models.** Example: twenty local authorities submit their bids for a government fund supporting projects that reduce carbon emissions. Each bid contains forecasts of emission savings. Ten bids are shortlisted since their models show the highest reduction in emissions, although the methodologies used are different. Even in those bids that used similar methodologies, different assumptions were made regarding the composition of the vehicle fleet. 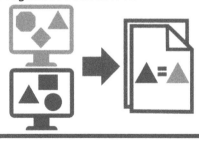

Figure 83: why and when models are misused

Reason 1: an incentive to present optimistic forecasts.

A company with appetite to make an investment might want the model to confirm an informal judgement already made. Local authorities bidding for funding have a better chance to win if their assessment of benefits is on the high side. An authority promoting a project they already approved will want to stress its positive sides.

Reason 2: pressure to satisfy someone.

A local or regional authority, when coordinating modelling work to agree funding priorities, will want the model to be perceived as a powerful broker, to establish their central role as a mediator. Consultants feel an obligation to present their clients' projects as having a strong case. Modellers in public sector bodies are under a similar pressure.

Reason 3: reducing external pressure.

Officers in national or local government are subject to less pressure from external interest groups if their funding  allocations can be presented as the result of a mathematical process, and not a matter of their own judgement.

Reason 4: scientific halo.

Many clients and colleagues are impressed by maps and figures with model outputs; they don't feel they have the skills to challenge them. When they have questions about the outputs, modellers will often answer using technical terminology which is hard to argue with. The halo effect of scientific-looking outputs can be equally impressive even if the modelling work wasn't good.

Reason 5: misunderstanding of what uncertainty means.

I often tell clients that the future will remain uncertain even if we work very hard on the model. A common reply is, "do you understand how important this is?". There's a common view that model outputs must give certainty because they are needed for an important decision. This view suggests that uncertainty is the result of bad modelling work. In reality, uncertainty is simply a feature of the world. It can be described, but it can't be eliminated.

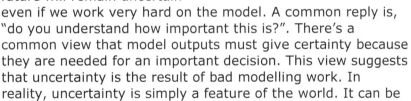

Reason 6: misunderstanding of the guidance.

In the UK, there's a common view that detailed modelling of many scenarios is a compulsory requirement, set by the formal guidance from government. The UK Department for Transport is actually clear that there's no such thing as "model compliance"; but the view that you must comply with a strict set of modelling rules is still very common. It has to be said that a more approachable guidance from government could help debunk this myth. Another common myth is that if you follow these formal sources of guidance, your model will tell you the future. Most sources of formal guidance don't clarify that this isn't the case.

Reason 7: an unrealistic vision of comparability.

Another view, which is common but flawed, is that applying consistent modelling practices will make the outputs of different models comparable to each other. This suggests you can look at projects assessed with different models and conclude which project is best. In reality, this view shows a poor understanding of the state of the modelling practice. Even if you represent exactly the same project using different models, any similarity between the outputs is a matter of luck. I dedicate section 11.3 later to this topic.

Reason 8: lacunas in the guidance.

There are cases where an investment gets support from senior politicians, and an instruction is given to approve it through a fast-track process. Formal procedures don't rocognise such cases even when they are perfectly legitimate. So there's a need to create an appearance of a standard approval process, which wasn't really followed.

Reason 9: the modeller isn't in the room.

Some of the issues covered here could be resolved by getting more intense feedback from the modellers themselves. To benefit from modelling expertise at the times when models are misused, modellers need to be involved continuously from the stage when modelling work has not yet been defined, until the stage when any interpretation of the results is complete. An even better solution would be if modelling, planning and management tasks were all done by professionals with varied skills, rather than by a full-time modeller. In practice, transport planning teams follow a tradition of recruiting full-time modellers, without much mixing of hands-on modelling with other tasks. Modellers are rarely involved in a project before it is decided to do modelling, since these project stages are seen as irrelevant to their job. The result is evident in my list of common model misuses.

Reason 10: diplomacy. Most issues I've listed here have been raised by many, over the years. The critique is usually expressed in a subtle diplomatic tone, which has so far not made a wide impact.

10.4 The expectations from transport models

Some readers might see this as a gloomy chapter, or think that I'm trying to undermine people's trust in transport models. But what I actually hope to do is refine your expectations. Throughout this book I try to suggest how you can make the most of what models have to offer; the main threat to doing this successfully is starting with unrealistic expectations.

Being knowledgeable about models can occasionally put you in dilemmas or conflicts. For example, when a model is expected to shed light on things that can't be modelled, or when clients require that the model confirms a pre-determined conclusion, it can be difficult to decide what's the most professional thing to do. Most of the time, being knowledgeable about models simply means that you can make wise professional decisions. In all these cases, if you're the only one in your work environment who can assess what a model can realistically achieve, it's important that you communicate this to colleagues.

I'm sure you'd like to know what can be done when so many pressures exist while the model remains limited. I'll return to this in chapter 12, with a list of practical recommendations. But before we get there, I'm not done yet explaining the risks of overstating model capabilities. In this chapter I spoke about the organisational perspective, and in the next chapter I'll summarise the things that models can and can't do.

Chapter 11
So is it accurate?

11.1 The tricky business of model accuracy

As a modelling advisor, I've often been asked about model outputs, "is it accurate?". My answer has usually been, "no, it's very inaccurate". Clients and colleagues hear this and say, "okay, but surely it's in the right ballpark?". If there's time for a discussion, I try to explain which of the outputs I find most helpful, and how they can be best used. But sometimes this is asked in a meeting with lots of senior people, and I'm expected to talk for no longer than 11.6 seconds. I clearly can't guarantee that model outputs are in the right ballpark.

Some colleagues are surprised that we do so much modelling work without knowing what it's worth. There are clients who don't believe me that the strength of the forecasts is so questionable; they prefer to speak to advisors that say "yes, it's fairly accurate".

How do you know whether or not model outputs are accurate? Some people see the results of the calibration and validation stages as evidence for how accurate the model is (see chapter 4 for a reminder). It's true that calibration and validation are stages that most models go through, and it's true that we produce in these stages detailed statistics about the model's goodness of fit. But these statistics are not an indicator of the general accuracy of the model.

We say that things are accurate if they are very close to the truth. But in the transport world, we don't know the truth. We calibrate and validate models based on limited data, which only gives us a random snapshot of things which are actually complex, dynamic and unknown. We can say that the model accurately replicates what's in the available data, but this would mean we're over-fitting the model to the data, which is a bad thing to do. See figure 55 for a reminder of over-fitting.

Since the real traffic volumes or travel times are unknown, and we cannot refer to their true values, the term "accuracy" in transport modelling remains undefined. It doesn't have any helpful meaning and I'd recommend that you don't use it.

Another reason why the calibration and validation results aren't indicators of accuracy is that we apply our models in new situations, where we analyse new conditions, some of which are in the future. The future doesn't exist in the calibration and validation data, so model outputs cannot be compared to it to determine their accuracy. Furthermore, even the past often doesn't exist in the calibration process, since we tend to use data from a fixed point in time, so the whole time dimension may not exist in the calibration process.

Since the work of building a model doesn't tell us whether it will be a good forecasting tool, an alternative is to examine how well models in the past performed in predicting things that happened afterwards. **Model evaluation** is what we do when we compare forecasts from an old model to what actually happened when the forecast year arrived. Evaluation can be powerful in showing the strengths and weaknesses of different models. But there are some real challenges in performing model evaluation:

- Authorities don't have a strong incentive to collect the data needed for evaluation. The project that the model was built for has been either approved or declined years ago. Funding is always limited, so authorities prefer to use existing budgets for new models and new projects.
- Some evaluation work is done and not published. Private sector companies who operate toll roads or run metro systems normally have good data about their own performance, but they don't publish it unless their concession obliges them to.
- There's a small number of published studies with model evaluation results. Most of them focus on relatively recent forecasts, which still attract political interest and haven't been forgotten. So there's more evaluation of short-term forecasts, and much less published evaluation of forecasts that go 10, 20 or more years into the future.

The few model evaluation studies that get published can be split into two groups. One group contains evaluation studies published by consultants and authorities who check their own models, and the other group contains studies where someone reviews the modelling work done by others.

Consultants and authorities who assess their own models always reach positive conclusions about their capabilities. Such studies are published mainly for marketing and positioning purposes, so they are less reliable; this is consistent with reason 1 and reason 2 which I described in figure 83. But comparative evaluation studies, where an auditor or a researcher looks at the models developed by others, show very different results. They show a systematic and significant over-estimation of positive impacts.

In short, there isn't much evidence on how models perform as prediction tools, and when there is such evidence, it shows that the models are too optimistic. Therefore, to make the best use of transport models, you have to acknowledge that they're not reliable tools for producing forecasts. Section 11.2 below contains a review of my reasons why you shouldn't see model outputs as forecasts. You can see this list as a summary of the points I made in part I of this book about model limitations.

Some of my friends in the transport modelling community would say, "true, models don't tell the future, but they are a good platform for a consistent options assessment". Unfortunately, I see this more as wishful thinking than as the truth. The idea that models can systematically identify the differences between transport improvements, providing some kind of sterile baseline, has no clear foundations. I dedicate section 11.3 to the question of models as comparison tools.

I hope you can bear with me while I make all these critical points. I'm covering them in this chapter so that in chapter 12 I can talk more positively about what you could do instead.

11.2 Why transport models aren't prediction tools

Before we start, allow me to share with you an ironic summary of a strongly related topic. This summary was presented by Professor Ron Smith from Birkbeck College, in a public lecture entitled "why economists cannot forecast" in 2013. The lecture was about any forecasting work done by economists, but it's very relevant to transport modelling.

Listed below are some actions that Professor Smith recommends to take if you failed to produce good forecasts, and some tips that can prevent this from happening in the first place:

- Give the client a number or a date, but never both.
- Have different forecasts in the text and the tables.
- Give different forecasts to different clients. Some of them will think you're good.
- Use vague definitions, and later explain them in a way that makes your forecasts look right.
- Forecast a large number of variables, and then focus on those you got right.
- Explain the work is no longer relevant: the forecaster was sacked and the model was changed.
- Blame your errors on stupid government policy, unless you work for the government.
- Blame the weather.
- Keep your forecasts close to the herd, so you can say everybody else made the same mistake.
- Say it was a self-defeating forecast: government responded to your warnings and this is what prevented a disaster from happening.

And now more seriously. There are different ways to describe what transport models can reliably do, but "forecasting what will happen in future situations" is not one of them. In the first part of the book I mentioned some of my reasons for saying this, and in this section I'll summarise these reasons.

In figure 84, I've listed my top 40 differences between the way models describe the transport system and the way this system really is. The selection of these top 40 is mine, but the list is made of items that are widely known. Each item in figure 84 is a factor or phenomenon which you cannot dismiss if you wish to predict future transport outcomes; but we do dismiss them.

Transport models either seriously simplify these factors or just ignore them. I don't know precisely how critical each of these factors is to our ability to estimate future travel demand, travel times and so on, because this hasn't been thoroughly checked. But I do know that each one of these factors further clarifies how limited our modelled representation of the real world is. The degree of simplification is so high, that it's illogical to see the modelled response as evidence for what will happen. You can use this list when trying to set the expectations of colleagues from a model at a sufficiently modest level.

To avoid any doubt, I'd like to stress again that I'm definitely not suggesting that models should improve to address these issues. I'm suggesting the opposite: no matter how large your development effort, your model will still provide a very partial picture of the real transport system, so you should better make a more modest effort. You'll save time, money and frustration, because much of the thinking that your project needs will have to be done outside the model anyway.

Figure 84: why models aren't prediction tools

Reason 1: model hierarchy. The way people travel in the model is based on the assumed model hierarchy. Most models assume that all travellers follow the same hierarchy. This assumption makes the modelling work less demanding, but it isn't realistic. The most common model hierarchy, with mode split above distribution, doesn't allow people to change their mode choice as a direct result of network changes. For more on model hierarchy, go to chapter 3.

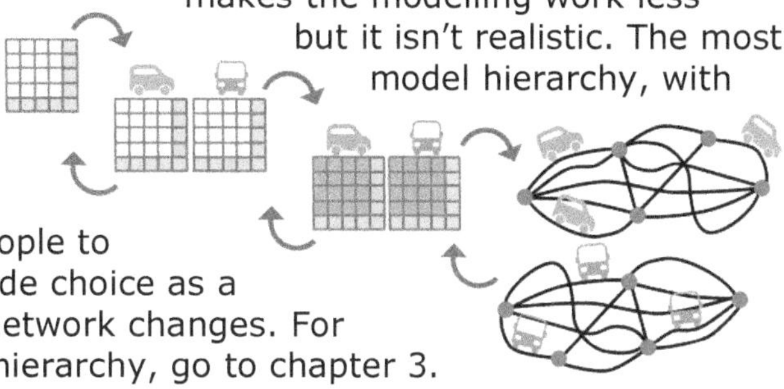

Reason 2: total demand. When developing matrices, the way we adjust the total demand involves drastic changes like doubling or halving the number of trips in an area. We do this due to conflicts between trip rates, traffic counts and other data sources. The decision on the total demand in each area is based on weak evidence. There's no way we can avoid double-counting some trips and ignoring others.

Reason 3: land use changes. Most modelling work takes the places where people live, work and shop as an external input, which isn't affected by their travel experience. Projects that use land use and transport interaction (LUTI) models handle this in a more realistic way, but LUTI models only partially deal with the complexity of land use changes. Only rarely we have a model that is sensitive to all the relevant factors.

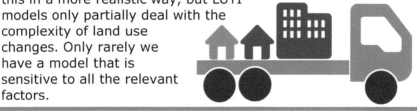

Reason 4: demographic changes. Travel and traffic patterns are influenced by demographics which are hard to predict. This book is written in England at a time when Britain's expected exit from the European Union, and a flow of refugees from Africa and the Middle East, feature in the news daily. These are two examples for issues that will clearly have demographic impacts, and will undoubtedly have some transport impacts too. But the models we develop have no means of taking these into consideration.

Reason 5: network changes. We test the impact of projects in future scenarios. Even if our project is delivered exactly as planned, other changes to the network happen in the background. When we work on a public transport project, for example, outcomes depend on the quality of service on many routes that either feed our project or compete with it. The service on these routes might change significantly in unexpected ways before our forecast year.

Reason 6: timing of new infrastructure. When we create a model for a future year, we take into account planned infrastructure that has already been approved and should be in place before the year we model. But the time when projects are implemented or opened in practice is often different from the original plans, and this could mean that the actual network in the forecast year is different from the one we assume.

2020   2021   2022

Reason 7: responsiveness to change. We have limited evidence on how people respond to changes in the transport system. If the behavioural responses are based on Stated Preference data, they might feature systematic bias towards or against specific behaviours (see figures 51, 52). If the responses are based on Revealed Preference data, the model often contains large alternative-specific constants that might be over-fitting the model to the data (see figures 53, 54, 55).

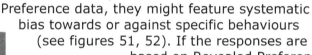
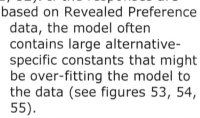

Reason 8: parking. I showed in section 9.8 and figure 73 how limited most models are in representing parking. We don't know where people park, how much it costs, how traffic is affected by cars searching for parking, how travel habits are affected by restrictions on the duration of parking, how this affects people's chance of using a car in the first place, and how all these things together influence people's choice of where to work and where to live.

Reason 9: network detail. A high level of detail in the modelled network makes it more realistic. But it also makes the model sensitive to data that we don't have, slower to run and harder to check. If model zones are too large then we can't provide clients with the information they want. But if the zones are too small then the outputs aren't statistically reliable.

Reason 10: coding errors. Modelled networks contain a huge amount of information, some of which is produced under time pressure. It's unfeasible to check the entire network coding regularly. I've never seen a modelling project without errors being detected very late; the last-minute rush to make correction sometimes undermines the value of months of earlier work. Errors are also found after the final results have already been reported. It's unlikely that all critical errors are found, and quite likely that in some projects, errors influenced investment decisions.

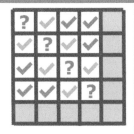

Reason 11: short trips. Trips made inside one zone may be critical for our understanding of urban traffic. But the number of these internal trips, their generalised costs, and the choices made by the travellers who make such trips – these are all estimated in a very simplified way.

Reason 12: trips by foot. Some models don't allow walking as a mode of transport, so they'll wrongly allocate walking trips to other modes. They also miss trips that can shift between walking and other modes. Other models do allow travellers to shift to or from walking; but due to limited data, they under-represent some trips and over-represent others. There currently isn't a widely-accepted methodology to link the different types of pedestrians on the street to the different types of trips in a transport model.

Reason 13: trips by bike. Modelling travel by bike is easier than modelling walking trips (see section 5.8), and there already are many transport models where cycling is represented. Still, in many cities, the demand for cycling goes through trends which aren't easy to explain in analytical terms. Modelling cycling is statistically sensitive to these trends because cycling forms a small proportion of overall demand, and is therefore subject to a high error.

Reason 14: combined trips. *I* explained in figure 56 how difficult it is to model trips where a car driver drops a passenger at a station, "park and ride" trips, "bike and ride", and other trips combining several modes. The way we model these trips is highly simplified, and this reduces our ability to assess the demand impacts of policies, projects or trends.

Reason 15: crowding. Many models have limited capability to represent the impacts of crowding on buses, trams and trains. The most common simplification is in not restricting how many passengers can board a crowded vehicle, and therefore not accounting for the additional waiting time to those that have no room left.

245

Reason 16: demand fluctuation. Changes in demand between days are a major issue in a busy transport system. But much of our data is only collected on specific days, so the modelled demand is "frozen" and doesn't fluctuate. Most models aren't built to analyse the impacts of demand variation. Even in traffic micro-simulation, where we can allow for such fluctuation, we rarely adjust the demand variation in the model are adjusted to match the level of demand variation in reality.

Reason 17: trip purposes. People's route and mode choices on a business trip are different from their choices on a personal trip. People's willingness to pay for tickets or tolls on a trip they make regularly is different compared to a one-off journey. Our assumption of how many trips are made for each purpose is based on limited evidence. Getting the split by purpose wrong could change model outputs substantially, even if everything else is right.

Reason 18: local behaviour. We sometimes use our model as if it was fully calibrated to the conditions and the typical behaviours of our study area. But almost every model relies on many parameters taken from other places or from outdated models. Whether or not these parameters can correctly describe current travel demand in our study area usually remains unknown.

246

Reason 19: microscopic factors. Some behaviours and choices have very clear reasons, which in principle we could include in the model, but they're too local and specific to be foreseen. For example, an improved road link may have low demand due to poor signage; a new station may have low demand due to poor lighting. Models for future scenarios rarely assume unclear signage or bad lighting.

Reason 20: variation in preferences. We use demand segmentation to represent different behaviours in the model (see section 2.7). To capture the behaviour of people in each segment (e.g. to describe driving styles), we use parameter values which are averaged across many different people. In reality there's a wide range of preferences and behaviours, including some extreme ones, also within each segment. The averaged parameters won't reveal the true impact of the real mix of behaviours.

Reason 21: complex willingness to pay. Most models assume that the impact of a price increase of $1 can be reversed by a price reduction of the same size. They also assume that a price increase from $1 to $2 will have the same impact as an increase from $6 to $7. There is a lot of evidence showing that people don't behave like this. See more on this topic in figures 17, 68 and 74.

Reason 22: major disasters. Transport models can't account for the probability and the consequences of large-scale traffic accidents, natural disasters affecting transport infrastructure, and terrorist attacks. Such disasters can have a significant and potentially long-term impact on travel behaviour, which we cannot foresee.

Reason 23: evolution of preferences. We observe how people behave now, and we then apply what we've learnt to new situations, in order to estimate future demand. But people's behaviour changes over time, sometimes because of external factors, and sometimes because of the same project we're exploring. There's a conflict between the idea of calibration-validation-application and the fact that people's preferences evolve.

2005 2015 2025

Reason 24: unexplained behaviour. People's preferences sometimes don't follow a logic that models can be trained to follow. People sometimes choose a route or a destination that don't have any visible advantage. Or they sometimes respond very differently to transport improvements which look the same from the perspective of planners and modellers. Experts in the financial sector remind us that the global financial crisis wouldn't have happened if everyone behaved logically.

Reason 25: imperfect knowledge. Most models assume that we make our travel and lifestyle choices by considering all available options. In reality, most people consider a small number of options – for example, those they've heard about first. People may be unaware of, or just ignore, the option which the model finds best.

Reason 26: response time. Models know that after we launch new transport infrastructure, the change in behaviour takes time. But does it take a month or a decade? The duration of the change, and the behavioural patterns as people gradually get used to the new infrastructure, are not much more than a guess.

Reason 27: travel trends. Travel choices are influenced by subtle cultural trends that have nothing to do with what's in the model. These cultural trends will have an impact, for example, on whether we think that cycling is cool, or whether we would even consider taking a taxi. We have no ability to say years in advance how such trends will develop.

Reason 28: local consumption factors. Some outcomes could be perfectly explained if only the model knew more about the consumption habits in the relevant area. For example, a tram stop can see the demand rising 1000% above the forecast if a popular shop relocates just next to it. Forecasting the relocation of this shop as part of the transport modelling process would be unrealistic.

Reason 29: wider consumption trends. In the wider retail and commercial sectors, there are continuous changes that have significant impacts on the transport system. We hardly have any ability to reflect these changes in the modelling of future scenarios. Increased demand for specific goods may result in more freight traffic to/from the places where these goods are manufactured or their distribution centres. This freight traffic may also have significant impacts on the general traffic.

Reason 30: shopping behaviour. Most past forecasts failed to predict the exact scale of internet shopping and the related rise in deliveries by van. It is likely that modelling work we do now will continue to fail in calculating the future relationship between shopping and transport, because consumers respond to new ideas introduced by technology and retail leaders, and we can't tell the outcome of this interaction before it happens.

Reason 31: wider economic factors. Even broader than these are any other changes in economic activity in the region, state or country where our project is. Growth or recession can occur in any sector, and every sector has its own relationship with freight movements, employee travel and other transport-related activities.

Reason 32: car ownership trends. There are places where every adult has a car unless they are very poor; modelling car ownership and its impacts is easy in these places. But there are places where car ownership goes through trends which are hard to predict. In England, for example, there are places which are now wealthier than they used to be, but their residents own fewer cars than before. Despite a lot of research on this topic, we sometimes struggle to predict the correct car ownership trends.

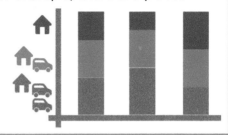

Reason 33: car sharing trends. The transport system is more influenced by how much we use our cars than by how many cars we have. This, too, is influenced by wider trends which aren't represented in the model. For example, at the time of writing this book, new forms of car sharing have only recently been introduced; nobody knows how successful they will be in the long term. When there's uncertainty about the share of one mode, it means that there's uncertainty also about the shares of other modes, since the different modes compete for the same total demand.

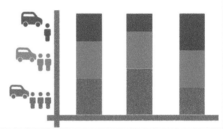

Reason 34: work legislation. Future travel will be influenced by changes in statutory labour regulations, such as the retirement age, the number of working hours per week, the number of working days per week, or even the minimum wage. We don't know whether, when and how these will change.

Reason 35: lifestyle trends. Cultural trends which are unlikely to be captured correctly by a transport model include where different kinds of families choose to live, what types of new houses are built, what kinds of schools people send their kids to, how many people at different ages decide to go to college or university, and what new activities people start doing in their evenings and weekends. All these trends influence the amount and nature of trip-making.

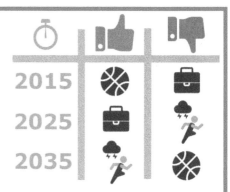

Reason 36: financial factors. Travel demand is sensitive to the cost of travel. This cost is influenced by a wide range of financial factors that can behave unpredictably. The price of one gallon of petrol, or of a single train ticket, are the combined outcome of dozens of different global factors, even if our model is built for one city.

Reason 37: remote working trends. There were times when we assumed that technology will soon make a large proportion of the workforce do their work from home. It is now accepted that this trend hasn't been so wide. It remains a mystery whether future technology improvements will lead to a larger increase in home working. Different views exist, for example that we'll see more use of general-purpose office spaces not far from home, to avoid long commute. But the likelihood and the impact of any such scenario are just a guess.

Reason 38: taxation. New taxes are sometimes introduced, and existing ones are sometimes modified or abolished. The political discussion that leads to such changes cannot be predicted, although the impact on travel can be significant. The transport-related impact can be direct, if the tax that changes applies to cars, fuel or housing. But there can also be secondary impacts on travel behaviour, for example if the taxation is on specific leisure activities.

Reason 39: vehicle technology. Many different improvements to vehicle technology can affect how people travel. For example, there can be a reduction in costs or an increase in speeds of either private or public transport vehicles. The biggest unknown, without doubt, is how quickly we'll see wide use of self-driving vehicles. Everyone agrees that autonomous cars have the potential to revolutionise travel, because they will use road space more efficiently, blur the differences between the existing modes, have different parking requirements, give car access also to those who don't drive, and allow users to make a more efficient use of their time while in transit. But the expected market penetration of such vehicles, the magnitude of the impact and the timing - these are a matter of wide speculation.

Reason 40: information technology. Technological improvements I've not mentioned yet include, for example, more intense use of real-time information to plan our journeys, so that congestion or crowding are avoided and the travel experience is optimised. Plenty of other initiatives are in different stages of development or testing, with very limited ability for us to reflect their impact in current modelling work.

11.3 Why transport models aren't comparison tools

It is understandable that many of us would like to see models as a source of objective, dispassionate figures about the impacts of transport projects. We would want to compare these figures between different options of one project, or between different projects, without worrying about how they were produced. Unfortunately, if you know enough about modelling techniques and the modelling process, you have to accept that there's no basis for seeing them as objective.

Model outputs are subjective and open for debate. They depend on the context in which they were created, and they can change as a result of conversation and persuasion. Outputs from your modelling work can't be straightforwardly compared to the outputs from somebody else's work because each modeller makes different judgements in their work.

Have a quick look again at figures 9, 15, 29, 32, 34, 38, 41, 43, 50, 53, 67, 68, 69, 70, 71 and 74. These figures are all about different approaches we need to choose from, when we model a project or a policy. All the alternative approaches shown in these figures are used regularly, and they're all correct. Using different methods will give you different outputs.

To illustrate the subjective nature of modelling in real projects, I've described eight different problems in figure 85. Each of them is a dilemma which came up during model development, and the figure shows different solutions suggested by experts. Some of the solutions in figure 85 are quite advanced, but it's not essential for you to go deep into the detail of each solution. My main point is that all the solutions are good, although not all of them will give results that will make the client happy. No source of guidance can tell you what's right and what's wrong in each case.

It's perfectly natural for different models to give different answers to the same question. The insight you need about your project shouldn't be based on simply accepting the model outputs as the answers. You get the most valuable insight by discussing the model outputs in the light of the limitations of the model and the modelling decisions that were made. The model, on its own, doesn't represent the scenario you're testing; how representative it is would be a question for you to discuss with colleagues.

Since the choice of a modelling approach can influence the model output, modellers vary the approach in order to get outputs that reflect their expectations. This might sound like cheating, but it isn't. There are so many technical decisions to make without knowing what is right, that modellers must make decisions so that they lead to logical outputs. This is a much better practice than accepting outputs that don't seem logical, given that illogical results could indicate hidden errors in the model.

The views and interests of clients influence what outputs the modeller finds logical. When model outputs don't match colleagues' expectations, modellers continue searching for a better approach until the team is happier. So when you see model outputs produced by a project team, they are likely to show an outcome that the project team wanted to see.

You already know that the ability of models to represent your actual scenario is limited. And you already know that this limited ability is an issue you need to think carefully about when looking at the outputs. Even if your scenario is modelled by two experts who use two copies of the same model, they'll probably get different answers.

Since the model gives limited evidence even when looking at a single scenario, it gives you even less when you compare those limited sources of evidence between different scenarios. Some people assume that model limitations cancel each other out in the comparison. In reality, when comparing scenarios or projects, the outputs of each one may be influenced by different limitations of the model, so we are piling up limitations one on top of the other. This makes the model more limited and less informative than for each scenario or project on its own.

The bottom line is that a comparison of model outputs between scenarios or projects has limited ability to tell you the differences between them.

Example 1: modelling a toll road. A new toll road is represented in a model in the common way of adding a standard, toll-free link, but making it longer. The added length is determined by converting the payment into additional travel time, using a standard value of time (see sections 2.8 and 9.9 for a reminder). But the result is that the toll in the model also applies to drivers that get a discount.

Martin

> Store the trips that get a discount in a separate matrix. Code a parallel road without the additional time. Allow only the demand from the new matrix to use this new road.

Polina

> Calculate the average toll that any driver pays, as a weighted average between the full toll and discount toll. Use this average toll to code the length of the toll road in the model.

Olga

> Keep the model as it is. Explain in the modelling report that discount drivers are modelled in a simplified way.

Example 2: project on a zone boundary. A development site is located on the boundary between two zones in the model. Each zone is connected to different streets and stations (see figure 8 for a reminder). So the estimated travel times to the site, which are important for the planning process, depend on which zone you link it to.

Laura

> Change the model coding so that the site is only connected to the zone with the lower travel times.

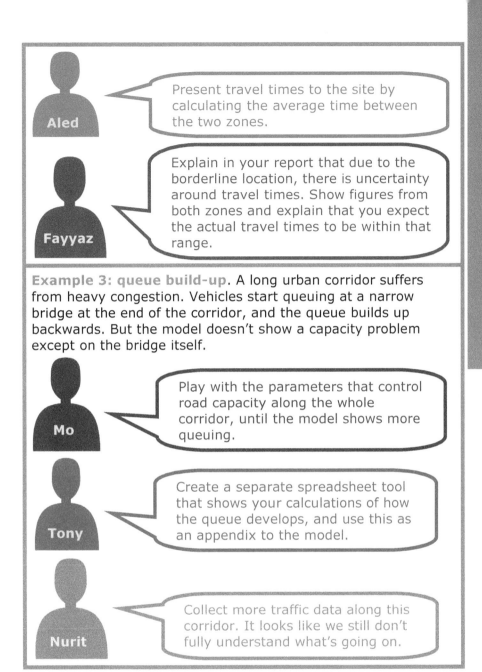

Aled: Present travel times to the site by calculating the average time between the two zones.

Fayyaz: Explain in your report that due to the borderline location, there is uncertainty around travel times. Show figures from both zones and explain that you expect the actual travel times to be within that range.

Example 3: queue build-up. A long urban corridor suffers from heavy congestion. Vehicles start queuing at a narrow bridge at the end of the corridor, and the queue builds up backwards. But the model doesn't show a capacity problem except on the bridge itself.

Mo: Play with the parameters that control road capacity along the whole corridor, until the model shows more queuing.

Tony: Create a separate spreadsheet tool that shows your calculations of how the queue develops, and use this as an appendix to the model.

Nurit: Collect more traffic data along this corridor. It looks like we still don't fully understand what's going on.

Example 4: cyclists in a junction. A high volume of cyclists in a junction causes delay to car users. But the model doesn't include cycling traffic, so the delay is not modelled.

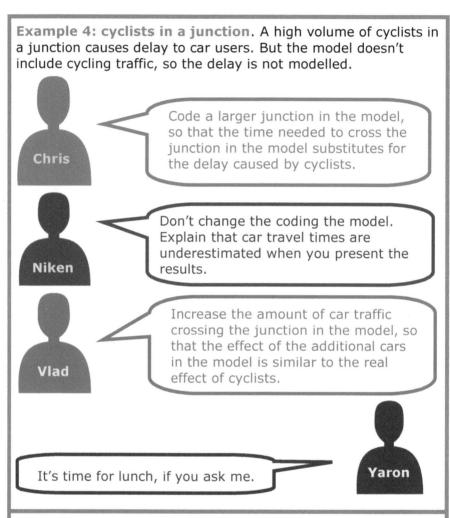

Chris: Code a larger junction in the model, so that the time needed to cross the junction in the model substitutes for the delay caused by cyclists.

Niken: Don't change the coding the model. Explain that car travel times are underestimated when you present the results.

Vlad: Increase the amount of car traffic crossing the junction in the model, so that the effect of the additional cars in the model is similar to the real effect of cyclists.

Yaron: It's time for lunch, if you ask me.

Example 5: segmentation by income. A model is developed to test options for improving a public transport network. Trips by travellers with high income and low income were merged into a single demand matrix. This was done because when stored separately, some zones had no demand data, so it was much harder to use procedures for adjusting the total demand using passenger counts (see figure 60). But with the income levels merged, the model shows travellers from deprived areas choosing the most expensive railway tickets.

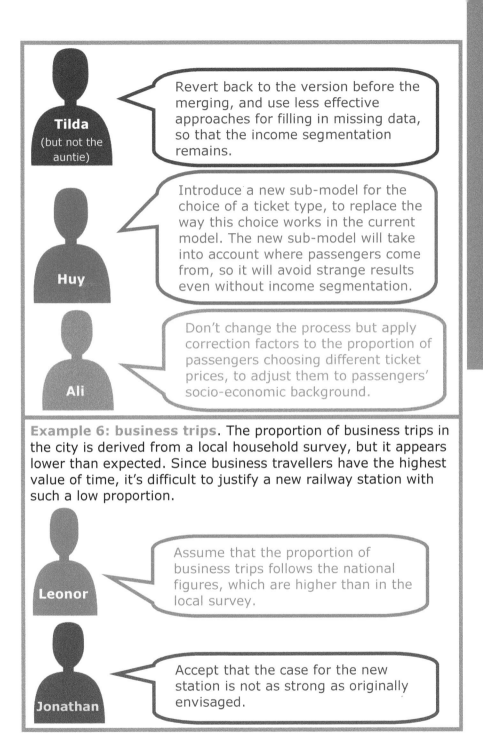

Tilda (but not the auntie): Revert back to the version before the merging, and use less effective approaches for filling in missing data, so that the income segmentation remains.

Huy: Introduce a new sub-model for the choice of a ticket type, to replace the way this choice works in the current model. The new sub-model will take into account where passengers come from, so it will avoid strange results even without income segmentation.

Ali: Don't change the process but apply correction factors to the proportion of passengers choosing different ticket prices, to adjust them to passengers' socio-economic background.

Example 6: business trips. The proportion of business trips in the city is derived from a local household survey, but it appears lower than expected. Since business travellers have the highest value of time, it's difficult to justify a new railway station with such a low proportion.

Leonor: Assume that the proportion of business trips follows the national figures, which are higher than in the local survey.

Jonathan: Accept that the case for the new station is not as strong as originally envisaged.

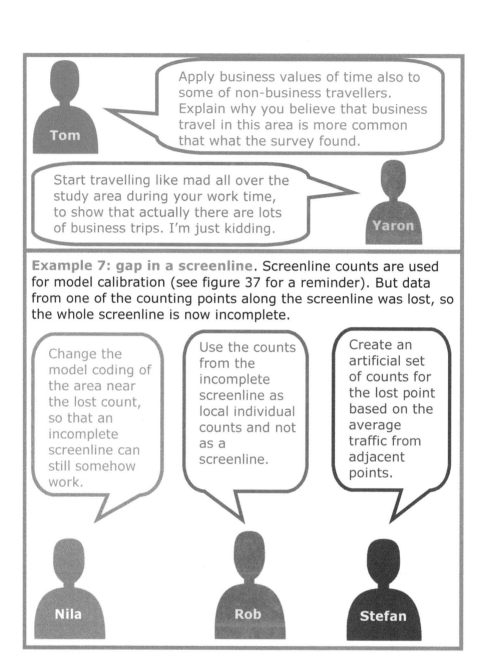

Tom: Apply business values of time also to some of non-business travellers. Explain why you believe that business travel in this area is more common that what the survey found.

Yaron: Start travelling like mad all over the study area during your work time, to show that actually there are lots of business trips. I'm just kidding.

Example 7: gap in a screenline. Screenline counts are used for model calibration (see figure 37 for a reminder). But data from one of the counting points along the screenline was lost, so the whole screenline is now incomplete.

Nila: Change the model coding of the area near the lost count, so that an incomplete screenline can still somehow work.

Rob: Use the counts from the incomplete screenline as local individual counts and not as a screenline.

Stefan: Create an artificial set of counts for the lost point based on the average traffic from adjacent points.

Example 8: mode split parameters. When estimating the parameters of a mode split model from Stated Preference data (see figure 51, 52 and 53 for a reminder), the parameter for "bus punctuality" comes out as statistically insignificant. But we must have a bus punctuality parameter in the model, because the model is built especially for a project that focuses on improving bus punctuality.

Alison

Nigel

Jide

Alison	Nigel	Jide
Undertake a literature review, to learn what parameters were attached to bus punctuality in other studies and whether others who worked on similar topics faced results similar to yours.	Re-define your model, so that bus punctuality is grouped together with other similar service features that did appear significant. Estimate a new single parameter for this group of features.	Analyse outside the model how punctuality can indirectly affect features that did come out significant. Use this analysis to demonstrate the impact of punctuality based on these features.

Chapter 12

Good modelling practice

12.1 Successful modelling

To be successful in the modelling industry, you need to work out regularly, eat healthy food, sleep well, look after your skin, and have a good agent. Sorry, I just had to make this joke somewhere in this book. In the transport modelling industry all these can help, too, but they are not sufficient.

In chapter 11 I explained that transport models can't tell you what will happen in the future. They also aren't safe tools for comparing between investment scenarios, to see which ones perform best. Earlier, in chapter 10, I described how different organisations and professionals develop expectations that models can't meet. Too often this results in pressures and perverse incentives to misuse the model, for example by saying that it provides evidence that it actually doesn't.

This book won't prevent model misuse from happening, but I'd like to at least present a clear alternative. The alternative is summarised in this chapter as a list of 10 recommendations. The idea of following these 10 recommendations is not entirely mine and not entirely new. Bits of this approach are used already by experts that I've learnt much from. But I'm not aware of any existing publication where these recommendations are summarised, so I hope that this chapter can fill in this gap.

The approach that consists of my 10 recommendations isn't a complete solution to all the problems I described in chapters 10 and 11. I don't know if there's a way to fix all these problems; the efforts some people make to continuously raise the expectations from transport models clearly don't help, since I believe these expectations are too high already. Still, if you follow the principles presented in this chapter, I'm sure this will result in a more sensible use of models.

262

The recommendations in this chapter aren't targeted at people with a specific role. You can bring up ideas from this chapter whether you are the person who does the modelling, their client, a manager, a colleague or an advisor. You can also do so if you're an external stakeholder who objects to the project they work on.

12.2 Looking for evidence

This book is dedicated to transport modelling, but models are clearly not the only source of evidence you should use to support your projects and decisions. I tend to split the evidence we can use in two different ways: by the type of evidence and by the purpose of providing it.

I use the following six categories for the type of evidence:

Data: facts and stats about the place we're looking at.

Precedents: facts and stats about places where similar infrastructure or policies have already been introduced.

Opinions: what people think about our project.

Context: things that have already happened regarding our project.

Forecasts: what models say about our project.

Theory: what theory says about projects like ours.

The importance of each type of evidence varies between projects, depending on the sources of information you have available. But I'd suggest the order of the list above as an initial indication of importance: direct sources of data can give you the strongest evidence, and the strength goes down from there.

You can see that as a first guess, without knowing the specific details of your project, I'd put model outputs towards the bottom of the list in terms of the strength of evidence they provide. However, my main point here is that ideally you should use all types of evidence.

I use the following three categories for the **purpose of providing the evidence**:

Need: evidence about the problem that our project targets.

Impact: evidence about what could happen in different scenarios, with or without our project.

Practicality: evidence about whether it's possible to deliver our project.

Each of these 6 types of evidence can be used for each of these 3 purposes. This gives us 18 ways of using evidence in our work. Depending on how much time you have and how important the project is, you should consider which of these 18 combinations you should work on. Even the smallest project should have something to say in at least several of these categories. Major projects, which try to address significant problems and are likely to have wide impacts, should ideally show evidence in all 18 categories.

Let's have a look at an example. I'll use an imaginary project in a place called Bridgetown. Three project options are being considered: a road bridge, a railway bridge, or no bridge at all. Figure 86 shows, under each one of the 18 categories of evidence, just one sentence to illustrate what kind of arguments this evidence can help us make.

Figure 86: mixing sources of evidence

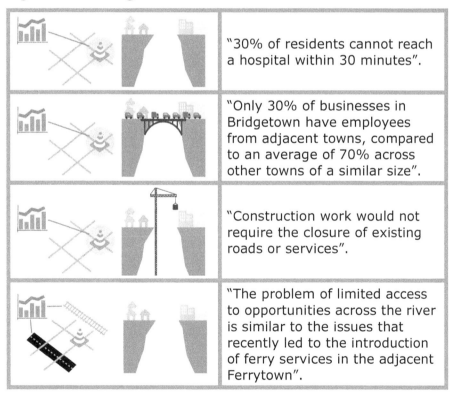

	"30% of residents cannot reach a hospital within 30 minutes".
	"Only 30% of businesses in Bridgetown have employees from adjacent towns, compared to an average of 70% across other towns of a similar size".
	"Construction work would not require the closure of existing roads or services".
	"The problem of limited access to opportunities across the river is similar to the issues that recently led to the introduction of ferry services in the adjacent Ferrytown".

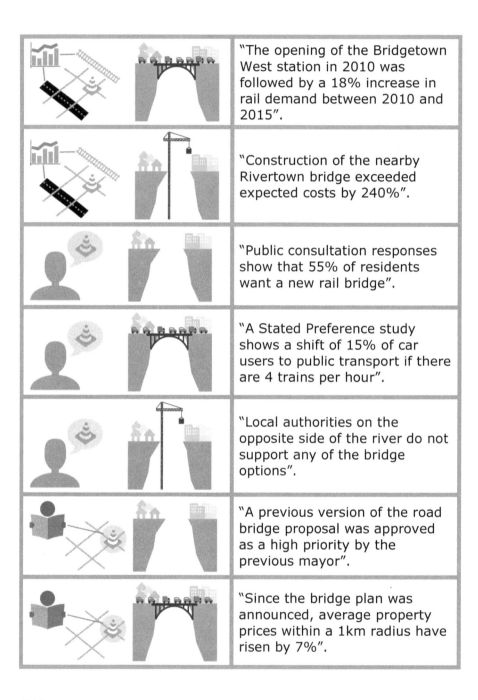

	"The opening of the Bridgetown West station in 2010 was followed by a 18% increase in rail demand between 2010 and 2015".
	"Construction of the nearby Rivertown bridge exceeded expected costs by 240%".
	"Public consultation responses show that 55% of residents want a new rail bridge".
	"A Stated Preference study shows a shift of 15% of car users to public transport if there are 4 trains per hour".
	"Local authorities on the opposite side of the river do not support any of the bridge options".
	"A previous version of the road bridge proposal was approved as a high priority by the previous mayor".
	"Since the bridge plan was announced, average property prices within a 1km radius have risen by 7%".

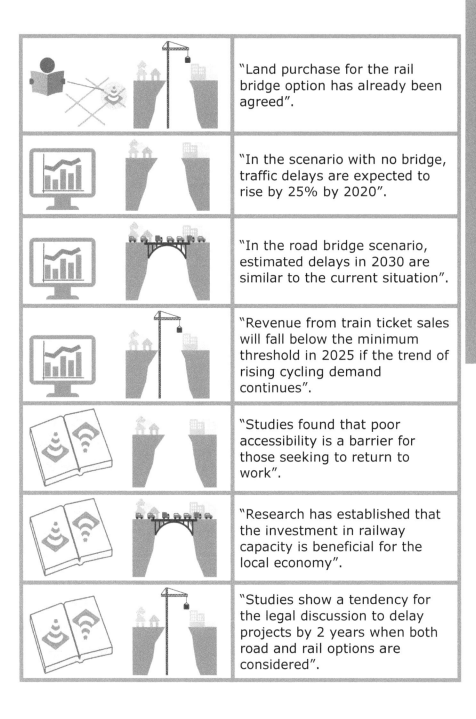

	"Land purchase for the rail bridge option has already been agreed".
	"In the scenario with no bridge, traffic delays are expected to rise by 25% by 2020".
	"In the road bridge scenario, estimated delays in 2030 are similar to the current situation".
	"Revenue from train ticket sales will fall below the minimum threshold in 2025 if the trend of rising cycling demand continues".
	"Studies found that poor accessibility is a barrier for those seeking to return to work".
	"Research has established that the investment in railway capacity is beneficial for the local economy".
	"Studies show a tendency for the legal discussion to delay projects by 2 years when both road and rail options are considered".

267

So in many cases, models shouldn't be your primary sources of evidence. The insight they provide is valid but relatively weak, for the reasons I summarised in chapters 10 and 11. The use of mixed sources of information means that you shouldn't dedicate too many project resources to work which doesn't provide strong evidence; I'll get back to this point later in this chapter.

You will have noticed I suggested that local facts and stats are an important source of evidence. When a transport investment is considered anywhere, there's a fundamental need to become closely familiar with the area and the people that the project will influence. So under the data category, it's worth exploring all the following:

- The locations of workplaces and businesses
- Residential locations and densities
- Social and demographic statistics
- Levels of deprivation and unemployment
- House prices, rents and how they vary with transport links
- Planned and potential new developments
- Levels of air quality
- Health, education and culture centres in the area
- Travel times for work, business or other activities
- The way any of the above varies by economic sector
- The way any of the above varies by demographic group
- How different scenarios may change any of the above.

Each one of these may help you explain the need for your project, its likely impacts and its chances of being delivered successfully.

Let's say you've done all the necessary work, and now you have evidence that includes all my recommended types: local data, information on relevant precedents, opinions about the project, local context, forecasts, and some theoretical references. How do you actually mix them? The way you combine all evidence doesn't need to follow any rigid structure. The only critical requirement is that it needs to tell a logical story about your project, what it's trying to do, and how you got to your conclusions and recommendations. All it needs is to make good sense.

The mixing of evidence from different sources isn't a quantitative stage where you apply weights to information of different types. It can't be a mathematical process because some of the most critical information is qualitative by nature; look again at all the arguments illustrated in figure 86, and you'll see that many of them won't benefit from being converted to numbers.

Furthermore, there will be cases where different sources of evidence will contradict each other. Some sources of raw data sometimes won't agree with other sources, as I've already discussed in chapter 4, and also in figures 53 and 60. The overall analysis of local data might result in conclusions that aren't in line with the lessons from similar previous projects, or with the opinions of people in the area. And any of these might imply different conclusions from what your model suggests.

To deal with such conflicts wisely, you need to neither dismiss them nor treat them in a formulaic manner. Combining evidence from multiple sources usually paints a complex picture. The inconsistencies between the different sources should help you explain what is known and what isn't, and this is an important finding in its own right. Describing this complex picture, including the conflicts in it and what you learn from them, is a more credible way of justifying your project than pretending that we know everything we want to.

Top tip 1:
Mix sources of evidence

The big bonus is that in some cases, most sources of evidence will actually lead to similar conclusions. The decision you reach in such cases is far more robust than a decision that would be based on modelling results only.

In some projects that require transport modelling, as soon as the work starts, the project leaders think: "modelling will be the most time consuming activity, so we must start immediately". They hardly spend any time considering the strengths and weaknesses of modelling in the context of their project; instead, their teams embark on a relatively standard modelling process in a way that is almost automatic.

When this approach is followed, the project has higher chances of falling into the common modelling pitfalls which I reviewed earlier. Such projects tend to over-state the strength of model outputs, make insufficient use of other sources of evidence, and bias the analysis towards things that can be modelled, even if things that can't be easily modelled are relevant to the project. The amount of time and money spent on modelling in such projects can become higher than necessary.

The approach to producing evidence needs to be tailored to the nature of the project. This should cover modelling and other sources of evidence jointly. It's better if the entire methodology for providing evidence is discussed, documented and shared with stakeholders before you actually do any of the work, with everyone understanding what questions it can answer and what questions it cannot. Examples of questions that should be covered at this stage:

- How to mix different sources of evidence (see figure 86)
- The scope of the modelling work (see figures 2, 81 and 84)
- Questions to answer without a model (see figure 3)
- The level of model detail (see figures 9, 10 and 70)
- Defining scenarios (see figures 12, 13 and 43)
- Defining demand segments (see figures 15 and 15)
- Behavioural responses to model (see chapter 3)
- Calibration and data sources (see chapter 4)
- How the model will consider money (see figures 17 and 74)
- The likely impact of modelling challenges such as parking (see figure 73).

Discussion and stakeholder engagement about all these questions, before starting any modelling, facilitate much smoother work later.

Top tip 2:
Don't start modelling too early

Just like we need sufficient time for planning and scoping at the start of a project, we also need sufficient time for interpretation and analysis towards the end. If your modelling plan only leaves a few days for interpretation after model outputs are ready, then this isn't a good plan. I've never seen a project where modelling activities follow the plan and finish on time; model development and application will take longer than expected in your project, too. For this reason, if your project plan suggests that you'll complete the modelling work just on time for some quick analysis before the project deadline, this means you're planning to do too much modelling.

12.4 Scheduling modelling activities

In many projects, the outputs from the modelling work are used as an input into other tasks. The post-modelling tasks may include:

- More detailed modelling work; for example, demand modelling outputs are the input into micro-simulation modelling
- Economic appraisal and cost-benefit analysis
- Environmental impact assessment
- Health impact assessment
- Engineering and structural design
- Architecture and urban design.

The project plan normally shows that these tasks start when modelling results are ready. However, modelling work commonly faces technical difficulties that take longer to resolve than expected. Since the post-modelling activities wait for modelling outputs to be ready, these activities often start too late, when there's not enough time left to complete them as planned.

271

While the wider team eagerly waits for model outputs, there can be extreme pressure on modellers to explain things they don't fully understand yet, or to show model outputs which are still work-in-progress. If the wider team decides to start the post-modelling activities using some interim model outputs, it's common that errors in the model are found after the post-modelling work has already begun. Various fixes and workarounds are used in such situations, and as a result, the remaining work is sometimes done in a rush. Only part of the planned work is actually completed, and what's completed goes through compromised quality control. This isn't healthy.

A healthier practice, is my view, is to be more relaxed about the level of alignment between modelling and post-modelling work. The desire for all parts of the puzzle to match each other is understandable, but the price is not worth paying. We can start the micro-simulation modelling, impact assessment or economic appraisal much earlier, without waiting for model outputs. To compensate for the lack of alignment with the model, we can look at more scenarios and potential outcomes in the post-modelling work (which is now no longer post-modelling). This can be much easier, and can be done more thoroughly, since we start this work earlier.

What this parallel approach gives us is a range of model outputs and a range of post-modelling work outputs, instead of a single fully-coordinated set of outputs. If we plan the work so that this range covers various interesting cases, then we can explain which of the outputs from the post-modelling work best match the latest model outputs, once they become available. A major advantage of this simultaneous approach is that we can pay more attention, in the (so-called) post-modelling work, to scenarios which can't be modelled. Given the limitations of every model, it's actually safer not to restrict the economic, environmental and other assessments only to scenarios that are based directly on model outputs.

If the (so-called) post-modelling tasks are done in parallel with the modelling, as I recommend, then the inputs can come from initial model runs, or from earlier versions of the model. You don't use them as they come but make various adjustments manually, to create a range of scenarios for the additional assessment tasks. You can even simply make these inputs up, so that they reflect scenarios which you find relevant, based on any source of available evidence.

Of course we should be able to explain how likely our assessment inputs are, why we created this range of scenarios, what we learn from each one, and which parts of the work are most consistent with model outputs. As long as we do this, then it's good practice not to let the model be the exclusive source of input into any subsequent work.

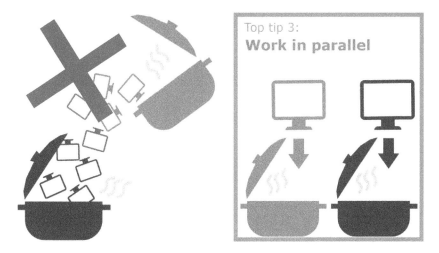

12.5 Allocating modelling tasks

A big problem in the transport planning community in the UK, USA and a few other countries is that modelling is done in too much isolation. I mentioned in figure 83 (under "reason 9") that some cases of model misuse could be avoided if the people who do the modelling were involved in all project activities, from start to end. But in reality, the majority of people employed as modellers only do modelling.

People are recruited to do modelling work because they have good analytical skills. Over time, many of them become aware of how limited transport models are, although they are still asked to provide answers to questions that models can't answer. There's not much they can do to change this, because:

- Over-ambitious modelling requests are sometimes made by senior colleagues, and passed to modellers without an opportunity to discuss.

- Making bold modelling promises to clients is sometimes seen as essential for commercial reasons.

- When modellers attend non-technical meetings, they are often expected to limit their contribution to a short summary, without challenging fundamental issues.

- Since modellers have few opportunities to liaise with wider stakeholders, over time some of them lose the habit of avoiding terms like "assignment", "link" and "matrix". By the time opportunities for wider engagement arise, modellers' contribution is seen as too technical and hence unhelpful.

- In many organisations there's a good understanding that a balanced mix of information sources should be used, giving models a more exploratory role, and using them less as prediction tools or comparison tools. However, the question is "when to start". Most projects don't seem the right time to start following this approach, due to various pressures.

- Occasionally there are organisational initiatives to get the wider team trained in modelling. These usually don't lead to a significant change, since the amount of training the wider team has time to attend doesn't take them as far as being able to do modelling work by themselves.

Top tip 4:
Don't allow anyone to do just modelling

These can all be alleviated if the same people who do the hands-on modelling are also intensely involved in other tasks. The right expectations from modelling work would spread wider, deeper and faster this way. The need to gain sufficient specialised modelling experience means that a modeller should still dedicate about half of their time to modelling. But there's no reason why in the other half, they couldn't be seen as fully fledged planners, designers, stakeholder engagement advisors, or whichever other role.

12.6 Defining scenarios

There is an implicit assumption, in many transport planning projects, that each scenario in the model corresponds to a planning scenario. For example, we assume that the model run "2030 with high economic growth and a new station on Main Street" adequately describes the real-world situation where the year is now 2030, recent growth followed the assumed pattern, and a new station is open on Main Street.

By now you should know that this isn't the case, even if you only agree with half of the 40 reasons I listed in figure 84. You should add modifications and reservations to the model outputs because of the limitations of the model; otherwise, you'd be using a scenario where some important things haven't been defined.

To make a justifiable use of model outputs in the context of a specific planning scenario, first you need to have a clear view about the differences between the real scenario and the one in the model. You can use figures 82, 83 and 84 as a checklist when deciding what your view is. For some aspects of your planning scenario, you'll decide that the simplification of the modelled scenario isn't a big issue. But if you're not concerned about any limitation of the model then you're not demonstrating a sufficiently critical judgement.

Identifying concerns about the modelled version of your scenario isn't meant to dismiss the model; it's meant to help you decide how to make the best use of the results. For every aspect of your scenario that was modelled in a simplified way, you should have an opinion on how the results would differ in the real world. Evidence not from the model can help you reach this opinion, as I explained earlier in this chapter.

In some cases, it may be justifiable to apply adjustments to the model outputs. For example, you could decide to increase travel times in some areas by 20% due to factors which weren't modelled. In other cases, it would make sense to leave the

275

outputs untouched but to say which outputs are more (or less) credible. As long as these are based on data, knowledge and common sense, I'm sure you'll make sensible decisions. The only case where I'd doubt the credibility of your work is if you decide categorically that you accept all model outputs.

If you are a stakeholder that reviews modelling results, I'd recommend that you use this as your initial rule of thumb. The guys who present the model outputs should win more of your trust if they show some self-criticism, and explain where and why modifications are needed due to limitations of their model. Don't easily trust modelling work that comes with no discussion of caveats and manual adjustments.

The distinction between model runs and planning scenarios has another important consequence. It means that you are free from the need to run the model for all the possible combinations of input assumptions. Let's use again the Bridgetown project, which I introduced in section 12.2, to illustrate this. In this example, a model is built to examine 3 project options (railway bridge, road bridge or no bridge). Let's say that the team follows the convention of developing models for 3 different years (2020, 2030 and 2040). There are also three demand growth scenarios (growth focused in the city centre; geographically dispersed growth; or negative growth).

The default plan in such a project would create 27 mega-scenarios that combine all combinations of the three years, three project options and three demand growth scenarios. The cost of developing 27 model runs would be very high, and it would take months to complete. We always discover modelling errors late in the process, and get some late requests for changes, so we'll need to run some scenarios more than once. Inevitably, the model development effort will come at the expense of the time left for analysis and interpretation of the results.

The fact that a model run isn't the same as a planning scenario means that there's no need to embark on such a gigantic modelling effort. We can plan, assess and discuss all 27 scenarios with a smaller modelling effort. A possible way of doing it, which the team may want to consider, is by only undertaking one or two runs with the negative growth scenario. These runs can be used for a general discussion about planning for the possibility of negative growth, without model outputs that examine this growth scenario in every year and with every project option.

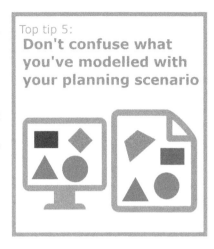

There would be alternative ways of reducing the 27 runs into a more manageable number. To avoid misunderstandings late in the project, the list of critical model runs should be discussed and agreed with stakeholders at the beginning of the project, before the work starts. The same discussion can also be used to draft a list of aspects of the planning scenarios which the model scenarios aren't likely to cover.

12.7   Dealing with uncertainty

There's one rule in transport modelling that is always correct, without any exceptions. The rule is that we know more about the base year (i.e. the current year, more or less) than about future years. This doesn't mean we know so much about the base year; the information we have is always full of gaps. But whatever we know or don't know about the base year, we always know much less about the future. The gaps in our understanding of the future include all the gaps from the base year plus many others. And the further we go into the future, the less we know, even if we spend years doing intense modelling work.

There's a habit of attaching similar importance in transport studies to every year we model. This habit isn't justified; you get more valuable insight from analysing the base year than any future year. A base year model for the scenario without the project can help your discussion about the need for the project, even without a similar future year model. A base year model for the scenario with the project can help your discussion about the impact of your project, even without a matching future scenario.

A simple way of putting more emphasis on the base year is by giving a high priority to the interpretation and visualisation of your base year matrix. Describing what we know about current travel demand should be the heart of your study, despite the gaps in our knowledge of this demand. When people see outputs from later stages of the modelling work, they can no longer separate what's actually known from all the additional layers of assumptions added by the model. It's important to extract as much insight as we can before these extra layers are added.

The hypothetical nature of modelling work is important to highlight when presenting outputs for future scenarios. I mentioned earlier that some clients believe that uncertainty results from bad modelling. The truth is, of course, that uncertainty is a natural feature of the world, especially when dealing with the future. But the limited certainty we can offer to clients is sometimes difficult for them to accept, especially if they are under pressure to prove that they invest in the right project.

For this reason, we have to educate our audience by putting uncertainty at the front. The point about uncertainty should be made from the start rather than mentioned apologetically when presenting results. You can't have a mature discussion about modelling outputs without agreeing with your audience what's uncertain; and since this is a complex topic, it has to be raised repeatedly and continuously, in all work stages, in every meeting and in every document.

There shouldn't be any mentioning of modelling without talking about uncertainty. Even when key model outputs are extracted from your report for a one-page summary, some commentary about your real level of confidence in the results needs to be there. It doesn't need to be technically complex, and it's not critical to use the word "uncertainty" itself if this scares your audience. But it has to be clear that much remains unknown even with a significant modelling effort.

It's also important not to confuse uncertainty with risk. When you do risk analysis, you show that there are several possible outcomes and you can attach a probability to each one. You can say, for example, that there's a 50% chance that a competing bus route will run in parallel with your new tram line. It's good to do risk analysis, but it doesn't remove uncertainty from the agenda. Things are uncertain if it's too complex to attach a probability to each event or factor. The number of factors that can influence our scenarios in transport analysis is very high, and there are complex interactions between them, so we can't possibly tell how likely or unlikely each scenario is.

Top tip 6:
Put uncertainty at the front

12.8 Explaining different choices

In figure 77 I showed some typical ways of presenting model outputs. A common problem occurs when the modelling team only presents assignment outputs on a plot of the network, and skips all the steps the model went through before the assignment. This is often done because clients only ask about levels of traffic or numbers of passengers in specific places, and not about earlier stages in the calculation.

Looking only at the assignment results is risky, because some important information is simply not there. For example, if you see a reduction in the level of traffic somewhere, this could be because of a change in route choices, a change in destination choices or a change in mode choices. If you look separately at the total demand by mode and the total demand by zone, directly from the demand matrices before they enter the assignment, you get the picture more clearly.

Top tip 7:
Present outputs of intermediate stages

Therefore, do have another look at figures 11, 61, 62, 63 and 64, and consider presenting such outputs whenever they are helpful.

12.9 Showing detailed outputs

I spoke a lot (too much?) earlier about various considerations to keep in mind when deciding how geographically detailed your modelling work should be. I won't repeat the full list here, but I'd like to include one of the main risks in my list of top ten tips.

Colleagues and clients will usually put pressure on modellers to present more detail than they can model reliably. The case for showing much detail, from their perspective, is obvious: they want to know exactly what will happen. The counter-argument, in favour of showing less detail, requires some understanding of basic statistics and therefore isn't intuitive to everyone. But the fact is that zooming in beyond the resolution of the input data, and beyond the geographical detail in which the model was calibrated, adds no new insight. Unfortunately, most modelling packages do not restrict your ability to zoom in excessively, but this is just an illusion which allows you to misinterpret what's presented as if it was a meaningful model output.

Most colleagues won't do it, so the pressure to avoid too much detail should come from you. You might be able to suggest a compromise. For example, say your client wants to forecast how traffic will split between different turns in a junction in a future scenario, while you think this is too detailed for your model. Maybe you could suggest using CCTV footage to see how traffic splits between the different turns today, and agree a set of assumptions about how this split would change in the future scenario; you'd use the model to estimate the total traffic through the junction and then apply your assumptions manually, outside the model.

Top tip 8:
Zoom out

Better yet, you might be able to convince your clients that this fine detail isn't suitable for modelling, and that the engineering and design work should acknowledge the uncertainty about the levels of expected traffic by turn.

12.10 Showing controversial outputs

If everyone agreed how we should improve the transport system, there wouldn't be a need to spend time on modelling. The problem is that sometimes people don't agree what's the right solution. A lot of work, including modelling, is done in an attempt to compare between alternative solutions or justify a specific solution.

When the modelling work is presented as a scientific comparison between options, it's misleading the audience. I showed in section 11.3 that the comparison is subjective, and that it's likely to reflect the opinions of the modellers' client. If a member of the public or a different organisation have a different opinion, and they haven't created their own model, their starting point in the debate would be weaker.

On one hand, this situation is not fair. On the other hand, those who develop a model can't do it without having an opinion about what it needs to show. Without knowing what to expect, they'd have to make important technical decisions without verifying that they lead to reasonable outputs. Since model development requires making subjective decisions, the only way to make the modelling work a bit more fair is by ensuring that it's open for challenge and criticism.

Top tip 9:

Present what people want to challenge

This requires that the most controversial model outputs are highlighted, so that they are easy for stakeholders to challenge. Many transport projects get disputed by stakeholders who promote different solutions, and those who do the modelling should make a particular effort to present model outputs that support the arguments of these stakeholders.

281

If the modellers simply show that the model can support the views of their own clients then they just state the obvious, and the model can't be seen as a fair source of evidence.

If you look at modelling work done by others, always check how much effort the modellers have made to accommodate views which aren't the views of their own clients. I tend to be suspicious with defensive presentations of model outputs, which focus only on how the model illustrates the advantages of the promoted project. By contrast, when those who present the modelling work are able to comment on controversial aspects of their work, and show how results would change if they took a different side in the debate, I see this as the most powerful sign of good modelling work.

12.11 Spending money

The time a team dedicates to transport modelling may be well-spent if the model is used appropriately. We use models appropriately in situations when they help stimulate our thinking. Transport models provide valuable inputs when we have time to play exploratory "what if" games, and when they help us brainstorm project options with clients, colleagues and stakeholders.

In many other cases, however, the time spent on modelling isn't effective. Figure 87 describes four general cases where, in my opinion, less time should be spent on modelling work. My final recommendation to those who wish to follow a good modelling practice is that they spend their time and money wisely.

Figure 88 closes this chapter with an overview of my ten top tips.

Figure 87: spending more than you need on modelling

When the input data doesn't explain the modelled behaviour. Models can help you estimate travel demand or traffic conditions if they were developed using data that can explain the relevant behaviours and phenomena. If the inputs into the model were coarser than the outputs you take from the model, you should better use other sources of evidence.

Top tip 10:
Don't waste money

When there's no time to absorb the outputs. Modelling is for projects where you have the luxury of spending time on exploratory analysis. It's neither for showing forecasts nor for judging which option is best. If a model is meant to support a decision, and decision makers will only read a two-page summary note, you should limit the work so that it can fit into these two pages. If the decision was made already, think again whether the modelling effort is worth making.

When there's no willingness to discuss subtle issues. Model hierarchy, uncertainty, over-fitting, level of detail: these are subtle issues. If your working environment disrespects subtleties, and there's pressure to provide succinct and unambiguous conclusions, then the model will certainly be misused (see figures 82 and 83). In such places it's better to avoid modelling, and only make direct use of data that shows the impacts of similar projects.

When the model needs to comply with inflexible criteria. Attempts to give generic guidelines on how to develop good models can cause the opposite effect. In England, for example, the guidance from government on the required model validation stats causes modellers to over-fit their models to the data in order to get good stats (read about over-fitting in chapters 7, 8 and 11). The time spent trying to meet generic guidelines, rather than tailoring a model to project-specific needs, isn't well-spent.

Figure 88:
my ten top tips
for wise
modelling

Top tip 1:
Mix sources of evidence

Top tip 2:
Don't start modelling too early

Top tip 3:
Work in parallel

Top tip 4:
Don't allow anyone to do just modelling

Top tip 5:
Don't confuse what you've modelled with your planning scenario

Top tip 6:
Put uncertainty at the front

Top tip 7:
Present outputs of intermediate stages

Top tip 8:
Zoom out

Top tip 9:
Present what people want to challenge

Top tip 10:
Don't waste money

Use this space to draw a smiley face.

Chapter 13
The future of transport modelling

13.1 Where do we go from here

If you've read the previous 12 chapters and you're still here, then surely you agree with me that nobody can tell the future. What we can do is explore what happened in the past, observe what is happening now, pay attention to trends and identify behaviours. In the previous 12 chapters I spoke about doing all this to estimate travel demand; in this chapter I'll do this in an attempt to guess what the models themselves will be like in the future.

If the future modelling trends I suggest here actually happen, then I intend to tell everyone "you see? I told you". If my suggested trends don't turn into reality then I'll tell everyone, "you see? I told you nobody can tell the future".

13.2 Self-driving vehicles

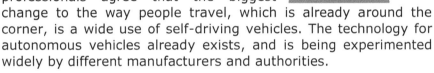

One of the reasons why transport modelling will change in the future is that the transport system itself will change. Models that describe the transport system will have to catch up with these changes. Many transport professionals agree that the biggest change to the way people travel, which is already around the corner, is a wide use of self-driving vehicles. The technology for autonomous vehicles already exists, and is being experimented widely by different manufacturers and authorities.

If cars don't require active driving, then some of the following may happen:

■ It may become easier to use the road space more efficiently. Vehicles on a busy highway could move closer to each other and at a higher speed, because the space between them today is determined by the typical reaction time of a human driver. If the car ahead of you slows down suddenly, or if a child runs into the road, then a machine will choose the best

285

response quicker, which means we'll need less space between cars.

- The faster and automated response should also allow narrower traffic lanes and more green time for everyone in signalised junctions. We might not need red signals at all, because the communication between vehicles would sort out the order in which they can efficiently cross a junction.

- The downside of automated responses is that there are things humans do better than machines. The human brain is better in telling the difference between a child on the road and the picture of a child on a large advertisement on a van.

- The efficiency gained by the automated responses will somewhat reduce if some vehicles are still driven by humans. It will probably take quite a while until each and every car is autonomous.

- It may become possible for people without a driving license, children and even blind people to travel independently by car. This can generate new types of trips and it can cause a shift of trips between modes.

- Parking space, which is limited today, could be used more effectively. It should be possible to let cars park themselves, with hardly any spaces between them. If there's no parking space nearby, the car should be able to drop you at your destination and find a parking space elsewhere.

- Self-driving vehicles could provide cheaper taxi services, either to individuals or on a shared ride with other passengers. The allocation of passengers to vehicles could be optimised in real time based on demand and on traffic conditions. Over time this might replace some forms of public transport.

What does all this mean for modelling? One piece of good news is that the behaviour of autonomous vehicles should be easier to forecast. The brain of a self-driving vehicle includes rules about what the vehicle should do in different situations; the same rules can be coded in a model, so that it accurately replicates the behaviour of the vehicle.

However, the model will need to know in advance everything the car learns in real time. Even if humans don't drive these vehicles, the behaviour of human beings will remain what causes a trip to be made. Human behaviour itself will not become more predictable than it is today, so the same uncertainty will remain regarding how many trips are made, whether people's trip destinations are affected by today's weather, and so on. In this sense, the fact that the car is driven automatically won't reduce the uncertainty around the model outputs.

A wide use of autonomous vehicles will require some serious re-calibration of existing models, but we should still be able to use the same modelling concepts:

- Using new data, we can re-calibrate the parameters that represent patterns of traffic flow and vehicle performance.

- Although self-driving vehicles may count as a new mode, the existing concept of mode choice modelling can deal with the introduction of such mode. The new mode will have its own generalised cost function, as I explained in chapter 2.

- The way we currently model parking is very limited anyway, so this too will just mean changing some parameter values.

- We may need to revised user segmentation if children, or others that currently don't travel independently, start making their own trips.

- The way we model signal settings in signalised junctions might need to go through a more radical change, depending on the extent to which communication between autonomous vehicles will replace the traffic signal.

A challenge much larger than including self-driving vehicles in the model is knowing when they'll become widespread. For this reason, now is the time when these vehicles cause the largest uncertainty. We keep developing models for 2020 and 2030 without knowing how dominant self-driving cars will be at these times, and without being able to observe any of the real-world impacts of mass autonomous traffic. The timing of the transition to autonomous driving is a matter of pure speculation, and therefore, a new dimension of uncertainty is added to any future scenario we currently model.

Will autonomous cars reduce the need for people to own a car? This, too, is a matter for pure speculation. Some people think it will, because it will be possible to subscribe to services that get any car you want to your doorstep whenever you want it, without having to worry about maintenance and parking. By contrast, others think that most people will still want to own their own car, because they attach a high value to the small perks that come with it, like having a stock of their preferred chocolate bars in the glove compartment.

Since there has never been such choice so far, the way car ownership will change is highly uncertain. But whether or not people will use a shared pool of autonomous cars, new forms of shared travel may become more common even without new vehicle technology. The sharing economy has gone through dramatic changes over the last decade, with notable examples in the transport sector (e.g. shared ride with Uber) and in other sectors (e.g. turning your home into a hotel using Airbnb).

It's becoming increasingly easy for people to share things with other users in a way that reduces prices, creates new opportunities, and at the same time, allows people to remain picky about what exactly they want. The ease of striking this balance is a result of advances in telecommunications and software. Since new software apps appear every day, offering new ways to share things easily, it seems likely that big changes in future travel behaviour will be driven by new software, and not only by traditional factors like new infrastructure.

From a modelling perspective, there are two separate challenges here. One challenge is to estimate the future uptake of these new forms of shared travel. Models are unlikely to be successful in doing this; the factors that turn a new technology or software app into a great success clearly aren't something we can include in a model. The best we can expect from a transport model is to be retrofitted after new travel habits have been established, so that the model reflects our latest understanding of these habits.

If some app-based sharing service becomes a common way for people to organise their travel, then the other challenge is for models to incorporate the same procedure that the sharing app uses. Whether it's based on sharing cars that belong to the app provider, or a clever way for people to give each other a lift, or anything else - models will need to know how it's organised, so that trips in the model can be shared like they're shared in reality.

Even when this procedure is known, getting transport models to allow new combinations of trips will cause much headache. See, for example, the trip sharing examples such as "kiss and ride" I mentioned in figure 56. Today we can ignore these ways of travel simply because their proportion of the overall demand isn't high. But if it becomes common for people to somehow coordinate their travel plans with each other, with or without the help of clever apps, then the way transport models work might need to change completely.

13.4 New data sources

The previous points were about possible future changes to the transport system, which will need to be reflected in models that describe the system. I now turn to future changes in how we do transport modelling even if the transport system stays the same.

In every profession and every sector, it has been a few years now that everyone talks about "big data". The world is full of computers, phones, sensors, detectors, and other communication devices. These different machines and the software that runs on them collect huge amounts of data. The availability of so much data is a relatively new thing, so in many cases the data piles up and doesn't yet get fully used. Many organisations and companies are busy these days improving the way they use their "big data". While doing so they are stretching the existing expertise in fields such as data science, information retrieval, data mining and software engineering.

The transport sector is no different. In figure 36, amongst the data sources used to develop transport models, I listed data from mobile phones and other mobile devices as a potential source. There are actually several types of "big data" that have some potential to improve transport models:

- Information about the location of a mobile phone based on the exchange of signals in a cellular network. This information is stored by the mobile phone operator.

- Information about the location of a phone, or another device, based on a GPS (**Global Positioning System**) technology. This information is typically available to companies that provide mobile apps for navigation, mapping or exercise.

- Information about the location of a phone, or another device, based on LPS (**Local Positioning System**) or IPS (**Indoor Positioning Systems**). Such data is collected, for example, when the device is connected to a WiFi access point.

- Information about the user's movement from other sensors, including sensors built into mobile phones. These include accelerometer to measure changes in speed, gyroscope to measure rotation, digital compass to measure orientation, barometer to measure altitude, and pedometer to count steps. The information becomes available to companies that provide apps who use these sensors.

These information sources seem very attractive because they contain people's location at different times, so they can tell us a lot about how they travel. The data is collected automatically, without the need to do surveys or collect data manually. Since this sounds so ideal, hundreds of projects over the last decade explored ways to turn such information into a standard data source for developing transport models. There's much enthusiasm to embed this data in the transport planning work.

Despite this, the use of the data sources listed above hasn't yet caused a widespread change to how we develop models. It hasn't even led to a significant reduction in the effort to collect the traditional types of data. There are many interesting case studies, but there isn't a standard practice with a complete methodology for embedding advanced location data in model development. To understand why this hasn't happened, let's talk about a few key characteristics of these new data sources:

- **User identity.** Some traditional data sources, such as household surveys or roadside interviews (see figure 36), have the great advantage of giving us individual information on the person who makes every trip. We use this information to understand their travel behaviour. When data comes from the cellular network, we are less sure who makes each trip. The phone company may know who pays the phone bill, but many people (e.g. children) don't pay their own bills.

- **User segmentation.** Segmentation by mode is critical in model development. Traditional data is collected separately for each mode, or if it's a general survey, respondents are asked which mode of transport they've been using. When using data from the mobile network, identifying which mode has been used on each trip becomes a major challenge. We need a sophisticated combination of data from several sources in order to distinguish trips by bike from trips by bus, for example, and the statistical confidence we have in the result is limited.

- **Amount of data.** When using traditional data sources, every survey has a known sample size. Getting a decent sample size can get costly. A major advantage with new sources, such as mobile phone data, is that information from a large number of people is collected without any physical fieldwork. However, with these new sources, the sample size can be misleading. Even if we know that 10% of the people use the network or the mobile application that collects our data, some data is only collected when there's good mobile reception, or only when the user is making a call, or only when they move between the catchment areas of different cellular antennas. This also makes it harder to derive the right factors to multiply the data by, when we want to convert the sample data to an estimate for the whole population.

- **Location accuracy.** With traditional data sources, there is little doubt about where exactly we observed each traveller or vehicle, although it can be expensive to undertake survey

291

fieldwork in multiple locations. With newer data sources, there are different cellular technologies with different levels of geographical detail. GPS is more refined than cellular data but the sample sizes tend to be smaller, because the number of users of any specific application isn't as high as the number of customers of a mobile network operator.

- **Data ownership and availability.** With traditional sources, we own the data we collect. With the new sources, it's common that we can only buy some analysis from the data holder. We don't own the data, and in most cases, we can't even see it. There are three reasons why new data sources aren't available for the client to view. First, there is commercial sensitivity in the competitive environment where mobile phone companies or app owners operate. Second, the raw data consists of very large files, which require specialised storage and processing capabilities. And third, owners of the data can't legally share it in its unprocessed form, because this can reveal personal information on users' locations and travel habits.

- **The data market.** Those who hold data from mobile phones and apps can sell insight from this data to a wide range of customers; transport modelling teams are only a minority amongst these. Customers in the transport modelling field have a limited ability to pay for the data, and their technical requirements are high. Hence, for the data owners, focusing on transport modelling customers might not be such a good deal, and this may be reflected in the way the data is priced. The result is that many of us see this type of data as unaffordable.

There's no doubt that data collected using location-based technologies will continue becoming increasingly central to model development. However, such data is not the magical solution that some have hoped it would be. There isn't a single data source that gives us everything we need in order to develop a transport model, and we need to constantly seek effective ways of fusing data of different types. This brings us again to the first recommendation I made in chapter 12: the best results are obtained by mixing information from multiple sources.

Model calibration is usually a one-off exercise. Although it includes some automated procedures, every time a model is calibrated we use different data sources and we need to make many decisions that are specific to the project we work on. Even in recent cases where new sources of "big data" feed into this process, each time we develop and calibrate a model is an independent, unrepeatable activity.

The much greater opportunity that "big data" brings to transport analysis is to have transport models continuously re-calibrated. The whole point about "big data" is that it keeps being collected automatically, all the time. This means that the insight that hides in the data remains up-to-date, and all we need is a methodology for extracting this insight on a continuous basis.

The real test for our ability to use new data science in transport modelling is whether we can develop models that refresh themselves and reduce the amount of manual work we do. This is a typical problem from the field of **machine learning**, since we want the model (i.e. the machine) to keep learning the best parameter values from a continuous feed of input data. This type of machine learning is the most common way of creating **artificial intelligence**.

Machine learning doesn't perform magic. It employs the same mathematical and statistical techniques which we use to calibrate models already. Machine learning isn't about leaving all the data in the right place and hoping that by the time you're back, the best model has been developed for you. A human modeller still needs to define how the model should be developed, and human judgement remains critical in interpreting any output. The difference from the traditional process is that it focuses on continuous improvement, rather than a one-off model development exercise. The model is self-calibrating in the sense that similar calibration tasks are performed repeatedly and the results get constantly refreshed.

The main current barrier to developing such clever solutions is logistic. Due to privacy issues, data holders cannot pass raw data to transport modellers. To use their data for model development we'll need to adopt a new process architecture, which allows modelling experts to define the methodology and apply it to an incoming stream of data, but without seeing the data itself. Developing such process architecture isn't that challenging, but it requires a considerable initial investment in setting everything up. There aren't many widely-known cases where organisations have been willing to make this investment.

You may remember figure 76, which focused on some specific characteristics of short-term prediction for the purpose of traffic control. I showed that this is a promising field of modelling, with fewer fundamental challenges. For the same reasons I explained in figure 76, traffic control is also the main area of transport analysis where artificial intelligence is likely to play a major role in the near future. Short-term predictive analysis, based on information collected in real time, can use machine learning to constantly improve how traffic light settings and road user charges are adjusted to reduce traffic congestion.

Artificial intelligence is already being used in such traffic control systems. Due to the immediate impact such systems have on traffic flow in urban areas, authorities and operators are willing to pay much more for this. And since there is willingness to pay, the largest companies in the technology sector invest in developing their offer in this area. The focus on the immediate future means that the forecasting element in these systems is relatively simple, so transport modelling isn't the primary challenge. These systems don't need to have meaningful parameters or strong behavioural foundations. If their suggested change to the timing of a traffic signal is bad, then this will have traffic impacts that can be observed immediately. The system will automatically learn from this experience, with no need to get into the painful topics of uncertainty or levels of future growth.

The use of artificial intelligence for the smooth operation of urban traffic strongly links to the **Internet Of Things** (IOT). The IOT is a common name for the concept of improving the automated communication between many types of devices, so that efficiency is achieved in many aspects of our lives. The entire technology sector spends millions every year on products and methodologies that will eventually make the IOT work. We already spoke about some key transport-related components of the IOT, including autonomous vehicles, automated parking and optimised signal settings.

The IOT concept goes far beyond transport infrastructure, and covers many aspects of how we work, shop, and interact with different services. Making the transport system an integral part of it also means that transport modelling needs to be better integrated into the latest practices in software engineering and data science. I'll get back to this point very soon.

13.6 **Data-driven decision making**

If we get to a point where data from the transport system gets continuously collected and analysed automatically, then we will need much less modelling. We can't start following such approach yet because the data we have isn't

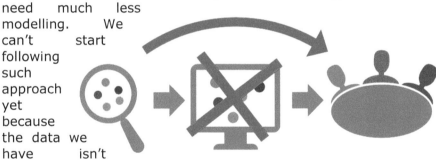

organised in a way that shows the impact of various factors. But if we get richer and more reliable data on the way people travel, and the way this changes over time, then we can focus on understanding the impact of these different factors, including projects and policies, directly from the data.

When different impacts can be observed directly, we can use what we've observed to support transport investment decisions without the lengthy model development process. For example, if our data shows that the rise in car traffic slowed down in the year after public transport fares were reduced, this gives some real evidence about the impact of fare reduction. If we wanted to model the impact of reducing fares, we would need to make dozens of assumptions which we have little certainty about.

This is similar to what I said in chapter 11, when I spoke about evaluation studies. Doing evaluation means that we investigate the actual result of a transport project directly from data we collect. In chapter 11 I spoke about evaluation as a way of checking the model, while here I talk about using data directly instead of building a model; but in both cases the key point is that data we collect is a more powerful source of evidence than a forecast from a model.

There are, of course, some downsides to the direct reliance on data. Isolating the impact of specific factors is statistically challenging. Say, for example, we build a new metro station and examine how road traffic changes in the subsequent months. The changes we observe could be a result of the new station, but they could also be the outcome of many other things that happened at a similar time. Traditional models have the advantage of allowing us to look at the impact of one change at a time. In addition, looking at the impact of projects in the past doesn't give much evidence on the impact of new types of projects or using new technologies in transport.

For these reason, I wouldn't expect the improved availability of "big data" to replace modelling so quickly; but I'd definitely hope to see more projects where more data is used more directly, more often.

Let's move on from the future of data handling to the future of the modelling software. Like every other computer tool and software product, the capabilities of transport models evolve very quickly. Two critical aspects of this evolution are the rise in computing power and the improvement in terms of graphical output format.

Models that took weeks to run in the 1970s can now run in seconds. If you compare how much modelling work can now be done in a given amount of time, the saving is tremendous, and this gives us an opportunity to do more comprehensive analysis in this timeframe. In practice, many of us don't do it. It's very common that due to the improved runtime of modelling tools, we decide to run more scenarios. We then wrongly assume that our projects are supported by better evidence, and we continue giving insufficient attention to critical thinking and interpretation.

The reduced runtime also leads modellers to increasing the level of detail and spatial complexity in the model, since this is now less costly than it was, even when the greater detail isn't supported by more detailed input data. Overall, the improved computing power has raised the expectations from transport models. I clarified in earlier chapters how risky this is.

There's no doubt that computer performance will keep rising in the future, so models will run faster and faster, to the extent that runtime itself will stop being a key consideration. The temptation to misuse the model, and state that it gives us more confidence than it really does, will rise accordingly. My own recommendation would be to use the improved computing power in the manner I described under "artificial intelligence" rather than intensifying the use of the traditional techniques.

Other important improvements relate to the visual side of transport modelling. Model outputs changed over the years from stark black and while text to high-definition coloured maps and infographics. I mentioned that the outputs from micro-simulation models are now often visualised as animated videos, and we are approaching the stage where model outputs can be illustrated in three dimensions through **virtual reality** and **augmented reality** techniques. These approaches make the modelled representation of the transport system less dry and more vivid. They are powerful in events where plans are presented to politicians or to members of the public.

Still, I need to poop the party again, by reminding of the risk that our audience will develop too much trust in the model outputs. It's too easy for people to believe that the model is a source of undeniable truth, given the confidence that radiates from these beautiful visualisations, which you can literally touch and feel. The more realistic the future looks, the less likely it is to be challenged, also in those cases where it's based on a flawed methodology.

Of course I wouldn't recommend making the outputs less clear on purpose. But I would highlight that any visualisation should still be subject to the principles I suggested in chapter 12.

13.8 Online modelling

Until quite recently, most software applications were independent programs that run offline on your computer. They were seen as a different creature from websites that you access using a web  browser (such as Internet Explorer, Firefox or Chrome). The high availability of broadband and WiFi, together with other trends, are gradually changing this. Desktop applications are being replaced with web applications that run in the browser, with continuous reliance on internet resources.

Most transport modelling tools still work as desktop applications. This is only natural, since transport models use a lot of information stored in large files on the local disk or a local network; the idea of sending or receiving such information over the internet during a model run seems unnecessary. But like other types of software, transport modelling tools will most probably turn over time into a form of web application. Some modelling packages already have online versions, and others are in development.

You may refer to a model that uses the internet and runs in a browser as a **cloud-based model**. The term "cloud" is sometimes used to simply refer to the internet, and sometimes used more specifically to indicate that your files are stored away from your office; both definitions are relevant here. Why will transport models move to the cloud?

■ Cloud-based tools are becoming more powerful than offline software. The performance of a package running on your own computer depends on your own hardware, whereas an online tool can use the power of many remote computers who run simultaneously.

■ Cloud-based tools can be upgraded more flexibly if you develop a more complex model, without having to change your own hardware. They can also be downgraded in order to save costs, when you no longer use them.

■ Models are often developed by several team members working in parallel. Working online can help transport modellers benefit from the advanced collaboration and version control tools that are in common use in the software industry.

■ Models that work online can benefit from some automatic updates using **application programming interfaces** (APIs). For example, parameters that are based on figures published by government sources can be updated by connecting to a government **web service** that provides the parameter value. A different API could be responsible for a feed of traffic data from a mobile app, as I explained earlier. An API to a mapping service (such as Google Maps) can save some network update work.

- With a cloud-based model, new functionality could be added to allow stakeholders to view model outputs online and create their own maps.

13.9 DIY modelling

One of the unwritten rules of transport modelling is that only specialists can touch the model. Stakeholders often ask whether they can get a copy of the model and play with it by themselves, and the answer is always a strict "no". For many years I supported this approach; I still think that with today's modelling tools, you can apply the model in different scenarios only if you are a modelling specialist and only if you were involved in developing the model.

However, I now think that this strict approach is essential simply because the modelling tools lack some important functionality. Once this gap is addressed, the model should be made available to any stakeholder; clients and other stakeholders should be encouraged to run their own scenarios. I also believe that it's only a matter of time before many modelling tools are upgraded to support this concept.

Let's talk first about why the current default is that only experts can access the model:

- Giving model access to people outside the modelling team involves a lot of logistical hassle, which modellers don't have the time for. This includes software installation, licensing, user-friendly documentation, and general user support.

- You've seen throughout this book how many specialised terms and techniques you need to understand in order to make a responsible use of a model. Letting an external user modify anything without sufficient knowledge will result in unreliable outputs.

300

- Requests to share the model always come in when the modelled project is at the heart of a debate. Giving some modelling capability to other parties in the debate means that the model owners give away some of their control over the outcome.

So why do I think that this will sometime change? Here's why:

- I showed in chapter 11 that model outputs mainly reflect what the modellers see as a logical outcome. This can easily be misused. The misuse can be eliminated by letting other parties exercise their own judgement and show how the outcome changes.

- Specialised modellers fear that an unqualified user would code illogical junctions or introduce all kinds of inconsistencies. But these fears can be allayed using a combination of pre-set defaults for common types of transport projects; automated network checks; a hierarchy of model permissions that specifies what end users can or can't change; and an effective user interface.

- The shift towards cloud-based tools reduces the burden of installation and file transfer when a new user is given model access.

- There are now examples in other fields, where a graphical user interface allows non-experts to play with complex models. An example is the Machine Learning Studio on the Microsoft Azure platform. This will not prevent some users from exploiting the tool, but such exploitation would be easy to detect. The benefit from allowing many others to use the tool in legitimate ways outweighs the risk.

- A more open modelling culture would facilitate interactive and creative engagement with stakeholders. Colleagues in the property, education, health and leisure sectors, as well as the wider public, would make extensive use of models that are made widely available. Original project ideas and solutions would be proposed through this channel. This would be a refreshing change to the way model outputs are presented in project consultations today.

I therefore no longer see any critical barrier to making future models widely available, for those who want to play with some "Do It Yourself" scenario testing.

13.10 Open-source models

In many fields of science, engineering, management, design and the arts, a lively community of software developers works voluntarily on open-source applications. Open-source software is distributed freely, and anyone is allowed to use or change it for any purpose. Some very common software products were built as open-source projects, including the Mozilla Firefox web browser and the Apache HTTP Server.

There are some open-source products in transport modelling, although I'm not aware of any such product that has become widely used. The highly specialised nature of transport modelling makes it difficult to find a large enough number of developers that would be willing to contribute to such a project. It's difficult to say whether this will ever change, but I can only hope that open-source software becomes sooner or later more dominant in this field.

A key reason why I look forward to prominent open-source initiatives in modelling is that it would encourage a culture of challenge, diversity and creative disruption. Transport modelling is too traditional and dogmatic. It took me the first 200 pages of this book to introduce you only to the core of the modelling tradition, but following this tradition doesn't prevent even the most fundamental types of model misuse. Since we don't have a common habit of rejecting weak parts of the modelling tradition, I'd be pleased to see a lively open-source community challenging things that don't work.

Another reason why open-source model development would be beneficial is that it would encourage transport professionals to engage in programming. Software development skills are not often used within a transport planning team, and important opportunities are missed since team members can't code.

Finally, I'd mention that open-source models could be developed not only by transport professionals, but also by community groups and individuals who aren't happy with the way transport-related decisions are made. Having the ability to present their own evidence on transport projects would give them more power, including in situations where the public today has limited ability to challenge decisions about transport infrastructure.

13.11 Same old tricks

The work of a transport modeller combines knowledge from all the following fields: economics; mathematics; statistics; market research; operational research; computer science; software engineering; geography; town planning; psychology; sociology; media and marketing; environmental science; medical science; physics; civil engineering; and design. I'm always puzzled by how little knowledge sharing takes place between transport modellers and experts in these other fields.

Transport models are developed and used by people that have limited exposure to forecasting and estimation practices in finance, commerce, biology, geography and medicine. The reverse is also true: transport models are not often shared with professionals who develop equivalent tools in other fields. Short-term work pressures and budget restrictions are the main reasons for the relatively isolated nature of transport modelling work, although there's also a lack of strategic vision.

With so little external exposure, transport models remain too dogmatic. The four-stage concept has remained surprisingly immune for decades, and hasn't been seriously threatened by any strong alternatives. The reliance on forecasts has grown over the years, despite the lack of evidence that these forecasts can be trusted. Opportunities to reduce complexity, or to introduce a better balance between modelling and evaluation, have not been pursued.

So there's a decent chance that transport modelling in the future will look the same as it looks now. Computing power will keep growing, so it will become easier for us to present dozens of model runs, argue that they tell us the future, show exactly how different scenarios compare to each other, display accurate forecasts for each street and junction, impress clients with dazzling visualisations, promise them that the model contains no coding errors, blur our long list of assumptions, dismiss any concern about uncertainty, hide factors which aren't modelled but might have a larger impact than what's modelled, and forecast also trends that we had no input data about. In short: the apocalypse!

But there's also a reasonable chance that something very good will soon happen to the transport modelling practice. If transport professionals are keen to embrace new opportunities, for example by using new data sources to create artificial intelligence in transport planning, then they'll have to make their work more similar to the work of software and data engineers outside the transport sector.

My own vision would be to see the isolated field of transport modelling disappearing off the face of the earth. I'd like to see this field peacefully dissolving itself into the broader field of data science, so that whenever an analytical need arises in a project, the solution isn't prescribed by tradition. The solution will be selected by professionals that have been exposed to many types of challenges in various different fields; they'll propose an approach that is entirely focused on the needs of the project.

When this happens, nobody will need to buy this book anymore, but if I'm still around, I'll write a new one.

CPSIA information can be obtained
at www.ICGtesting.com
Printed in the USA
LVHW072025280622
722299LV00008B/131